HERETICS

HERETICS

The Creation of Christianity from
the Gnostics to the Modern Church

JONATHAN WRIGHT

HOUGHTON MIFFLIN HARCOURT
BOSTON   NEW YORK   2011

For information about permission to reproduce selections from this book,
write to Permissions, Houghton Mifflin Harcourt Publishing Company,
215 Park Avenue South, New York, New York 10003.

www.hmhbooks.com

Library of Congress Cataloging-in-Publication Data
Wright, Jonathan, date.
Heretics : the creation of Christianity from the Gnostics to the modern
church / Jonathan Wright.
p. cm.
Includes bibliographical references and index.
ISBN 978-0-15-101387-6
1. Christian heretics — History. 2. Christian heresies — History.
3. Church history. I. Title.
BT1315.3.W75 2011
273 — dc22   2010043049

Printed in the United States of America

DOC 10 9 8 7 6 5 4 3 2 1

For Peter Taylor

CONTENTS

1. THE HERETICS   1

2. THE INVENTION OF HERESY   14
    Ignatius   14
    Marcion and Gnosticism   19
    The Montanists   30
    Blunting the Challenges: Christian Unity   34
    Persecution   39
    The Church   44

3. CONSTANTINE, AUGUSTINE, AND THE
   CRIMINALIZATION OF HERESY   50
    The Seven Sleepers of Ephesus   50
    Constantine   54
    Who Was Christ?   58
    Donatism   69
    Augustine   74
    Whence and Whither?   78

4. THE HERESY GAP   83
    Heresy Redivivus   85
    Iconoclasm   89

5. MEDIEVAL HERESY I   95
Orléans, 1022   95
Popular Heresy   102
Valdes   106
Popular Heresy: Reality   115
Popular Heresy: Myth   126
The Cathars   130

6. MEDIEVAL HERESY II   135
Francis   137
Where to Draw the Lines?   140
The Beguines   142
All the Others   145
Hus   150
The Fabled Road to the Reformation   156

7. REFORMATIONS   160
The Revolution   160
The Reformation Muddle   169
The Other Reformation   171
Reformation Certainty   181
The New Heresies   188
Drowned Without Mercy: Anabaptists   196
Servetus   200
Plus Ça Change?   204

8. THE DEATH OF HERESY?   212
Caution   212
Pragmatism   221
The Great Leap   225

9. AMERICAN HERESY   238
New England   241
Hutchinson   245

Williams   251

Quakers   255

Revolutions Great and Small   262

Jefferson and Madison   264

The Republic   271

10. THE POLITE CENTURIES   276

Emerson and Parker   278

The Sum of All Heresies   284

11. CONCLUSION   291

ACKNOWLEDGMENTS   303

NOTES   305

SUGGESTED READING   317

INDEX   323

HERETICS

1

THE HERETICS

OVER THE PAST two thousand years Christian heretics have
been likened to whores and lepers, savage beasts and demons, sexual perverts and child killers. So far as the sixteenth-century Jesuit
Francis Coster was concerned, they had a great deal in common
with "the filthy dregs that flowed through the outhouse." Warming
to his theme, Coster added that just as phlegm was expelled from
the body, so heretics were to be banished from "the heavenly body
of saints . . . as if religion became sick and vomited them out."[1]

Behind the unsavory rhetoric there was often an assumption
that heresy ought to be obliterated. It was not simply pesky, it was
utterly pernicious and, as a character in Thomas More's *A Dialogue
Concerning Heresies* opined, it was the obligation of the righteous
"to sit upon the mountains treading heretics under our feet like
ants."[2]

Sometimes God was touted as the chief executioner. Stories
would be told of the fourth-century heresiarch Arius (about whom
we'll hear much more) going to the lavatory one day only to witness
his bowels gushing out. Into which disgusting mess, so Saint Ambrose reported, his head fell "headlong, besmirching those foul lips
with which he had denied Christ." This, Ambrose crowed, was no
random accident, no "chance manner of death." It was the Almighty
inflicting vengeance upon "wickedness."[3]

Sometimes, the ant treading was left to human beings, as when hundreds of medieval Cathars were slaughtered by crusading armies at Béziers in 1209; or when (so legend tells) North African Donatists were herded onto ships at Carthage in 347, weighed down with casks of sand, and dumped far out at sea; or when poor old Giulio Cesare Vanini's tongue was cut out ahead of his being strangled at the stake in 1619 Toulouse. Many heretics made it through the vale of tears unharmed, but this did not necessarily exempt them from punishment. They could be condemned after death, at which time their bones would be dug up and destroyed or, like the sixty-seven deceased heretics in Mexico in 1649, be burned in effigy.

These were not the only sanctions available to the syndics of orthodoxy, however, and the historical landscape of heresy is not nearly as corpse-strewn as might be imagined. From the perspective of the ecclesiastical establishment, to kill a heretic was to fail. The murdered heretic was someone who, despite all the threatening and cajoling, had obstinately refused to recant his errors. Worse yet, he could look a lot like a righteous martyr to his followers and confreres. It was far preferable, therefore, to win supposedly errant Christians back to the supposedly true path by means of corrective justice. This, in terms of theological logic, was deemed to be charitable (you were only trying to save people from eternal perdition, after all). If this was *caritas,* however, it was often of an extravagant, sometimes brutal variety.

Medieval heretics were made to go on penitential pilgrimages (often in chains), their clothes were bedecked with stigmatizing, stitched-in symbols, and they were sentenced to grueling service in the king's galleys. In sixteenth-century France they could be whipped or made to endure the most public humiliations: standing in their penitential gowns in the church or the public square, bareheaded and shoeless, holding a lighted candle, abjuring their errors, and begging the community for forgiveness. If they were errant clerics, their heads might be shaved (removing all sign of their tonsure), their priestly vestments ceremonially stripped off, or, if they were especially unlucky, their flesh cut from the thumb and index finger: a symbolic way of removing their right to celebrate the Eucharist.[4]

An obvious question springs to mind. What was this thing called heresy and why was it so detested? To indulge in such lavish persecutory measures must surely have required a great deal of certainty on the part of those doing the persecuting.

An important first step was to define this most heinous of crimes: it had to be identified before it could be stamped out. An awful lot of theological ink was spilled in this pursuit but, for our present purposes, a sentence from the medieval theologian Robert Grosseteste is as good a starting point as any. Heresy, he wrote, is "an opinion chosen by human perception, contrary to Holy Scripture, publicly avowed and obstinately defended."[5] At first blush, this looks fairly straightforward but, once it is unpacked, the definition turns out to be quite sophisticated. Religious truth, so the theory went, was divinely inspired, objective, and fixed — soaring far above the fleeting speculations of human opinion. There was room for reined-in theological interpretation (at least for learned clerics), the variable nuts and bolts of worship could sometimes be tinkered with, and some concepts and rituals might take several centuries to emerge. When it came to basic Christian dogmas, however, these were all contained within the New Testament message. They had been righteously pored over by the fathers of the early church and codified in a succession of creedal statements, church councils, and, so far as the Western half of Christendom was concerned, papal pronouncements.

There was no good excuse for any reasonably well informed Christian to dissent from these supposedly eternal verities. To do so was to threaten the unity of Christendom: it was to trample on the memory and sacrifice of Christ. Heretics often advertised themselves as holy men but, so far as the church was concerned, they were madmen, prideful scoundrels addicted to the exercise of their addled imaginations, or, more than likely, the minions of Satan.

Grosseteste's talk of public avowal is also crucial. The heretical mind in which dangerous thoughts secretly festered was beyond the reach of the church militant. There had always been vipers in the nest: hypocrites and dissemblers who harbored heretical opinions. It didn't really matter. God could tell the difference and would deal with such wretches accordingly. In the here and now, so long as the heretic did not spout his blasphemies in the street, the tavern, or the pew, then others were not at immediate risk of infection.

Obstinacy, another of Grosseteste's keywords, was just as important. There was no need to rush to judgment when confronted with a seemingly heretical deed or utterance. To be guilty of full-fledged heresy a person had to be aware that his behavior contradicted orthodoxy, and he had to persist in that behavior. The theological term for this is pertinacity. Often, the suspected heretic might simply have been acting out of ignorance, confusion, or habit. Perhaps he was brought up by heretical parents and had never been exposed to what the established church regarded as pure doctrine. The obvious litmus test for distinguishing between unintentional and willful heresy was to inform the supposed heretic of the church's acceptable teachings and see how he reacted. If he agreed to conform, then that, after the exaction of suitable penances, was usually the end of the matter. If, however, he clung to his heterodox notions, then the more gruesome punishments could be unleashed.

Problem solved and terms neatly defined, then. To be a heretic was to dissent publicly and repeatedly from genuine Christianity. The heretic was far worse than the pagan, Muslim, or Jew. Such people had never had the chance to embrace the Christian message. The heretics, by contrast, had been shown the way toward eternal bliss, but they had traveled other roads. They had betrayed Christ and, during the many centuries when Christianity was intimately connected with political power, they had also threatened to undermine social order and cohesion: they were as treacherous as regicidal maniacs and more infectious than the most virulent pandemic.

⏗

This anti-heretical logic, and it prevailed throughout most of Christian history, possesses a certain uncompromising elegance, but we might wonder if it didn't rest on some very shaky foundations: at root, the notion that there was a single, obvious, and authentic version of Christianity to which all true believers should subscribe. Such an idea, at least from our modern perspective, is very hard to countenance.

The thorny issue of what Christians ought to believe has never been resolved to everyone's satisfaction. Almost from the outset, as soon as the apostle Paul began scurrying around the towns and cities of the ancient Mediterranean, divisions, theological fault lines, and unseemly animosities began to emerge. Over the course of the next twenty-one Christian centuries, the chasms only grew deeper and the rows only became more boisterous. Instead of a united Christian commonwealth, there would be factions, rivalries, schisms, and reformations.

The fifth-century cleric Vincent of Lérins famously declared that it was the good Christian's duty to adhere to what had been believed everywhere, always, and by everyone. This fits perfectly with the enduring campaign to expunge heresy. There was a default Christian position and those who headed off down alternative devotional, ecclesiastical, or theological avenues were heretical. The trouble is, given the manifest diversity of Christian musing and practice, it becomes hard to discern what Vincent's talk of "everywhere, always, and by everyone" could possibly mean.

This raises an intriguing possibility. Perhaps heresy was sometimes little more than a convenient construct. Theological battles

were fought, certain ideas emerged victorious, and they were gar-
landed with the name of orthodoxy. Other ideas were cast upon the
heretical scrap heap. The process was very useful (it helped to stave
off chaos by providing a theological anchor and it certainly helped
the Christian church to emerge as a neatly defined powerhouse),
but it was sometimes decidedly arbitrary.

To be fair, some heretical deeds and musings were so outrageous that they were always likely to be condemned. Take Aldebert of Soissons, who, in the eighth century, managed to convince a
band of followers that he was a divinely inspired prophet and gave
them clippings of his fingernails as if he were dispensing precious
holy relics. Or Tanchelm of Antwerp, who denounced every clergyman in twelfth-century Christendom, rejected all Christian rituals,
and encouraged his acolytes to drink his bathwater. Or the band
of fourteenth-century Swiss heretics who, so the (most likely apocryphal) story went, preached that the soul of a louse was worth as
much as the soul of a man, that communion bread should be fed
to pigs, and that having sex on an altar during Mass had as much
salvific value as partaking of the holy sacrament.

Sometimes, heresy was clearly the product of unsettled minds,
as when Leutard of Vertus, around the year 1000, claimed that a
dream about mischievous swarming bees had inspired him to start
smashing crucifixes in his local church. After being taken to task
by the local bishop, Leutard killed himself by jumping into a well.
The advice of the medieval cleric Geoffrey of Auxerre sometimes
seemed appropriate: heretics, he suggested, should be made to
drink a tonic derived from the hellebore plant — a tried and tested
palliative for insanity.[6]

These were only the most outlandish, most aberrant examples
of heresy, however. Heresy was not the preserve of wild-haired
prophets. As we will see time and again in what follows, it was also
something in which priests, erudite theologians, and sober-minded

Christians regularly indulged. It was the pastime of serious and devout people at the heart of the Christian establishment who had simply fastened onto alternative ways of interpreting the malleable Christian message. As one concerned third-century theologian asked, "What if a bishop, if a deacon, if a widow, if a virgin, if a doctor, if even a martyr, falls away from the rule of faith. Will heresies on that account appear to possess the truth?"[7] It was a very good question.

Heresy was often in the eye of the beholder, and the Catholic writer Hilaire Belloc, for all his flaws, was on to something when he observed that the term has always been used in many different ways because it can represent any one of fifty things.

This realization allows us to pose some searching questions about the fundamental nature of Christianity. We have to ask why there has been so much Christian heresy (far more than in any of the world's other great faith traditions). Perhaps dissent and unregulated speculation were bred in the Christian bone and perhaps that is quite easy to explain. Christianity's founding texts are crammed with potential contradictions, they discuss extraordinarily confusing ideas (a god becoming a man; a godhead split in three), and they represent a heady mix of Judaic tradition and Greek philosophical nostrums. They also fail to provide much concrete advice about how to build a church. It is hardly surprising that Christians have disagreed so often and so passionately.

Heresy allows us to prod and probe these tensions, all the way from the ancient era down to the present day. Over the course of this book we will see heretics conjuring up alternative ideas about the nature of God, Christ, and the universe, about how to achieve salvation, about the best ways to worship, and about the advisability (or lack thereof) of harnessing faith to political power. What were the right rituals, should there be an elevated priestly caste, which texts should be regarded as sacred? They argued about whether it was better to baptize mewling children or theologically well versed adults and over the question of whether holy images are wonderful devotional aids or loathsome commandment-breaking atrocities.

The story of heresy exposes all of these Christian squabbles, and many more besides. It provides a ringside seat at a two-thousand-year battle over the meaning of Christianity, and it also reminds us that if ancient and more recent theological conflicts had fallen out differently, the complexion of mainstream Christianity might have been very different. Happenstance often played a starring role.

∽

This is a short volume about a vast subject. You should think of it as a primer, but I hope it achieves a few important goals. First and foremost I want to tell some of the fascinating heretical stories (some familiar, many neglected) that have energized and confused the Christian enterprise. I also plan to emphasize the extraordinarily creative role that heresy has played. It was important in its own right (a veritable breeding ground of religious speculation) but, with no small amount of irony, it also did many favors to the cause of orthodoxy. Heresy was always orthodoxy's grumpy but indispensable twin. The heretical challenges forced the Christian majority to clarify its positions. When some ancient heretic announced his latest ruminations on the nature of Christ, the champions of emerging shibboleths were obliged to leap into action. When some medieval heretic questioned the role of the clerical establishment, the powers-that-were had little choice but to defend their status. Oddly, heresy was one of the best things that ever happened to orthodox Christianity.

Finally, I will be obliged to take you into some very choppy interpretative waters. When confronted by the story of Christian heresy it is very hard to resist the temptation to sit in judgment. Our hearts bleed and we wonder why countless centuries' worth of Christians found it impossible to bask in the glorious, seemingly inevitable confusion of their faith. Why did differences of opinion have to lead to foulmouthed catfights, scatological imagery, executions, banishments, and ash-making exhumations? We might even be persuaded to construct a narrative of heresy populated by heroes and villains: the nasty, ingenuity-smiting church versus the plucky, freethinking heretics.

This is a very understandable response. To us, the assault on heresy can seem ridiculous and vindictive. Just think of that medieval definition of heresy: the heretic's great crime was to follow an "opinion chosen by human perception." To chastise something as laudable as intellectual curiosity strikes us as loathsome. Almost instinctively, we want to agree with the Quaker Benjamin Furly who, back in 1694, offered an alternative definition of heresy: it was one of the "most pernicious words that have, for one thousand years, obtained amongst mankind." It was, he said, a concept that had been used to attack honest, generous-spirited people who had been so bold as to profess and practice what they believed. The heretics were those who had sought to cast out "the bugbear of authority — tradition."[8]

I would caution against joining this chorus of disapproval too eagerly, however: at least in our role as students of history. It is worth remembering that current, rather cozy definitions of intellectual and religious freedom, pluralism, or ecumenism are inventions of the modern age. The later parts of this book will trace their emergence, but the undeniable fact is that during the sixteen hundred years before Benjamin Furly hardly anyone was interested in a theological free-for-all in which differing religious visions could happily coexist.

Yes, there was sometimes grumbling about the excesses of the heresy hunters. When Conrad of Marburg embarked upon a vicious crusade in thirteenth-century Germany he left a legacy of trumped-up accusations and communal burnings in his wake. When those who balked at his reckless behavior assassinated him in July 1233, there was general rejoicing. This only meant that Conrad was deemed to be taking things much too far: it did not signal a rejection of the dream of imposing cohesion and uniformity of belief, preferably by gentler means, on the Christian world.

There were also those who sought to limit the number of essential Christian doctrines and practices. There was no point falling out over every last detail of worship, and when it came to matters indifferent (*adiaphora* is the technical term) there was room for latitude. But this never did much damage to the idea that there was a central, orthodox core (however you happened to define it) that should never be assailed.

The key point is that searching for antecedents of modern philosophical assumptions in the past can be a perilous undertaking. Past individuals sometimes complained about their beliefs being insulted and assaulted (of course they did!) but it would be erroneous to position them as champions of a *human right* to religious freedom. Similarly, people sometimes objected when their thinking was curtailed, and others argued that there should be more room for speculation than the prevailing cultural mood allowed. It is even possible to locate instances of earlier figures bucking the trend and suggesting that coercing anyone into a particular belief was a fool's errand: any genuine belief, especially of the religious variety, had to be freely developed. Again, however, this was all a very long way from supporting a *right* to intellectual freedom. The whole concept of human rights, let's remember, is a construct (albeit an excellent one) of the modern era.

Finally, we have to recognize that those rare ancient, medieval, and Reformation-era moments when different faiths managed to coexist were almost always created by pragmatic necessity (the quest to sustain social and political order, to find some temporary

mechanism for "getting along"), not some principled, latter-day belief in liberty or pluralism.

The past, in sum, had different attitudes and, crucially, they
were not limited to those who happened to wield ecclesiastical
and cultural power. It was often the mob that led the anti-heretical
charge and, while the established church was intolerant of supposedly heretical movements, such movements were equally intolerant of the established church and, crucially, of each other. It could
even be argued that the so-called heretics were often more irascible
and more theologically snooty than anyone: they simply lacked the
wherewithal to carry through their exclusivist vision.

I only ask that you bear all this in mind. Asking why these vanished eras saw things so differently is a far more nourishing pursuit
than slamming down our judge's gavels. This introductory chapter
began (rather shamelessly) with a wealth of poignant tales and, unless your heart is calcified, you doubtless began to feel sorry for the
heretics. It ended with a raft of caveats and a reminder that the past
(as it was perfectly entitled to do) interpreted and encountered religious belief in ways we'd now find deeply puzzling. This, assuredly,
is to throw a spanner into the hermeneutic works, but it serves an
important purpose: it reveals just how confusing and difficult interpreting the history of heresy can be.

Here is the rule of thumb. We can still feel sorry for those who
were broiled alive, we can recognize that many people in the past
would have preferred to live quiet lives in which religious animosity
was kept to a minimum, and we certainly do not have to think of
our ancestors as mindless automatons dutifully following the party
line. What we should avoid is any concept of an ethically nourishing, millennia-long moral conflict in which individual freedom was
pitted against authoritarian repression. The terms of such a narrative (and the outrage it provokes) are our own. If we adopt it, we run
the risk of promoting an unhelpfully triumphalist perspective in
which our moral assumptions (every bit as contingent and histori-

cally determined as those of our forebears) are mistaken for superior inevitabilities: stupid old them, we might say, and wonderfully evolved new us. This really won't do.

∽

Instead, let us utilize the history of heresy as an extraordinary prism. It shows us what happens when a fledgling, persecuted faith turns into a politically sanctioned, world-girdling religion; it takes us deep inside the engine rooms of Christian power; and, above all else, it reveals just how fascinating, supple, and boisterous Christianity has been.

A second-century philosopher called Celsus had many mean-spirited things to say about the upstart faith that was steadily winning over converts across the Roman Empire. One of his favorite tactics was to pour scorn on all the divisions and dissensions that were cropping up within the Christian fraternity. He equated Christians with squabbling frogs, croaking their versions of the truth in a marsh. He was absolutely right, insofar as he saw, very early on, that heresy and Christianity were destined to walk hand in hand. He also missed a crucial point. The thing about a marsh is that it can be fertile. Life isn't easy there, the potential to get bogged down awaits you with every step (or hop), but if you somehow manage to carve out an existence (even for a little while) then you have done very well and, if you are lucky, you might even thrive. That, in the nutshell that Celsus never intended, is the story of Christianity, and the history of heresy reminds us of just how treacherous and fecund the waters could become.

This book is neither an apology for orthodoxy nor a rallying cry for the virtues of heresy. There are enough of both already. It is an examination (hopefully one that steers toward objectivity) of the Christian muddle. Enter, then, Gnostics dreaming up a spellbinding, myth-rich cosmos created by a mischievous demiurge, fourth-century clerics quarreling about the identity of Jesus Christ, emperors in eighth-century Byzantium blinding those who dared to paint religious images, the heresiarchs of the Reformation upsetting every theological apple cart in town, and the colonists of seventeenth-century New England reinventing heresy in their brave new devotional world.

If we want to know why Christianity turned out as it did, why some battles were won and others lost, and why the battles had to be fought in the first place, we could do much worse than walk alongside the heretical cavalcade. Our first port of call is the early church. It was there, in the buffeted communities of cities like Carthage, Antioch, and Ephesus, that heresy was invented. It was there that the search for Christian unity took root. It was also where everything began to unravel and where Christianity began to prove just how fragmented, puzzling, and enthralling it could be.

2

The Invention of Heresy

Ignatius

> Man by man, become a choir, that being harmonious in love, and
> taking up the song of God in unison, you may with one voice sing
> to the Father through Jesus Christ, so that he may both hear you
> and perceive by your works that you are indeed the members of his
> Son. It is profitable, therefore, that you should live in a blameless
> unity, so you may always enjoy communion with God.
>
> — Ignatius of Antioch, Letter to the Ephesians

In about 107 c.e., Ignatius, bishop of Antioch, was hauled before the Roman emperor Trajan. "Who are you, wicked wretch," the
furious emperor asked, "to set yourself up to transgress our commands?" Call me Theophorus, the bishop calmly replied — the God
bearer who has Christ in his heart. The seventy-year-old Ignatius
was in provocative form. Every last god in the Romans' pantheon
was a demon, he declared, and he would never offer sacrifices to
them. "There is only one God, who made heaven, earth, and sea
and all that are in them; and one Jesus Christ, the only-begotten
son of God, whose kingdom I hope to enjoy." And enjoy it he soon
would. Trajan ordered that Ignatius "be bound by soldiers, and carried to the great city of Rome, there to be devoured by the beasts
for the gratification of the people." Ignatius, so we are told, cried out

with joy: he clasped the chains as they were fastened around him and, delighted by the prospect of martyrdom, he departed "like a distinguished ram, the leader of a goodly flock."[1]

He took a winding route from Antioch (in present-day Turkey) to Rome, journeying on foot through Macedonia and traversing the islands of the Adriatic. His days and weeks were arduous — he described the brutish imperial troops who accompanied him as vicious leopards — but he found great solace in writing letters to the scattered Christian churches that had begun to spring up over the past few decades: to the wealthy port of Ephesus, on the west coast of Anatolia, to the mineral-rich region of Magnesia, and to the churches of Tralles, Smyrna, and Philadelphia.

These letters had one resounding aim: to inspire concord and solidarity between (and within) distant Christian communities. They were saturated by pleas for unity and fierce denunciations of heterodoxy and, as Ignatius knew full well, this was the most urgent of tasks. The growth of Christianity had been spectacular or, at the very least, surprising. In short measure it had expanded its reach from the Jewish heartlands of the Middle East to gentile communities across the empire, but even at this early stage squabbles and divisions were beginning to appear. Ignatius was not best pleased with this development.

As he informed the Christians of Ephesus, it was vital "that you may be perfectly joined together in the same mind, and in the same judgment, and may all speak the same concerning the same thing." They must all "run together in accordance with the will of God." As for how this was to be achieved, Ignatius recommended trusting and obeying the bishops: the people who, since they were God's representatives on earth, should be looked upon "just as we would upon the Lord himself." Those who dissented were to be cast out: "No sect has any dwelling place among you." As Ignatius warned Tralles, "Use Christian nourishment only, and abstain from herbage of a different kind: I mean heresy." Heretics were those who "mix up Jesus Christ with their own poison, like those who administer a deadly drug in sweet wine."[2]

Close to the end of his journey, Ignatius wrote one final letter to the Christians of Rome. He took special pains to dissuade them from showing "unseasonable goodwill toward me." If they were overly kind, or if they urged him to try to escape his impending death, then he might succumb to their pleas. He was fearful that the love of brotherhood would hinder his zeal toward the Lord. Far better, Ignatius advised, to treat him as "the wheat of God, and let me be ground by the teeth of wild beasts that I may become the pure bread of Jesus Christ."

And so, on the thirteenth day before the calends of January (December 20), after praying with his brethren that persecution might one day cease, Ignatius was killed in a Roman amphitheater, in the shadow of one of the pagan temples he so despised. His remains were wrapped in linen and sent back to Antioch "as an inestimable treasure left to the holy church by the grace which was in the martyr." Back in Rome, on the night following his death, some Christians reported having visions of Ignatius, "still dripping with sweat, as if he had just come from his great labor, standing by the Lord."[3]

ↄ

We will never know how reliable the surviving account of Ignatius's condemnation and martyrdom is, but in many ways this doesn't matter a jot. It was an exercise in hagiography, after all, so it is the awe-inspiring, propagandist content that truly counts. That mighty image — the recently slaughtered martyr dripping with sweat, standing in paradise alongside Christ — is hard to forget. Ignatius, a solicitous bishop since his thirties, the man who snubbed his nose at a Roman emperor, the martyr who went gleefully to his death, seemed to sum up everything that was best about the very early church.

Thanks to people like Ignatius of Antioch, Christians of many different stripes would look back on the church's first centuries as a golden age. Many of them still do. It was, so the oft-told tale would have us believe, an age of simplicity, when Christ's unsullied teachings held sway, and before all the endless bickering became too rancorous, or too debilitating. There was (as Ignatius would certainly have insisted) a single, self-evident Christian message, and if false prophets sprang up, they were eagerly denounced and driven out. It was also an age before the worldly compromises with political power, before church and state became embroiled, before corruption set in. Christians were righteous victims, strangers in the world, constantly being assayed in the furnace of persecution. There was cogency, purity, and valor back then, before it all went so terribly wrong.

This has proven to be an extraordinarily resilient image but, when all is said and done, it is distorted. Hankering after a pristine Christian era has always made excellent strategic sense. Those who have done so (and they have existed in every Christian century) have been able to denounce contemporary corruption, conflict, and backsliding, and they have been able to portray themselves as the people who can finally set things back on track. Authentic Christianity has been there all along; its message simply has to be rediscovered and fulfilled. We simply have to complete the work of the apostles and brave men like Ignatius of Antioch. It is a very powerful myth, the stuff of reform and reformation, but, in many ways, a myth is all it ever was.

The period of the early church was actually one of the most befuddled and contested in Christianity's history. Almost everything was in flux and the notion of a single Christian truth had already proven itself to be chimerical. Men like Ignatius of Antioch might have yearned for a constant, regnant orthodoxy but, as Christians from Antioch to Rome to Ephesus were proving every day, it simply didn't exist. Christianity did not fall, fully formed, from the sky, and a cohesive, affable Christian commonwealth was, and would remain, a distant prospect. Dreams of concord had to be invented, and they were hammered out on the anvil of heresy.

In the different corners of what would come to be known as Christendom — whether western Europe, the eastern Mediterranean, or North Africa — divergent Christian identities were emerging, replete with their competing theological passions. The thriving centers of early Christian thought (places like Alexandria and Ignatius's own Antioch) were always likely to be bitter rivals as much as bosom allies. There was endless competition for political and intellectual influence and there were countless bones of theological contention.

Arguments about doctrine, privileged texts, the puzzling issue of how to confront the Jewish past, and the very identity of the Son and the Father were all gathering momentum. Even the precise role of Ignatius's much-loved bishops was still unclear to a persecuted faith whose members often had to worship clandestinely and whose ecclesiological structures were still being determined. Ignatius's bold suggestion, that the bishop of Rome deserved ecclesiastical primacy, often rang hollow. Saint Peter, the rock upon whom the Christian edifice was built, had happened to die in the city, but this hardly altered the fact that much of the new faith's dynamism and intellectual energy resided in cities that lay several hundred miles to the east.

Ignatius was every bit as good a flatterer as he was a martyr, and in his letters he was sure to praise the people he was addressing: of course they would follow his advice, of course they would readily identify and expunge heresy, of course they would heed their bishops and deacons. The trouble was, many people were doing precisely the opposite and it was awfully difficult to tell the difference between orthodoxy and heresy: the stark division between Christian truth and Christian error was still *in ovo*.

Ignatius could bravely inform Trajan of his belief in "one God, who made heaven, earth, and sea and all that are in them; and one Jesus Christ, the only-begotten son of God" but, for many, this didn't answer the fundamental questions of who God and Jesus Christ actually were and what relationship they enjoyed. It certainly did not provide a blueprint for what the fledgling Christian church should look like. Christians would struggle with such conundrums throughout their first centuries and the earliest stirrings of these ferocious disputes were well known to Ignatius himself.

The letters that Ignatius wrote are beautiful. They encapsulate the peril and the passion of the early church like few other documents but they also have a whiff of desperation about them. If defining Christianity was really so straightforward then Ignatius would not have been obliged to spend his final tragic weeks barking at his co-religionists to fall into line.

Many of the things Christians now take for granted — a satisfying elucidation of the Trinity, an accepted canon of scripture — lay decades, even centuries in the future. Given all this, it is hard to discern what Ignatius's talk of "running in accordance with the will of God" was supposed to mean. The existence of two groups at the heart of the early Christian enterprise makes this point particularly well.

MARCION AND GNOSTICISM

> I have had a brush with this sect myself . . . women who believed this nonsense offered it to me . . . What is more, they tried to seduce me. I was young and this made me attractive to them . . . Outwardly [they were] very charming, but all the devil's ugliness was in their vile minds.
>
> — EPIPHANIUS[4]

The great North African theologian Tertullian would have his own flirtations with heterodoxy (he would become enamored of the provocative Montanist movement — a phenomenon to which we'll turn in a few pages' time). Before this descent into what many re-garded as heresy, he had been something of a paragon of Christian virtue. After being converted to Christianity during his thirties he began to deploy his extraordinary rhetorical skills (unmatched in the early church for their vim and venom) in praise and defense of the new faith: exploring its spirituality, lauding its martyrs, and excoriating its heretics.

He had despised one heresiarch above all others. In one of his most bilious works Tertullian wrote some deeply unpleasant things about the Black Sea province of Pontus. "The fiercest nations in-habit it," he explained, "if indeed it can be called *habitation,* when life is passed in wagons." Such people had no fixed abodes, their life had "no germ of civilization," and they indulged "their libidi-nous desires without restraint." Worse still, as Tertullian's rabid rant continued, "They cut up the dead bodies of their parents with their sheep and devour them at their feasts." And yet, Tertullian con-cluded, "nothing in Pontus is so barbarous and sad as the fact that Marcion was born there." He was colder than its winter, more brittle than its ice, more craggy than the Caucasus Mountains. Marcion, dubbed the "firstborn of Satan" by his enemies, was perhaps the most despised heretic in the early church, and also among the most dangerous since, as Tertullian lamented, his teachings had filled the whole world. Across much of the Roman Empire, his followers, like swarms of wasps, built their heretical honeycombs in imitation of bees.[5] His alleged crime was twofold: he had renounced the entire legacy of Jewish scripture (what Christians would now refer to as the Old Testament) and he had invented a second god. He was bold, if nothing else.

A wealthy ship owner from Sinope, Marcion traveled to Rome in or around the year 140 C.E. At first, he made an excellent im-pression on the local Christian community, not least through his contribution of 200,000 sesterces (a very generous sum) to the church's coffers. Very quickly, however, eyebrows began to be raised at Marcion's radical cosmological vision. Determined to cast off the Jewish heritage, Marcion suggested that the Christian God, the father of Jesus, a God of love, was an entirely different entity from the fickle, wrathful deity of the Hebrew scriptures.

Marcion was articulating (in exaggerated, sometimes unsavory form) Christianity's determination to distinguish itself from the Judaic past. Christianity was often very keen to portray itself as a radically new religious tradition: a legitimate spiritual alternative rather than just another Jewish sect. Given the subsequent, often unedifying relationship between Judaism and Christianity, we might imagine that this was easily and instantly accomplished. Not so. Christ, after all, was a Jew, as were his disciples, and his ministry was aimed almost exclusively at his fellow-religionists. He was, by all accounts, the fulfillment of the messianic prophecies of Jewish scripture. Had Christianity never moved beyond Palestine, the new faith's Jewish credentials would doubtless have continued to receive suitable emphasis but, with the odysseys of the apostle Paul, the Christian message spread out across the largely gentile eastern Mediterranean.

This provoked an almighty headache. How were gentile converts to behave: Were they to adopt the dietary and ritualistic habits of Judaism? Were they to undergo circumcision — the ancient ritual sign of Abraham's covenant with God?

Paul said no, and at the Council of Jerusalem in about 50 C.E. (less a council as we would now understand the term, and more an ad hoc meeting of local luminaries) a momentous decision was reached. Gentile converts to Christianity would not be required to abide by most of the tenets of Jewish ritualistic law. There was a new covenant, one that supplanted Abraham's, and Christianity was set on course to be a novel, distinctive religion. This certainly didn't please everyone within the Christian fraternity, and the first century saw the emergence of numerous groups (the so-called Ebionites being the most discussed example) who sought to sustain a conspicuously Jewish Christianity, insisting upon the continued dominance of Mosaic law and denouncing Paul's encounters with the gentile world.

Ultimately, however, such groups garnered a great deal of criticism (some of the very first accusations of Christian heresy, in fact) and the notion of a necessary break with the Jewish past became the majority position within the fledgling church. So far, so palatable for Marcion but, by his reckoning, the rupture was still not sufficiently radical. Very few Christians were unwilling to turn their back on the whole Jewish inheritance. The Hebrew scriptures were avidly recruited as earlier signposts to the brave new Christian future, while the deeds of Jewish heroes and the musings of Jewish prophets continued to be a source of Christian inspiration. As our friend Ignatius of Antioch put it, it was time to lay aside the old, sour leaven, and be "changed into the new leaven, that is Jesus Christ" but, as Ignatius was careful to add, while the new Gospel was of a different, better caliber — "transcendent," as Ignatius put it, and "the perfection of immortality" — the Jewish prophets were not to be abandoned.[6] Christians (like the Ebionites) who clung too tenaciously to Jewish practices and theological nostrums — Ignatius called them Judaizers — were to be vilified, but in spite of their excesses it was still important for Christians to take cognizance of the Jewish legacy. This allowed the new faith to construct a millennia-old historical narrative and pedigree, one that stretched back to the time of Adam, and one in which the arrival of Christ represented the fulfillment of ancient salvific promises.

This is precisely what Marcion found so objectionable. In his scheme, Christ had nothing whatsoever to do with the Jewish days of yore, and he insisted that the Jewish scriptural canon should be thrown out in its entirety. In fact, his list of acceptable Christian texts included only a bowdlerized version of Luke's Gospel and ten of the Epistles of Paul (Marcion's great apostolic hero). Marcion had deployed extreme editorial violence (using the knife, not the pen, as Tertullian put it) in deciding which scriptures were legitimate.

Even more unsettling was Marcion's suggestion that the whole material universe was the creation of this non-Christian Old Testament god, and that all the matter within the cosmos was evil. Christians were to have as little as possible to do with this fleshly realm; they were to shun sensual pleasure and live lives of extreme asceticism. This also meant, by Marcion's calculation, that Christ (the son of the true God) could not possibly have defiled himself by assuming creaturely form. Instead, Marcion adopted the position known as Docetism, whereby Jesus had only appeared to take on a physical body: the "likeness of sinful flesh," as Romans 8:3 (one of Marcion's approved texts) helpfully put it.

Docetists (from *dokein,* a Greek word meaning "to seem") were a common sight in the early church (it is likely that they were just the sorts of heretics that got Ignatius of Antioch so riled up in his letters). Uncomfortable with the idea that a god could really assume human shape, they made the radical suggestion that Christ's incarnation had been little more than an illusion. He had no human flesh or intellect, no rational soul. Christ was a mirage. The body that was crucified had not been divine; Mary had not given birth to a god. The divine essence had simply and spectrally taken on the appearance of a man. Perhaps the clearest signal of Marcion's sympathy with this theological position was his removal of the familiar birth narrative from Luke's Gospel: for Marcion, such a sordid event as Christ's emergence from the bowels of a human being, Mary, was repugnant.

Needless to say, many corners of the Christian world found much to object to in all this (although it is important to stress that it went down rather well in others). Marcion seemed to provide powerful ammunition for those, like Tertullian, who argued that the worst heresies were the progeny of overly speculative imaginations. At a time when Christianity was trying to impress Greek speakers, there was considerable advantage in seeking out some synthesis with the fashionable tenets of Greek philosophy. Deciding how far this dialogue ought to be taken was the cause of bitter debate within the Christian fraternity, however.

Some Christian theologians — Origen and Clement of Alexandria are perhaps the most obvious examples — were delighted to turn Christianity into a sophisticated, jargon-rich philosophical undertaking. Others were not so sure and they came up with a resonant rallying cry: "What has Athens to do with Jerusalem?" or, as Tertullian put it, "What is there in common between the philosopher and the Christian, between the pupil of Hellas and the pupil of heaven?"[7] For many, the wayward thought of some Christians, Marcion included, was a direct result of the deleterious impact of Greek philosophical ideas. Marcion was being far too clever for his own good.

The idea of a noncorporeal Christ was especially problematic because, if Christ's sacrifice on the cross was to be of genuine benefit to mankind then, as most theologians agreed, it was paramount that he had actually suffered as a human being. In the human part of himself he had to be just like the people for whose sins he was atoning. Anything less would have represented an empty redemptive gesture. As for the notion of an earlier, competing Old Testament god, this obviously flew in the face of Christianity's monotheistic message. Unsurprisingly, Marcion was excommunicated by the church in Rome in 144 C.E. (though at least his generous donation was returned to him), but in the coming years his ideas won over large numbers of recruits.

Something approaching a rival Marcionite ecclesiastical structure grew up, which dealt a blow to Tertullian's point that heretics were always "motherless, houseless, creedless outcasts, wandering about in their own essential worthlessness."[8] On the contrary, Marcionites were very well organized, self-confident, and possessed of a creed, and they continued to thrive after Marcion's death in 160 C.E., surviving in some places until well into the third century. People continued to moan about Marcion in Crete, Cyprus, and Rome, and across Anatolia. It has even been argued that Marcionism was among the first varieties of Christianity to firmly establish itself in some eastern towns and cities: a further challenge to any concept of an original, orthodox core at the center of the Christian tradition. "In all cases," Tertullian argued, "truth precedes its copy," but in some places it seems possible that Marcion's ideas came to prominence very early on.[9]

∽

Marcion was one of the first thinkers to articulate an abiding theme of Christian heresy: the troublesome dualistic notion of two gods (or, at least, one true God and an imperfect demiurge who created the material universe). The idea would recur among the Bogomils of the tenth-century Balkans and among everyone's favorite medieval heretics, the Cathars. It would also inspire the Gnostics.

Marcion is routinely grouped together with leading Gnostic thinkers such as Valentinus (c. 100–c. 175) and Basilides (c. 120–c. 145), although it is vital to stress that his idiosyncratic vision lacked many of their more exotic theological concoctions. Full-fledged Gnosticism, if we accept it as a coherent heretical movement (and we'll see in a moment that this is up for debate), went to far more elaborate lengths to flesh out its mythos and populate its universe with a bewildering cast of divine and semidivine characters.

In the beginning, as one school of Gnostic thought explained, there had indeed been only one God: a being of pure spirit, unknowable, unapproachable, inhabiting an infinite realm. Ages passed in stillness and inaction, but then God's seed entered the womb of silence and a host of emanations, or spiritual forces (mind, truth, reason, prudence among them), emerged. Unfortunately, the last of these forces (Sophia, or Wisdom) turned out to be something of a cosmological disaster. She had the arrogance to emulate God's powers and to do some creating of her own. For this crime she was cast out of the infinite realm (*pleroma*). Alone and adrift, Sophia could manage to fashion only a monster, who in turn created a demiurge. This demiurge was flawed, limited, and a decidedly unreliable workman (more an inept journeyman than a skilled master craftsman), but this did not deter him from creating mankind and the universe that we all still inhabit.

Here, the overlap with Marcion's ideas is clearly visible. This universe, just like Marcion's, was chaotic and disjointed, a place of sin, natural disasters, and disease. The entire material world — every atom of it — was corrupt and repulsive: and, crucially, it had nothing whatsoever to do with the original God of the *pleroma.*

All was not lost for mankind, however. Some human beings retained a spark of the original divine spirit, of the infinite deep. Salvation consisted of acquiring secret knowledge (gnosis) so that, at the time of death, this spark could escape the prison of the material world and, via an extraordinary journey through the stars, return to the *pleroma.* Making this possible had been Jesus Christ's great achievement. He had been sent to impart this arcane knowledge so that at least some of humanity (by most accounts a tiny minority) might be saved.

It is immediately obvious that much of this has little to do with Marcion. It is also important to realize that this tidy (slightly caricatured) account of just one variety of Gnostic cosmology collapses the diversity of Gnostic thought into a single, relatively digestible schema: it is exotic, but at least we can get the gist. The truth was far more discombobulating. Within the divergent Gnostic "schools" there were many different variations on a creation myth, many different ways of interpreting the role of Christ, and many competing casts of divine and subdivine characters. The vision of one Gnostic was likely to be different from the vision of another and, as some recent scholars have convincingly argued, this calls the whole concept of Gnosticism into question. Gnosticism, to borrow one of its most eminent historian's phrases, is a dubious category. It is a later attempt to impose a false unity on a staggeringly wide-ranging religious phenomenon. As another historian, Karen King, puts it, "The literature defies attempts to force its theological diversity into snug categorical cubby holes."[10]

Until the middle of the twentieth century, our understanding of Gnosticism relied heavily on its enemies: the first great heresiologists of the early church. In the absence of a reliable corpus of genuine Gnostic texts, all we had to hand were the negative caricatures of what has reasonably been called a "severe and cantankerous genre."[11] Trawling through such books is an entertaining but ultimately bewildering proposition for the modern reader. Our heads inevitably spin when confronted with the bizarre compendia of sordid allegations and claims that Gnosticism represented some clumsy collision of Greek philosophy, sorcery, and astrology.

Fortunately, everything changed in 1945. In December of that year, an Egyptian peasant farmer headed into the hills near Nag Hammadi to dig for fertilizer. He discovered a clay jar containing twelve complete papyrus codices and a few leaves of a thirteenth: they contained no fewer than fifty-four authentic Gnostic-looking tracts — new sayings of Jesus Christ, alternative gospels, divergent creation myths, and a host of hymns and prayers. It was the most sensational of accidental discoveries (one that ranks alongside the unearthing of the Dead Sea Scrolls). Over the past few decades, scholars have been diligently translating and editing these texts and they reveal just how diverse Gnostic thought could be.

It still makes sense to talk of recurrent Gnostic themes — a differentiation between the true God and the creator god, a stark distinction between soul and body, the importance of attaining secret knowledge — but simplistic caricatures of Gnosticism have been sensibly abandoned.

All this recent work has also bolstered the idea that we should not dismiss Gnosticism as nothing more than a heretical offshoot from the Christian mainstream. It is better, perhaps, to think of it as a distinct, though far from cohesive, religious phenomenon. The great Gnostic thinkers undoubtedly regarded themselves as Christians — that was what so irked their critics — but they were also part of a far broader tradition: one that drew influences from trends in Greek philosophy and various Near Eastern religious movements. Gnosticism managed to articulate a theme that transcended the narrow concerns of Christianity: what the modern philosophical lexicon might describe as a sense of alienation from the material world and a considered attempt to explain evil and suffering.

Christianity has always struggled to account for the existence of evil in a universe purportedly created by an all-powerful, loving God. It has been suggested that evil is a necessary part of creation, something that Christians need to encounter if they are to enjoy spiritual growth, or that evil is entirely the result of mankind's misuse of its God-given free will. None of these solutions ever provided fully satisfactory answers to the nagging question of why God didn't fashion a perfect universe rather than one filled with earthquakes, murderers, and cancer victims. The Gnostics posited a far more satisfying answer: evil and suffering had nothing to do with God. Someone else (the incompetent demiurge) was to blame for their existence.

The depth and sophistication of ancient Gnosticism make it all the more depressing that it has been hijacked by the half-baked theorizing of the modern New Age movement. However, so far as its role in the history of Christian heresy is concerned, it was the caricatured version of Gnosticism that mattered most at the time. Many Gnostic leaders undoubtedly regarded themselves as Christians. They would have claimed that they were simply adapting the Gospel message in a different, but entirely devout way. Moreover, and this must certainly have convinced them of their legitimacy, they won over significant numbers of followers. Even in places that now stand as bywords for Christian orthodoxy, not least the city of Rome, active Gnostic communities flourished.

Because of all this, those of more conventional Christian sensibilities saw Gnosticism as an internal problem, not as an external threat. It was a movement that seemed to jeopardize the sustainability and cohesion of the entire Christian enterprise. From the second through the fourth centuries a succession of theologians penned detailed, ferocious attacks and the campaign against Gnosticism represented the first sustained attempt to systematically define and denounce a Christian heresy. It was hardly surprising that such theologians — Hippolytus (170–c. 236), Irenaeus of Lyon (c. 130–c. 200), and our old friend Tertullian — were so energized. There was, from their perspective, much to object to within the Gnostic vision.

The Gnostics' demiurge could sometimes look a lot like another, albeit lesser, God, another creator, which obviously queered the monotheistic pitch. Gnosticism also threatened to turn an avowedly inclusive religious tradition into the preserve of that minuscule minority who retained a spark of divinity, thus making Christ's sacrifice on the cross (in which he had atoned for the sins of *all* humanity) into an irrelevance. For the Gnostics, Christ's purpose had been the imparting of secret knowledge: events on Mount Calvary simply lost all significance. As for God the Father, again the Gnostics boldly undermined Christian notions of an interventionist, caring creator who could be encountered, or at least communicated with, via prayer, ritual, and devotional practice. For many Gnostics, the true God was still entirely out of reach: he was most likely uninterested in the events of a world he had not created, enjoying, instead, the splendid isolation of the infinite realm. For all Gnosticism's ingenuity, it is very difficult to see how — especially in the straitened circumstances of the early church, especially within the context of a proudly monotheistic religion — such a radically different interpretation of the Christian message could have gone unanswered.

In any event, the existence of Gnosticism certainly reminds us just how pliable early Christianity could be. If people could erect such extraordinary theological visions upon its foundations, then anything must have seemed possible. At two thousand years' distance it is very easy to conclude that Gnosticism, with its talk of two gods, its reevaluation of Christ's role, and its extravagant cosmology, was entirely aberrant. It is sobering to remember, however, that many of the earliest Christians looked at Gnosticism very differently: for them, it represented a feasible, if always slightly outlandish, Christian alternative.

〜

Heresy was not always about migrating toward radical theological extremes. Just as often, groups and individuals seized upon a broadly acceptable aspect of Christian belief or practice and explored it in new ways. In a sense, this was even part of the Gnostic enterprise: hatred of the world, since the world was a place of persecution, pervaded the early church, and the Christian penchant for asceticism arrived very early on the theological scene. Gnostics merely pursued this notion of alienation and world-weariness to its extreme.

The perfect example of the heretical ability to investigate and expand an otherwise unexceptionable idea can be found in the movement known as Montanism — our next ancient heresy and the one that appealed to as upstanding a theologian as the Gnostic-hating Tertullian.

THE MONTANISTS

> It was about the middle of the second century of Christianity that Montanus, the Arch-Heretic, and Proto-Patriarch of all Enthusiasts, made his appearance in the world. He was a native of Phrygia, and was no sooner converted to the Christian faith, than he appeared very zealous for the honour and improvement of his new religion . . . He began (as all heretics and schismatics . . .

generally do) with accusing and complaining of the bishops and
their clergy as careless and negligent in their duties, and remiss
in their discipline. He taxed them with want of zeal, and with
falling from their first love; with neglecting the spirit and life of
Christianity, and contenting themselves merely and only with the
bare and outward letter, and form of it. In a word, he confidently
charged them with being entirely void of the Spirit, and with
leading mere animal and physical lives.

— *Montanus Redivivus*[12]

During the mid-second century, news began to spread through the
towns and villages of Phrygia (a province of western Asia Minor)
of new Christian revelations. Two prophetesses, Maximilia and
Priscilla (or Prisca), had abandoned their husbands and families
in order to follow the religious leader Montanus — a man, according to the hostile historian Eusebius, who "in the unbounded lust
for power . . . became obsessed and suddenly fell into frenzy and
convulsion." In moments of spiritual possession and ecstatic frenzy
they saw visions of Christ's imminent second coming, of the beginning of his thousand-year rule on earth. Or, as Eusebius put it, they
had been filled with a bastard spirit, "so that they spoke madly, im-
properly, and strangely."[13]

In preparation for these last days Montanus and his followers
began to plan for a New Jerusalem in the east (on sites that modern
archaeology has only just begun to unearth) and to preach the most
strident of Christianities. The faithful were to practice chastity and
abstinence, to lead lives of strict asceticism (surviving on repasts
of radishes, as their critics alleged). Above all they were to resist
persecution with all their might, even to the point of seeking out
martyrdom when occasion arose. The Montanists were responding to what they perceived as a softening of Christian values: they
feared that a formerly rigorous faith was becoming complacent.
Far better, they suggested, to embrace deprivation, extreme penitential discipline, and, above all, persecution: the fan that cleansed

the Lord's threshing floor, separating the grain of martyrs and the chaff of deceivers. As one of their oracles put it, "Desire not to die in bed, nor in the delivery of children, nor by enervating fevers, but in martyrdom."[14]

There is room to wonder why any of this should have offended the early church. As we have seen, reputations were made through the embracing of persecution (just think of Ignatius of Antioch), and many early Christians subscribed, just like the Montanists, to the notion that Christ's second coming was imminent. Ultimately, though, it was the unregulated and extreme nature of Montanism that provoked such a fearsome backlash, especially as Montanist ideas began to spread westward, reaching as far as Italy and France. The Montanists seemed to be actively provoking the Roman authorities and relishing the bloody consequences. For those responsible for the preservation of a precarious church, it was very easy to denounce the Montanists as suicidal lunatics whose immoderate zeal brought Christianity into disrepute and unnecessary danger.

Worse yet, they were acting without the approval and oversight of clerical leaders. Montanism seemed to strike deeply at the emerging (and much cherished) notion of an apostolic succession of priests and bishops: they were allowing for the possibility that people other than priests (even women, for heaven's sake!) could play a role in discerning the will of God. Montanism dwelled on the unsettling notion that the Bible did not contain the entirety of the Christian message and that new revelations (as enjoyed by the likes of Maximilia and Priscilla) might be necessary. This was deemed offensive and, as one of Montanism's most strident critics put it, there was no place in Christianity for "novel furies . . . and mad dreams of new doctrines dreamed by mad women."[15]

The Montanists were charged with arrogance and pride, of suggesting that they were nothing less than the vessels of the Paraclete — the spirit, mentioned in John's Gospel, that Jesus had promised to send to instruct his disciples. As Hippolytus explained, only the stupid Christian could possibly be "captivated by wretched women . . . overrun with delusion" and think that they had learned something from them that was unavailable in scripture. The so-called Montanist prophets were following the dangerous example of Montanus himself, described by Jerome as the "the mouthpiece of an unclean spirit."[16] Theologians penned their denunciations of the movement, while orthodox bishops seized Montanist prophetesses and set about exorcising the restless demons who had supposedly possessed them.

The surviving statements of Montanists (though their authenticity is a matter of debate) do often seem to drip with hubris: "I am the lord God Almighty who has descended in a man," "I am the Paraclete," and so on. As most historians now agree, however, Montanists probably didn't expect such statements to be taken literally: they were merely suggesting that they were being used as an instrument, a vehicle through which God could speak. As that most memorable of Montanist oracles put it, these new prophets and prophetesses were the humble plectrums of the Lord playing his lyre. This was radical, but not nearly as radical as was often suggested. Nor, as much recent scholarship has demonstrated, were the Montanists trying to demolish the role of the priesthood: they were only seeking to put that role in context, suggesting that there was still some room for individual initiative in the religious experience. This was controversial, but it did not spell disaster: over the coming centuries, a good many Christians who never came close to being implicated as heretics espoused very similar ideas.

Thinking about Montanism in such terms is very useful. The Montanists latched on to ideas that would continually resurface within Christianity. Their embrace of persecution and asceticism only exaggerated an existing and widespread tendency: which is precisely why someone like Tertullian was won over to their cause. Throughout Christian history, the mystic or the self-flagellating hermit would sometimes be deemed acceptable, sometimes adjudged heretical. The decisions were often ludicrously arbitrary, but it usually came down to whether an individual was willing to come under clerical supervision. It was about regulation and containment, and in this regard the Montanists were perceived as deeply troubling. The fact that, in purely theological terms, it is possible to conclude that they weren't really heretics at all was easily overlooked. We will see this happening many times again.

BLUNTING THE CHALLENGES: CHRISTIAN UNITY

Montanism enjoyed considerable popularity. As late as the reign of Justinian, a sixth-century bishop of Ephesus would still be ordering the destruction of a shrine that was said to contain the remains of Montanus, Maximilia, and Priscilla.[17] Even some of Christianity's most doted upon martyrs — the Roman noblewoman Perpetua and the slave Felicitas, who perished in Carthage in 203 C.E. — have sometimes been suspected (though the case remains unproven) of harboring Montanist sympathies. But this was precisely the problem. The stubborn persistence and broad appeal of movements like Marcionism, Gnosticism, and Montanism heightened Christianity's sense of fragmentation, and some within the new faith were determined to blot them out. The more cracks that appeared, the greater the need to impose an artificial unity. Or so, at least, some eminent Christians decided.

We have already seen Ignatius and the anti-Gnostic writers engaged in this pursuit, but no one made a more elegant and enduring effort than one of Tertullian's fellow North African Christians, Cyprian of Carthage. Just like Ignatius, Cyprian would also perish at the hands of the Roman authorities: murdered in 258, though not before graciously tipping his executioner with twenty-five pieces of gold. Cyprian wrote his famous treatise on Christian unity, *De unitate ecclesiae,* as a response to specific historical circumstances, but his soaring phrases would transcend their local circumstances and be constantly invoked by later Christians.

For Cyprian, it was very simple. There was no salvation to be found outside the church, there could be only one church, and someone had to be in charge. As Christ had explained to Peter, "I will give unto you the keys of the kingdom of heaven: and whatsoever you shall bind on earth shall be bound in heaven; whatever you shall loose on earth shall be loosed in heaven." And from the apostles, the keys were passed on to a distinct priestly caste: the sole possessors of the church's *magisterium,* or teaching authority. This was the fully thought out version of Ignatius's old logic. The person who challenged this, who sought out other paths, or challenged the always precarious status quo was, said Cyprian, "a stranger, profane, an enemy," not unlike dust shaken by the wind, blowing randomly about, making not an inch of progress toward heaven. Heretics and schismatics — terms that were quickly beginning to mean those who dissented from clerical authority — were, by one account, "cut off, like branches from the vine, marked off for punishment like dead wood, for the fires of hell." They were, as the rich storehouse of abusive biblical texts made clear, akin to ravening wolves or rocks that caused shipwreck.

Unity was all. There was room for imagination and proscribed diversity within this framework, but some ideas were beyond the pale. There were many rays of the sun, Cyprian explained, but, ultimately, only one true source of light; there were many branches of a tree, but only one true source of strength based in its "tenacious root." Break a branch from the tree and it would not be able to bud; grow a feeble tree, and it would be overthrown "by the onset of the whirlwind." Cyprian could always coin a winning phrase and, for many of his contemporaries, he also made a compelling point. There was simply no room for unnecessary argument. This only led to animosity and, as Cyprian insisted, the whole point of Christianity was to achieve concord: the love of Christian brotherhood was supposed to be "gentle and meek," in imitation of the doves. It was not intended to replicate the "savageness of dogs."[18]

That Cyprian was living in cloud cuckoo land is immediately obvious. At the risk of repetition, it was incredibly hard to define orthodoxy in the circumstances of the early church, especially in Cyprian's own North Africa. The idea that was contentious to one Christian constituency was theological mothers' milk to another. That men as brilliant as Ignatius of Antioch and Cyprian of Carthage realized as much seems certain. And yet they still tried to construct a myth of orthodoxy, to hammer out universal articles of faith to which all reputable Christians were expected to subscribe. However mighty the sentences they deployed might have been, and however rich their metaphorical imaginations obviously were, their entire effort runs the risk of striking us as misguided. Which brings us back to that nagging question: Christianity was always going to be a divided faith, so why did it try to impose an artificial unity upon itself?

There are many unedifying reasons why this happened. Barking about orthodoxy was often an exercise in asserting power: if your version of Christianity ruled the theological roost, then you would gain authority and prestige. Better yet, you would be in a position to trample on your rivals. That this was one of the enduring motivations behind the invention of heresy and orthodoxy is beyond question, and it continued in perpetuity. Erasmus, the great early modern humanist whom we'll meet again and who could always make a telling caricature out of a depressing reality, talked about the misuse of heresy by the small-minded cleric: "If anyone across the dinner table calls him a fathead or a drunkard, he in turn will announce in his next sermon that the man is a heretic." If his cook served up his meat overdone, Erasmus continued, then that same cleric would probably spread the word that she was harboring heterodox opinions.[19] Erasmus wasn't very far from the truth, and time and again Christians (popes, kings, and emperors among them) abused the potential of a word like *heresy* in order to smite their enemies.

For all that, there were also valid, or at least understandable, reasons for aspiring to Christian harmony. First, we need to think in terms of intellectual satisfaction. If a religion was truly inspired by God, if it truly had the potential to bring salvation to all of mankind, then, so the theory went, it could have only one genuine identity. A multiplicity of forms, let alone the preponderance of heretical sects, dented the notion of Christianity's authenticity. If there was only one God, as Christians believed, and if he was omniscient, as Christians also held, then he would obviously know his own mind. He surely intended his children to believe one thing, and if they didn't, then they were presumably at fault. There are a dozen ways to challenge this line of reasoning, but within the paradigm of an exclusivist, monotheistic religious it had an obvious appeal. From a theoretical standpoint, a craving for unity of belief was not illegitimate. One God, one providential plan, one route to salvation, so one church. It's not for nothing that this was precisely the stance that many Christian thinkers (both in the early church and ever since) have adopted.

We should also remember that, for those who anticipated the imminent return of Christ, it was reasonable to suppose that he would not want his church to have descended into chaos during his absence. This is one of the aspects of the early church that seems most alien to us: these days, millennial expectations are often regarded as the preserve of cultish sects. Back in the first Christian centuries they appealed to a much wider constituency and, in such an environment, the prospect of confronting the returned Christ and coming up wanting was likely a source of great trepidation.

Next, and this is an idea that is sometimes underemphasized, Christians were especially sensitive about the issue of unity because many of their most vocal critics reveled in pointing out the new religion's incoherence and glaring divisions. As we have seen, such adversaries did not have to look very far for evidence. We have already mentioned the Platonic philosopher Celsus, who wrote in the third quarter of the second century about a fragmented Christianity. For someone of his philosophical cast of mind, this instantly signaled illegitimacy. Just like the Jews before them, Celsus crowed, it was best to liken Christians not only to "frogs holding council in a marsh," but also to "a flight of bats, or to a swarm of ants issuing out of their nest, or worms crawling together in the corner of a dunghill, and quarreling with one another as to which of them were the greater sinner." At first, when Christians were "few in number," they "held the same opinion, but when they grew to be a multitude, they were divided and separated."

Celsus had many unflattering things to say about Christianity: it was a pushy, irrational religion that mainly appealed to the ignorant and those on the lowliest rungs of the social ladder. The very apostles, Celsus pointed out, had been "tax gatherers and sailors of the vilest character." Christ, meanwhile, had been little more than a huckster who "by means of sorcery was able to accomplish the wonders which he performed." But it was the characterization of Christianity as a self-imploding, bickering entity that smarted most of all, especially at a time when a great deal of Christianity's time was taken up winning over philosophically sophisticated Greek speakers who would have instantly appreciated Celsus's point.[20]

Origen — who took the trouble to produce a blow-by-blow refutation of Celsus's argument (the only source, in fact, of what Celsus may or may not have written) — took the philosophical high ground. The fact that people twist and bastardize an idea, he argued, does not, in and of itself, discredit it. Healing people, for instance, is a useful enterprise, but the fact that there are quacks doesn't mean that well-trained, conscientious doctors are any less necessary and well intentioned. Aristotle and Plato had lots of wise things to say, Origen continued, but the fact that other thinkers have bowdlerized

and abused their theories does not invalidate their initial speculations. By exposing a fallacy at the heart of Celsus's argument, Origen did very well, but the suggestion that Christianity's divisions
signaled its illegitimacy was still a fertile polemical avenue for
Christianity's enemies to explore.

It can at least be suggested, then, that people like Ignatius and
Cyprian were being astute. There was theological common sense
and propagandist advantage in portraying Christianity as a coherent, unified religion: it was a myth, but a very useful one. Not that
any of this should make us forget the other, towering reason behind
the obsession with unity. When Cyprian talked about the Christian
tree having to sustain a whirlwind, he was not simply reaching for
an attractive image. These were troubled times, and the idea that
martyrs were all dying for the same cause provided a much-needed
boost to Christian morale. There was strength, not merely intellectual satisfaction, in the dream of solidarity.

PERSECUTION

One facet of the mythical early church has a solid grounding in
reality. It was an age of persecution: not quite so swingeing and
not quite as ceaseless as is often imagined, but an age of persecution nonetheless. It was clear that Rome detested Christianity and,
while it couldn't really help the fact, this was largely Christianity's
own fault. If you erect a religion that characterizes all other faiths
as false, and if some of your brethren refuse to make any compromises with the religious world around them, you are behaving very
bravely. You can also expect baleful consequences.

Let us return to Cyprian of Carthage who, in the middle of
the third century, sat down to write a letter to a friend. Apparently
(though we might suspect that this was merely a literary conceit)
Cyprian had been remiss in keeping his promise to discuss divine
matters. Now, though, "when the vintage festival invites the mind

to unbend in repose and to enjoy the arrival and appointed respite of the declining year," he dedicated a lazy afternoon to fulfilling his pledge. Cyprian explained that he had managed to escape "the unrestrained clatter of a noisy household" and had sought out a bower where "the pleasant aspect of the gardens harmonizes with the gentle breezes of a mild autumn in soothing and cheering the senses." In these idyllic surroundings he launched into a withering attack on the morals of the Roman Empire.

There had been a time, Cyprian began, when the prospect of conversion to Christianity had seemed very distant. We are all the products of our circumstances, he confessed, and we all find it hard to overcome what is "deeply and radically engrained within us." How does a man learn thrift, Cyprian asked, when he has "been used to liberal banquets and sumptuous feasts?" Cyprian had always sensed that Christianity offered a better path, but he had often found himself "lying in darkness and gloomy night, wavering hither and thither, tossed about on the foam of this boastful age." He had finally seen the light, however, and this represented nothing less than a new spiritual birth. The society he had left behind was rotten to its core. "Consider the roads blocked up by robbers, the seas beset with pirates, wars scattered all over the earth . . . the whole world is wet with mutual blood." It was a place of brutal gladiatorial games, where savagery "may gladden the lust of cruel eyes," and a place of perversion, where male actors wore women's clothing and reenacted "the old horrors of patricide and incest" celebrated in classical drama.[21]

It goes without saying that Christianity's cause was not always helped by this tendency to launch into damning indictments of the ethical and social milieu of the Roman Empire. This model of radical separation — an almost world-hating outlook — permeated the thought of many early Christians. In its most radical manifestations, epitomized in the later writings of Tertullian, it went so far as suggesting that, to escape the world, radical action was required. It might even be best to languish in a Roman prison: there, "you have no reason to look on strange Gods . . . you have no part in heathen holidays . . . you are not annoyed by the foul fumes of idolatrous solemnities; you are not pained by the noise of public shows, nor by the atrocity or madness or immodesty of their celebrants; your eyes do not fall on stews and brothels." Prison, in fact, "does the same service for the Christian, which the desert did for the prophet."[22] Tertullian was extreme, but his basic theme resounded throughout early Christianity.

Christianity was insisting that it was the world's only legitimate faith and that its followers should have no involvement with other religious traditions. As the story of Ignatius of Antioch reminds us, and as Cyprian would learn to his cost, this truly appalled the Roman authorities. An empire as vast as Rome's was well used to absorbing and, for the most part, tolerating different religious ideas. So long as a person was willing to make public sacrifices to the gods of the Roman pantheon — sacrifices that were seen as the guarantor of political stability and economic well-being — then his core religious beliefs could go largely unscrutinized. This was a compromise that Christianity was usually unwilling to make.

Jews within the empire suffered many indignities and disadvantages but, provided they paid their taxes, they could enjoy exemptions from imperial sacrifices and cultic observances: a grudging recognition by the Roman authorities that they were members of an ancient, established faith. But since, as we've seen, the early Christians had decided to distance themselves from Judaism, such indulgences were not available to them. In consequence, several centuries' worth of persecution came down upon the heads of the faithful. They were pursued as political criminals, which, under the terms of Roman law, is precisely what they were.

It is very easy to over-egg this persecutory pudding. It is often forgotten that, for long stretches of time, many Christian communities went unmolested. When persecution did arrive, it was more often a local initiative than an imperially sponsored project. Even the emperor Trajan, however wicked he seems in the narrative of Ignatius's martyrdom, was actually relatively relaxed in his attitude: if Christians behaved provocatively and refused to recant, then he was keen to punish them, but he saw little advantage in actively seeking them out.

Nor was the gap between Christianity and Roman culture quite as wide as someone like Tertullian insisted. On the contrary, the church continued to win over converts in the empire's heartlands and even some of those who failed to adopt the Gospel message were still intrigued by Christianity's ideas and impressed by its resilience.

On the Christian side, many thinkers worked very hard to make their religious ideas more palatable to the philosophy-loving elites of the Greek-speaking Mediterranean. Church fathers like Justin Martyr went as far as composing fully worked out apologias for Christianity and addressing them to the Roman emperor and senate. Very often, however, Christianity seemed to exhibit a condemnatory attitude to the world in which it found itself. This was courageous and quite possibly a matter of theological necessity but it undoubtedly caused rankles among the empire's intellectual and political elites.

The backlash was predictable. Some commentators contented themselves with rhetorical ripostes or with spreading unseemly rumors about Christianity. Marcus Cornelius Fronto, famed orator and erstwhile Latin tutor to Marcus Aurelius, offered this sordid account of Christian worship: "After much feasting, when the banquet has heated up and the flame of lust and drunkenness has been lit, a dog tied to a lampstand is incited to jump and dance." The lights were extinguished and "under cover of the shameless darkness [they all] embrace one another in their unspeakable lust as chance brings them together."[23] Such accusations were commonplace. Christians used the word *agape* to describe their communal meals: this translates as "love feast," which made life easy for those who wanted to charge Christians with incest and sexual excess. Christians also had their Eucharist, founded on Christ's making a sacrament out of the spiritual consumption of his body, which allowed Christianity's critics to dream up accusations of ritualistic cannibalism.

It did not stop with the slander, however. As the historian Tacitus reported, in the wake of the burning of Rome in 64 c.e., the emperor Nero required scapegoats, and Christians fitted the bill perfectly. Followers of Christ, Tacitus went on, were clad in the hides of beasts and torn to death by dogs, or set on fire to illuminate the night. Over the next three centuries, in many of the Roman Empire's territories, outbreaks of brutal persecution would come to define the early Christian experience. The persecution, as mentioned, was fitful and localized, but a healthy roster of martyrs was quickly established and, as devastating as this was, it also opened up a tempting propagandist possibility.

Christians were dying horrible deaths (or, at the very least being punished and lambasted), but this only demonstrated how committed they could be. They were willing to give their lives and this was a sure sign that they had truth on their side. And how much more spectacular if it could be proven that they were all dying for the same cause! Their sacrifices would make more sense and the Christians who had to read and hear about their punishments would be suitably impressed and emboldened.

Take the story of the French martyrs of Lyon and Vienne, for instance. Just like the letters of Ignatius, this famous narrative had two overriding objectives: to demonstrate how cruel the Roman authorities could be — "the fury of the heathen against the saints" — and to inspire awe and unanimity. Sometimes, we are told, the punishments had been trivial (exclusion from the forum and the public bathhouses) but sometimes Christians had been made to endure all the "mockings, beatings, draggings, robberies, stonings, and imprisonments" that had come from the infuriated pagan mob. The martyr Blandina had been savagely tortured: "Her whole body was mangled and broken." Red-hot plates of brass had been placed on the "most delicate parts" of another Christian's body. Some had been confined in the darkest and most foul smelling cells of the cities' prisons, and when they died of suffocation they were thrown to the dogs; others had been exposed to wild beasts in amphitheaters; many had simply died in their cells, after which their corpses were burned and their ashes swept into the river Rhone.[24]

As with the story of Ignatius, it is impossible to know how accurate any of this is, but it seems reasonable to suppose that the Christians of Lyon and Vienne weren't making it all up. Being a Christian in ancient Gaul was not the easiest of devotional wickets, and the churches of Lyon and Vienne seized upon such events and included them all in a letter sent to "the brethren throughout Asia and Phrygia." This letter was intended to bring news — comforting and devastating all at once — to those "who have the same faith and hope of redemption as ourselves." There's the key phrase: the same faith. It was Ignatius all over again. It was meant to reveal how heavy the shared burden was and to remind everyone that there was a correct way to confront persecution and a single, righteous cause for which to fight.

For good or ill, this was certainly the image of the early church that Christianity opted to cherish and publicize. There was to be a belief in orthodoxy even before orthodoxy existed and, as the famous phrase put it, the blood of the martyrs (people who, so the story went, all believed the same thing, even though they manifestly didn't) was to be the seed of the church. In such circumstances, the very existence of theological diversity made the search for unity seem all the more important.

THE CHURCH

We can marvel at the exuberance and inventiveness of groups that would come to be known as heretical, but we can also sympathize with the Christians who tried to carve out the myths of unity and orthodoxy. These early centuries are among the most jumbled and most fascinating in the church's history and, unsurprisingly, they have received a huge amount of scrutiny in recent decades. Not so long ago, many scholars followed the lead of the influential German historian and theologian Walter Bauer (1877–1960), who energized a stagnant debate by trying to explode the myth of early Christian cohesion. And he made quite a decent fist of it. One of his suggestions was that, from the outset, there were many competing Christian agendas and worldviews. This idea of Christian diversity is still very compelling. In many particulars, and as a general interpretative model, it is impossible to gainsay, in fact.

Other aspects of Bauer's thesis have undergone substantial correction and readjustment. Careful studies of the cities of ancient Christianity have challenged the parts of Bauer's chronology that insisted on the precedence of various heretical groups in various cities and communities, and there have also been efforts to refine the notion of an *imposition* of orthodoxy. Historians have quite sensibly asked who was doing all this "imposing" in a church without any meaningful political power, in which bishops and lowlier clerics relied on the approval of their local congregations to secure election and sustain their careers. The tools of coercion available to later church leaders were conspicuous by their absence.

These days, some historians talk a lot about something called nacent orthodoxy, and it is an idea that at least deserves our attention. Some versions of Christianity did, in fact, win out, and it is very hard to decide whether they were foisted on the Christian masses or whether they triumphed because they were inherently more popular, cogent, and loyal to the Gospel message. In this scheme, a sensible category of heresy (essentially, one that encompassed ideas that were simply too outré) existed long before Christianity became an accepted and imperially sponsored faith.

It could be argued, for instance, that something like Gnosticism was assaulted and, for all intents and purposes, done away with, on purely intellectual and theological grounds. Perhaps, meanwhile, the Christians of Rome banished Marcion simply because they did not like what he was saying. In all this, there was a distinct lack of crusading armies; just a preponderance of Christian thinkers penning tracts and preaching to their flocks. Perhaps some ideas were genuinely beyond the pale.

This is an interesting idea, but there is a risk of abusing the logic. It might lead us to suspect that, from the outset, there was a fixed, sensible, and coherent way of being a Christian. Perhaps orthodoxy, in an embryonic way, existed all along. This is certainly an attractive proposition — it allows the Christian to adopt a sanguine "the truth will out" approach — but it is surely flawed. Even if some Christian ideas were rejected simply because they were too outlandish (and this is hard to demonstrate, not least because of the crowds they sometimes drew), it doesn't follow that there was an all-encompassing standard of orthodoxy, waiting in the wings from the very beginning, against which they could be measured.

It did not require too much effort to decide that talking about two gods in the context of a monotheistic religion was glaringly unacceptable (though it is worth bearing in mind that such a notion recurred time and again within Christianity), but that didn't bring anyone much closer to definitive decisions about a host of other conundrums: the nature of Christ; the need to balance ecclesiastical discipline and the individual's impulse to seek out personal encounters with the divine; the rituals that Christians ought to observe and the books they ought to read; whether they should think of Plato and his Greek philosophical cronies as helps or hindrances in the business of theologizing. In all these areas, and many more besides, the notion of nacent orthodoxy is either too slim or too shaky to be of much interpretative value.

It is possible (if perilous) to talk about the Gospel's ethical core (loving our neighbors, cherishing the meek, and various other nourishing platitudes), but beyond that most issues were up for grabs. The next several centuries, in which such knotty problems were endlessly discussed, amply proved this point.

It's not for nothing that the early Christian era is a hotbed of scholarly disagreement. Identifying the birth pangs of heresy and orthodoxy is difficult. The most obvious conclusion is that we'll never really know just how confused and conflicted early Christian communities were and we will never be sure if Christian orthodoxy and its mirror image, heresy, were destined to emerge as they did.

It would surely be erroneous to cast someone like Cyprian or Ignatius as dimwitted or malevolent. Such people were dying for their faith and if their tempers were sometimes frayed it is easy to see why. Across the theological aisle, it would be equally inappropriate to denounce all those who were demonized as heretics in the early church as deluded troublemakers — or, conversely, to lionize them as bold freethinkers. All we know for certain is that the concerned parties were in the thick of things and their fluctuations between chipper certitude and bewilderment are perfectly understandable.

∽

If Christianity had stuck to its meandering, persecuted route, we would now be in a much better position to reach firm conclusions on these sorts of issues. We could treat it like any other bold ancient religious experiment that grabbed the headlines for a while then petered out or, at best, clung on as a healthy minority sect. It is fascinating to ponder what might have happened if the martyrs had continued to stack up and if, in perpetuity, local religious leaders had been obliged to pander to the shifting agendas of their congregations. All things considered, it seems highly unlikely that a single Christian orthodoxy would have emerged. Instead, to be counterfactual for a moment, there is an overwhelming probability that dozens of regional, competing Christian communities would have blossomed, and some of them would have sneered at the notion of a single font of ecclesiastical authority.

The persecution would have continued, Christianity would have stumbled on, and it is highly likely that subsequent Christian generations would have lived, at least for a much longer while, in a proudly pagan world because the Roman emperor would still have invoked Jove, not Jerusalem. And then, assuming Islam had arrived on schedule, its extraordinary expansion would have been even more world-changing: it wouldn't have had an established Christianity with which to compete, and where there are now churches there would probably be many more mosques.

It is an interesting, sobering supposition and, in the hundred or so years that followed the heretical musings of people like Marcion and Montanus, it came closer to becoming a reality than we might imagine. By the middle of the third century, Christianity was entering the most lamentable period in its history. During the reigns of the emperors Decius and Diocletian, fitful, localized persecution evolved into a systematic attempt to eradicate the Christian religion. The first years of the fourth century would witness the widespread destruction of Christian churches, the confiscation of scriptures, the mass imprisonment of clerics, and, in 304, a decree that any Christian who refused to make public sacrifices risked the death penalty. When priests weren't being killed, they were being put to work in the mines. Christianity was in peril.

Then, however, everything changed. Suddenly, against all expectations, Christianity was transformed from a despised sect into the doted-upon religion of the Roman Empire. Constantine arrived and he told everyone that Christianity was acceptable. Because of this, the Christian church had a very bright future ahead of it.

An obvious assumption would be that this made the quest for Christian unity—the aspiration that had both damaged and sustained Christianity through the worst of times—far less important. In happier days, the quarrels would not matter quite as much. In fact, the opposite turned out to be true. Imperial approbation turned the need for concord into the most pressing issue imaginable. Heresy became even more unappetizing to some Christian palates: it became a political crime. Previously, religious ideas that were thought unsavory had been caricatured and castigated: now they were seen as a threat to political and social stability. Where they had previously been attacked by the pen, they were now, on occasion, assaulted by the sword of imperial power.

This momentous change — one that defined (some would say blighted) Christendom for the next sixteen centuries — is perhaps best summed up by the fictional story of the Seven Sleepers of Ephesus, one of those towns, fittingly enough, to which Ignatius of Antioch had written one of his pie-in-the-sky letters as he headed contentedly toward his death. It was a story that, from the sixth century onward, came in many guises. The next chapter, which charts the great transformation in Christianity's fortunes and the momentous consequences this had for heresy, begins with an especially poignant Anglo-Norman version from the poet Chardri.

3

CONSTANTINE, AUGUSTINE, AND THE CRIMINALIZATION OF HERESY

THE SEVEN SLEEPERS OF EPHESUS

> May He who dwells in Holy Trinity keep us all as one, and may He grant us by these saints the joy to be with Him. And may He grant that through their prayers He will keep us in peace in every land; that neither misbelief nor heresy may set us awry in folly. May He grant in our time joy and sweetness, and may He deliver us from the moans and stench of hell.
>
> — CHARDRI, *La Vie des Set Dormanz*

CHARDRI TELLS US that during the reign of Decius the faithful Christians of the venerable city of Ephesus confronted a stark choice between offering sacrifices to pagan gods and embracing martyrdom: being hanged, burned, and hacked to pieces, after which their severed heads would be paraded on pikes through the city. Those who survived had to endure the effrontery of new Roman temples being built in their midst, so that the city "was filled with blood and smoldering smoke and the stench of entrails which came from their butchery." Many Christians proved themselves to be cowards, handing over sacred texts and partaking of idol worship. Neighbors accused neighbors, sons and daughters informed on their parents, and the entire Christian community of Ephesus was split asunder. There had been persecution before, but it had never been so swingeing.

Seven noble young men behaved with conspicuous valor, however, continuing their religious services in secret and refusing to pollute themselves with pagan ceremonies. When confronted by the emperor, the men boldly declared that they despised the Roman gods more than the lowest dog, and cared not if Roman idols were found in sewers or in the loftiest temple — they were wooden atrocities, best used as fuel for the furnace.

Realizing that they had incurred the emperor's wrath, the seven decided to flee into the mountains. One of their number, Marcus,[1] occasionally ventured into town in disguise to gather food and report back on the emperor's activities. The situation only worsened, with more insults being inflicted on Christianity and more of its acolytes falling away. Worryingly, the emperor had ordered his generals to seek out the seven Christians and one night, after they had fallen asleep, troops found their isolated cave and blocked up its entrance with limestone — effectively burying them alive.

Seeing this, God put his seven dedicated followers into a deep sleep that lasted for more than a hundred years. Then, one morning in the last decades of the fourth century, a group of local workmen who were scouring the mountains for rocks came across the isolated cave and set about unblocking its entrance. The seven noble youths were awakened and, so far as they were aware, only a single night had passed. Marcus set out on another of his furtive trips into Ephesus. He was as terrified as ever, but when he reached the city gates he was startled by the sight of a beautiful cross. He saw yet more crosses as he moved through the city, and glistening Christian churches, and he even heard people talking openly of the Virgin Mary and swearing by the Holy Ghost. Marcus assumed that he had gone mad or was dreaming, but he continued on his way to buy provisions for his friends.

He came to a stall and proceeded to buy some bread, only the coins he handed over bore the image of the long-dead emperor Decius. The vendor asked Marcus where he had come across such precious artifacts, and when a befuddled Marcus could provide no satisfactory answer, he was put on trial as a thief who had obviously stumbled upon a cache of buried treasure. All that was left to Marcus was to recount his story: that, so far as he knew, it was a hundred and more years earlier and he and his friends had recently moved into a cave in the mountains to evade the Christian-hating troops of the emperor.

Understandably, the Ephesians were skeptical, but they allowed Marcus to lead them to his cave and there — with God's providence at their backs — a startling discovery was made. When the cave had been sealed up all those decades earlier, two covert Christians had concealed a small leaden tablet close to its entrance, so that future generations would not forget the sacrifice of the seven Christians trapped inside. This tablet was now unearthed, making Marcus's bizarre story suddenly more credible. When the Ephesians went inside the cave they found Marcus's six friends huddled together in a corner, terrified by what they assumed was the arrival of blood-thirsty imperial troops.

The people of Ephesus were now entirely convinced that they were witnesses to a miracle, and they invited the ruling emperor, Theodosius, to visit their city. He arrived without delay, and when the Christians went out to meet him, they did so not in chains, but with dancing and singing accompanied by harps, viols, and pipes. Roman emperors were no longer the persecutors of Christians, but their devoted protectors. They were Christians themselves. On meeting the seven young noblemen, Theodosius fell to his knees and "worshipped them humbly," basking in the light of their faces, which glowed "as does the sun's heat at midday in the month of May." But then, with their travails over, the seven young men suddenly "laid themselves down without grief or pain and rendered their souls to the Lord God Almighty." Theodosius was desolate: "Whosoever saw a noble emperor so stricken by grief?" He wept profusely, kissed each of the young men in turn, placed his silken cloak over their bodies, "and bade them rest in peace." Grief soon gave way to reverence, however. The emperor decreed that the bodies of the seven men should be placed in golden reliquaries and that a church of marble and limestone should be built around the cave. These men were saints, he declared; their memory was to be celebrated each year by feasts and celebrations.[2]

༄

There can be few fictions that better encapsulate the extraordinary improvement in Christianity's fortunes. In the long decades during which the seven young men of Ephesus had been slumbering, Christianity had been turned from a persecuted sect into the established faith of the Roman Empire. As late as the early fourth century, Christians had made up perhaps 5 percent of the empire's population, the vast majority of them concentrated in the Greek-speaking cities of the eastern Mediterranean. They were usually obliged to worship in secret, they were vastly outnumbered by pagans and Jews, and, as we have seen, the first decade of the fourth century had witnessed the most brutal persecution Christianity had yet endured.

Only a few years later, it was a very different world. Christianity would first be tolerated, then it would become politically sanctioned and embark on the road to becoming culturally dominant. It all began with Constantine: the ancestor of Theodosius and the man who, for eminently self-serving reasons, allowed Christianity to survive and, better yet, to thrive. This would have epochal consequences for the cause of Christian unity. As soon as Christianity won imperial approval, the crushing of heresy would no longer simply be a matter of theological purity or solidarity. It would come to be seen as a political necessity.

CONSTANTINE

The Christian-hating Diocletian, an enlightened and progressive emperor in many regards, abdicated in 305. He was succeeded as leader of the western half of the empire by Constantius, who in turn died at York, in northern England, a year later and passed on the reins of power to his son, Constantine. Constantine would turn out to be the most influential of emperors, the man who built a city in the east, Constantinople, that rivaled and then succeeded Rome, but his route to plenitude was not straightforward. At his father's death, Constantine's political ascendancy was secure throughout Gaul and Iberia, but in Italy he faced a significant rival in the person of Maxentius. After fighting southward in the following years, Constantine finally joined battle with Maxentius at the Milvian Bridge in October 312. Despite being severely outnumbered, Constantine was victorious and went on to take the city of Rome: he had no doubt about who was responsible. The chroniclers tell of Constantine seeing a cross of light in the sky the day before battle, or having dreams in which Christ promised his support if Constantine convinced his soldiers to wear Christian symbols. In the wake of victory, not wishing to offend his new benefactor, Constantine pledged to lift all prohibitions against Christian worship, to return property seized from Christian communities, and, in effect, to turn Christianity into one of the approved religions of the empire. This was all enshrined in Roman law by the Edict of Milan in 313.

The events at the Milvian Bridge did not represent quite so damascene a moment as the chroniclers suggested: in fact, long before 312, Constantine had proven himself to be relatively tolerant of Christianity. Nor should we assume that Constantine simply switched his entire religious allegiance to Christ. The complexities of his spiritual imagination should not be underestimated. He was the inheritor of a Roman polytheistic tradition and it seems likely that the Christian God was only ever one deity in his personal pantheon.

But if, for the time being, Christianity was only one among many religions that shared the benefits of political approbation, this still brought huge advantages. Suddenly, imperial troops began to wear Christian symbols on their helmets, clergymen were granted generous tax exemptions, and grandiose basilicas were constructed across what was quickly turning into something called Christendom. A very welcome die had been cast and while there was some backsliding among Constantine's successors, rival faiths were supplanted by the Gospel with extraordinary dispatch. By the year 381, Christianity was not merely tolerated: it had become the empire's only legal form of religious worship.

Such a staggering transformation did not come without a cost. We are apt to forget that it tolled the death knell for pagan religions, which had served the Roman Empire for centuries. In 386, a man named Libanius, who was devastated by the piecemeal destruction of the old faiths, pleaded with the sitting emperor to rein in the excesses of Christian officials. They "hasten to attack the temples with sticks and stones and bars of iron, and in some cases, disdaining these, with hands and feet. Then utter desolation follows, with the stripping of roofs, demolition of walls, the tearing down of statues and the overthrow of altars, and the priests must either keep quiet or die. After demolishing one, they scurry to another, and to a third, and trophy is piled on trophy." Libanius sought to remind the emperor that the newly unfashionable gods had overseen the rise and expansion of Rome. Many was the peasant in the fields who still looked upon those gods to "bless their labors" and, on a more practical note, it was surely foolish of the emperor to demolish some of his most precious real estate.[3] There is a neglected tragedy here, and also the often overlooked story of how the ancient faiths of Rome struggled for survival during the coming centuries.

As for Christianity, the arrival of imperial support was undoubtedly a boon, but it also made the subject of heresy more potent than ever. In such a context — one in which the enduring, albeit troubled, relationship between church and state first emerged — unity of Christian belief took on a colossal importance. In the interests of preserving the social and political stability of his dominions, it was now the emperor's duty to stamp out any divisions and dissensions within the Christian community. Heterodoxy, and so it would remain for more than a thousand years, was now a political problem, and the heretic was comparable to the traitor. Deviance from orthodoxy was no longer a simple theological transgression. As Constantine had informed his empire, heretics were to be treated as the pests of society and the pernicious enemies of the human race.

Such thoughts would gather considerable pace in the century after Constantine, and no document sums up the new political ramifications of heresy quite as well as the Theodosian Code: a digest and refinement of the previous century's legislation, promulgated by the emperor Theodosius II in 438. As book sixteen of the code announced, all citizens of the empire were to "believe in the single deity of the Father, Son, and the Holy Spirit, under the concept of equal majesty and of the Holy Trinity." "The rest," the code continued, who tried to "sustain the infamy of heretical dogmas," were to be "adjudge[d] demented and insane." "Their meeting places shall not receive the names of churches and they shall be smitten first by divine vengeance and secondly by the retribution of our own initiative." People who behaved badly, who continued to attend pagan sacrifices, were to be denounced, and those who approved of their deeds "shall be beaten publicly with clubs," unless, of course, they were of sufficiently lofty social rank to avoid such indignities, in which case they were to be punished with hefty fines. Any who betrayed their faith and profaned their baptism would be unable to give testimony in court, make wills, or receive inheritances. Christians who behaved well, by contrast, were to be showered with privileges. Priests, along with their families and servants, were to enjoy exemptions from taxation and were not expected to make financial contributions to the post wagons that sent correspondence across the empire. This was fitting recognition of the fact that "our state is sustained more by religion than by official duties and physical toil and sweat." It was a fine time to be a member of the First Estate.

These were very confident pronouncements and, by the year 438, they had garnered a staggering level of support: quite why it had all been so easy, quite why Christianity just seems to have won the day, remains one of the great historical mysteries. Beyond doubt, part of the answer resides in the fact that the fourth century was teeming with heresies. There was an obvious need to impose order on the Christian world, and Constantine and his successors (if we ignore the occasional fourth-century heretical or pagan emperor) were more than happy to step into the breach. They were quick to realize the political potential of launching campaigns against troublesome groups of Christians. Constantine, who set the tone that generations of kings, emperors, and rulers of third-rate palatinates would dutifully follow, reveled in his new role as arbiter and protector of the Christian faith.

This was where power began to dominate the heretical equation. There was a huge difference between persecuted priests in Antioch and Alexandria falling out with one another and the ruler of an empire becoming vexed by the unseemly squabbles of his subjects. The stakes had been raised, and the empire pounced, not least when heresy threatened to undermine the emperor's authority. One of the first victims of this new dispensation was, once again, not a deviant or a lunatic, but an austere, devout Libyan cleric named Arius (c. 250–336). He had made the fateful decision to formulate a provocative answer to the most basic theological question of all: just who was Jesus Christ? As we have seen, people had already been providing rival solutions to this conundrum for centuries. Now, however, they would be answerable to the emperor of Rome, and the massed bishops of the Christian world gathered, under that mighty emperor's auspices, at the first of the church's great councils. Nicaea happened, and heresy would never be quite the same again.

WHO WAS CHRIST?

It might be supposed that reaching firm conclusions about so fundamental an issue as the identity of Jesus Christ would have been one of Christianity's first and most urgent priorities. The notion of a god becoming a man and walking among us was, after all, Christianity's boldest and most controversial claim. In fact, down to the fourth century, many different theories percolated in the minds of the faithful. There were two towering difficulties: how to achieve a balance between Christ's divinity and his humanity, and how to conceptualize Christ's relationship with the Father. Getting Christ just right was terribly important, and this area of divinity, known as Christology, was destined to become one of the most hard fought arenas of Christian theology. It wasn't resolved in the era of Ignatius of Antioch, it still wasn't resolved by the time of the Unitarian Bostonians of the nineteenth century, and even Constantine could not quite manage to impose a solution that pleased everyone — though he did try very hard indeed.

Offering a palatable account of early Christological debates is extremely difficult, not least because the subject is saturated with a host of confusing Greek philosophical terms and some of the most abstruse theorizing that Christianity ever managed to fashion. Perhaps the best approach, though it runs the risk of simplification, is to keep in mind the idea of a theological pendulum, swinging between two trends: ideas that concentrated a little too hard on Christ's divine attributes and those that overemphasized his human aspects. When the pendulum lurched in one direction there was an almost inevitable reaction, which, with alarming regularity, again swung too far toward the opposite extreme. Along the way, and at different times, those who fell out of favor, whose theologizing was adjudged unacceptable, were often accused of heresy. Since we have already mentioned Arius, it would be sensible to begin, in medias res, with his story.

One of his fiercest critics, Epiphanius, described Arius as "very tall in stature, with downcast countenance."[4] He also thought of Arius as a "guileful serpent" who, with his gentle words and humble clothes, adopted a veneer of piety and holiness in order to hoodwink the gullible into accepting his dangerous theories. It might be more evenhanded to think of Arius as one of those people who exposed the root-deep perplexity of Christianity's big idea: that God could become a man and save our souls.

Regrettably, we know very little about the specifics of Arius's thought: all we have directly from his pen are a handful of letters and a few fragments of his rather odd poetry. What he believed has to be largely reconstructed from hostile sources (which isn't ideal) and, to make things even more confusing, there are long-standing arguments about the origins of his theology: historians talk about the influence of Neo-Platonism, or the impact of Origen, but no one can ever pin Arius down with precision. Most annoying of all, it is almost impossible to disentangle Arius's original ideas from the meditations of those who came after him and who were tarred with the Arian brush.

Still, and with all this in mind, we can at least venture an informed guess about Arius's basic agenda. He seems to have thought that treating the Father and the Son as co-equals (both existing, as divinities are apt to do, for eternity, and both made of the same divine substance) was a colossal error. There was only one God, "alone unbegotten, alone everlasting, alone unbegun, alone true, alone having immortality, alone wise, alone sovereign."[5] In this scheme, Christ was to be thought of as a creation of the Father: a subordinate being who, until God had deemed it necessary, had not existed. There was nothing eternal about Jesus Christ. As Arius allegedly put it, there was a time "when Jesus Christ was not." Christ was still far superior to any human, of course, and his deeds had undoubtedly played a huge role in humanity's salvation. He was most certainly a cut above and he deserved all the devotional plaudits being lavished upon him, but to suggest that he was, like the Father, eternal and unbegotten — a god in every sense of the word — surely threatened to send an avowedly monotheistic Christian religion down the path of polytheism.

It is useful to think of Arius as representing one of those aforementioned swings in the Christological pendulum. During the second and third centuries there had been a recurring theological tendency to stress Christ's divinity at the expense of his humanity. We have already encountered one example of this in Docetism. You will remember the proposition (hated by Ignatius of Antioch, embraced by Marcion) that there was only ever one God and that, by the means that are available only to a deity, he had stepped into mortal fancy dress and convinced everyone that he was a bona fide human being. Think of it as a divine con trick — a very clever one — the Docetists might have argued, but don't think of Christ as a person who suffered toothaches, who was possessed of human rationality, or who had a prenatal past in the innards of a woman called Mary from a town in Palestine. That, so the Docetists insisted, was not how a god behaved.

Another school of thought, a version of the ever-puzzling heretical category known as Monarchianism, also talked a great deal about the oneness of the divinity. For the Roman cleric Sabellius, as just one example, the components of the Trinity — Father, Son, and Holy Ghost — were best understood as convenient ways of expressing different "modes" of the one God. Thinking of the Father doing the creating, the Son doing the redeeming, and the Holy Ghost going about its post-crucifixion business allowed us feeble-minded humans to comprehend the various tasks of the Godhead, but that didn't mean that there were three distinct divine persons. Thinkers like Sabellius preferred to talk about three aspects or three energies of a single divine entity. If nothing else, this line of reasoning owned up to the fact that the nature of the triune God is beyond our understanding and that the terms we use to describe it are our own invention. They represented a clumsy attempt to fathom the unfathomable, but that didn't grant them a metaphysical reality.

Such ideas caused much grumbling. In a sense, they were attractive theological approaches: insisting on the unity of one single God in a monotheistic religion always made good sense. However, they also did considerable damage to safer analyses of the Trinity and, most worrying of all, they opened up troublesome consequences for the human element in Christ's atonement. It was vital, many Christian thinkers insisted, that Christ had been, in a very real sense, a human being: if he died for our sins, and if that death was to have any redemptive value, then he had to have been one of us — the nails had to hurt as they were hammered in.

Arius, attracted by the concept of Christ's human aspects, can sensibly be understood as part of the backlash to such divinity-and-nothing-else ideas, but, according to many onlookers, he pushed things much too far. His critics growled that Arius was suggesting that Christ was really just an exceptional human being, lacking the eternal attributes of a true divinity. This was seen as throwing the theological baby out with the bathwater: it looked, to some, like an echo of an old Christological heresy, subordinationism, which, during the church's first three centuries, had insisted that only the Father was a genuine deity and that Christ always had to be understood as subdivine, or subordinate. Right or wrong, Arius was deemed to be making Christ into little more than a creature, however lofty and exceptional.

During the first decades of the fourth century, Arius's ideas caused mayhem. A local theological squabble in Alexandria spread out across the entire eastern church, with bishops taking up positions in the competing Arian and anti-Arian camps. A local episcopal council denounced Arius's position in 321 — asking, "What man of any piety is not horror-stricken, stopping his ears against such filth?" — but this official statement apparently took little heat out of the controversy. Arius moved on to Palestine and Syria and began to win support (or at least sympathy) from churchmen as eminent as Eusebius of Caesarea and Eusebius of Nicomedia.

At first, the emperor Constantine did not seem to grasp the significance of the Arian crisis. He was content to send letters to Arius and his main antagonist, the bishop of Alexandria, urging them to stop discussing such confusing, intricate points of theology. "It becomes us on such topics to check loquacity," he advised. After all, "how few are capable either of adequately expounding or understanding the import of matters so vast and profound?" Quarreling about such matters, Constantine concluded, was "vulgar . . . [and] not suitable to the intelligence of priests and prudent men."[6] It was very much hoped that the rival camps could simply agree to differ and let peace return to the eastern church.

They could not, and it began to dawn on Constantine that resolving the Arian crisis provided a signal opportunity to assert his newly minted authority over the Christian faith. So it was that, in 325, the very first of the great councils (those described as ecumenical, which in this context simply means representing the "whole church") was staged in the city of Nicaea, in present-day Turkey.

It is one of the great tragedies of Christian history that we have so little detailed evidence of what transpired. We can be certain of one thing, however: it was all a very long way from the decorous church councils of more recent times. As many as three hundred bishops accepted Constantine's invitation, forming — as the contemporary church historian Eusebius put it — "a vast garland of priests, composed of a variety of the choicest flowers."[7] Many of them bore the scars of persecution and torture inflicted in less happy times and, so far as we can tell, they were determined to bicker unendingly.

Constantine was having none of it. From the outset, he tried to turn the entire assembly into an exercise in propaganda and show-manship: into an assertion of his God-given authority. At the first opportunity, as Eusebius remembered it, Constantine entered the council's debating chamber "like some heavenly messenger of God, clothed in raiment which glittered, as it were, with rays of light, re-flecting the glowing radiance of a purple robe and adorned with the brilliant splendour of gold and precious stones." The awestruck as-sembled bishops, Eusebius dutifully continued, had downcast eyes, barely daring to look at Constantine, at "the blush on his counte-nance, his majestic dignity and invincible strength and vigour."

Constantine's message was made abundantly clear. "Internecine strife within the Church of God is far more evil, far more danger-ous, than any kind of war or conflict." "The first object of my endea-vours," he announced, "[is] the unity of faith, sincerity of love, and community of feeling in regard to the worship of Almighty God."[8] Arius and his ideas were interrogated in sessions across the city's churches and in the chambers of the imperial palace and — through what must have been a heated process of debate and browbeat-ing — a consensus emerged: one from which, rather surprisingly, only a handful of bishops dissented. An indication, perhaps, of the tremendous political pressure that had been brought to bear. Arius was deemed a heretic. Orders were issued to burn any surviving copies of his books, and the heresiarch himself was banished to Illyria.

In direct refutation of Arius's teachings, the council composed what would come to be known as the Nicene Creed: a statement of belief that, with the inclusion of some alterations made at subsequent councils, remains operative within much of the Christian church to this day. "We believe in one God," it begins, in roundly monothe-istic terms, "the Father Almighty, maker of heaven and earth, of all that is seen and unseen." We also believe, it continues, "in one Lord, Jesus Christ, the only Son of God," and he was "eternally begotten of the Father" — not, in other words, an entity that had only come into existence when the Father had created him — and he was "true God from true God . . . of one substance with the Father . . . begotten, not made."

It was an idea that would endure (and for perfectly sound reasons) but, for many people (both then and subsequently), it looked a lot like a fudge and it certainly failed to dampen down Christological speculation. Arianism itself was not quite so easily silenced. Constantine's own sister was won over to its arguments, as was a subsequent emperor, Constantius II (r. 337–361). And even when Arianism was effectively eradicated within the ranks of the imperial political elite, it still enjoyed a thriving afterlife among the tribes — the Ostrogoths, the Visigoths, the Vandals, the Lombards and all — who were shortly to tear the western half of the empire asunder.

Just as important, many Christians were unconvinced that Nicaea ought to be the final word in the long and winding Christological debate. Constantine and his apologists endeavored to put a decidedly optimistic spin on the events that had taken place there: "At the command of God, the splendour of truth has dissipated all dissensions, schisms, tumults, and deadly poisons of discord."[9] It was not quite so straightforward. Not everyone within the Christian fraternity was happy with the message of the Nicene Creed. Many were flabbergasted that a word drawn from Greek philosophy — *homoousios*, a word that did not appear *once* in scripture — had been used to explain how the Father and the Son consisted of the same substance. Others, largely in reaction to Arius's musings, began, yet again, to lay exaggerated stress on Christ's divinity, and a whole new batch of Christological heresies emerged during the decades after Nicaea. The pendulum began to swing once more.

A heresy known as Monophysitism quickly entered the fray. Harking back to third-century ideas, it insisted that, after the incarnation, Christ only had one (*mono*) entirely divine nature (*physis*). As one of its most radical followers, Apollinarius of Laodicea, argued, Christ had simply not possessed a human soul or consciousness: he was all God. Such notions were, in their turn, condemned (at a council in Constantinople in 381), but they continued to gain adherents. The pendulum began to swing back, and a theologian like Nestorius, made bishop of Constantinople in 428, started to talk about the importance of distinguishing (in some way) between Christ's divine and human attributes. Christ was made up of two separate, entirely distinguishable persons conjoined in a metaphysically unique way. Yet again, eyebrows were raised (not least those of Cyril, Nestorius's great rival over in Alexandria). Someone like Cyril was committed to the ideas of Christ's divinity and equality among all members of the Trinity. Nestorius was a rather rash and clumsy thinker and at one point he took aim at an increasingly well established term for the Virgin Mary: *theotokos*, God bearer. His enemies were not impressed. By rejecting this coinage and by attempting (by his rivals' calculation) to make two Christs, he came under fire. In 431, another of the church's councils in Ephesus descended into farce as two of the Christian world's most eminent leaders exchanged bitter accusations of heresy. Cyril, the patriarch of Alexandria, and Nestorius joined battle. For Nestorius, it was the end of an illustrious career and, after a period languishing in a monk's cell at Antioch, he was banished.

Not that this resolved anything, and only a few years later, in 451, the church felt obliged to mount another council, at Chalcedon. Here, something approaching a workable solution (though some would call it a compromise) was hammered out. The extremes of Arius (who had been accused of paying too much attention to Christ's humanity) and the extremes of the Monophysites (who had all but ignored Christ's humanity in order to highlight his divinity) were both rejected. Instead, Christians were now informed that Christ was fully human and fully divine. He had a divine nature *and* a human nature, but — despite what the Nestorians might think — they were joined in a *single* divine person by means of something called the hypostatic union.

The Monophysites were not pleased, and that is why the Monophysite Copts of Egypt seceded from the rest of Christianity and established a church of their own: one that still survives today. This was one of the more dramatic early examples of a recurrent tendency in the history of heresy: an allegedly heretical group of Christians setting up their own theological stall, which, so far as they were concerned, represented authentic Christianity.

All of these Christological debates had confused and divided Christianity for more than two centuries. We stand amazed that such theological technicalities had such an impact, but they possessed extraordinary power in the early church. As Vincent of Lérins put it (and at this point we might remind ourselves of his neat and tidy "everywhere, always, and by everyone" catch phrase), "Not only relationships by marriage and by blood, friendship, and family, but cities, provinces, nations — even the whole Roman empire — were shaken and uprooted from their foundation."[10] As the bishop Gregory of Nyssa explained, it had been impossible to buy a loaf of bread or ask for some change in Constantinople without someone engaging you in Christological debate.

The solution, this mystical idea of a hypostatic union, was far from perfect and, as we'll see, arguments about Christ's identity would rumble on down the centuries. The decrees of Chalcedon — ideas to which the vast majority of Christians would still subscribe — can best be understood as an attempt to find some middle ground: an attempt to stop the pendulum swinging quite so violently. Too many people had ignored Christ's humanity, too many people had questioned his divinity, so why not let him have both, in some strange and wonderful way. Whether or not this made theological sense, it had significant political advantages. And that, so far as the history of heresy is concerned, is the crucial point. It was the process, as much as the outcome, that mattered.

သာ

At the Council of Nicaea, a political mechanism for responding to heresy, for imposing religious conformity, was inaugurated. Much was achieved in the name of unity in 325. Arguments over how to calculate the date of Easter were settled (more or less), rules about episcopal elections were codified, it was agreed that no clergyman ought to live in the same house as a woman unless she was his sister, mother, or aunt — the taproot of an enduring Christian obsession with clerical celibacy, and (as a reminder of just how long ago and far away Nicaea was) it was announced that priests who had been castrated by barbarians against their will should be allowed to retain their jobs, while those who (eager to become eunuchs) had done the castrating themselves ought to be dismissed.

The most epochal development of all, however, had been the enshrining of the idea that it was the duty of political leaders and churchmen to work together in the pursuit of "our common peace and harmony, and in the cutting off of every heresy." This is what Nicaea and all the subsequent councils of the early church were all about. Some have seen this as a tragedy but this does not diminish its significance. For the next twelve centuries, churchmen would gather at their councils: events, so an awestruck medieval observer once noticed, where "the senate of the whole Christian republic comes together, to consider and give judgment to the universe." The participants, dedicated to declaiming truth, were convinced that the eradication of heresy was as much a political duty as a theological one and, from the year 325 onward, temporal rulers would always be at their backs.

This was bad news for heresy. Previously, theological tussles had produced little more than acrimonious tracts, bitter sermons, and the odd exorcism or two. Now, because political power had intervened, the stakes had been raised. Local populations, when a council materialized in their midst, knew this very well.

They would sometimes gather outside the churches and palaces in which debates raged about the nature of God and the quiddities of mankind. They would cheer their champions and spit out venomous accusations of anathema at those churchmen they despised. When decisions went well at such councils, the local people would escort clerics home to their lodgings with joyful, drunken, torch-lit processions. When decisions went badly they would burn men in effigy and make bonfires of their books. In better moods the crowds would hold placards aloft. In worse moods they would fight bloody battles in the streets. Nor should we suppose that events were any more decorous inside the halls of power. At council after council, from the fourth century to the sixteenth, churchmen would trade accusations of heresy, and the eastern and western halves of the Christian world would play out their ancient rivalries. Armed guards would sometimes be drafted in to prevent eruptions of physical violence.[11]

The only question remaining, and it cropped up almost immediately, was what steps these politicians and churchmen were entitled to take in order to eradicate the heretical menace. Was the burning of books sufficient, or excommunication, or banishment to Illyria?

In the decades after Nicaea, clear signs showed which way the wind was blowing. A flood of anti-heretical legislation made its way onto the statute book. Regional governors were instructed to exile any heretics they encountered or, at the very least, to close down their churches, seize their property, and trample on their political and economic privileges. At different times, heretics were forbidden from disposing of their property in their wills, from owning slaves, from holding office, from conducting business transactions, and from receiving poor relief.

All of which raised a crucial issue. When confronted with heresy, was it appropriate to employ coercion or, at the very least, the threat of force? As we are about to discover, this was another question that was asked and resolutely answered during the reigns of the first Christian emperors, and the answer would hold good for more than a millennium. Matters came to a head with the Donatists of North Africa and the impassioned response of the most famous church father of them all, Augustine.

Donatism

In Europe and North America, we have an unfortunate habit of conceptualizing Christianity as a solidly Western enterprise. This is as about as legitimate as portraying Jesus Christ — as so much of our devotional art does — as a bearded, white-skinned, flowing-cloak-wearing individual who bears a striking resemblance to a citizen of a Renaissance Italian city-state. That he was an olive-skinned Palestinian is easily forgotten. So too is the fact that, during its first five centuries, Christianity was a decidedly un-European affair. As we have witnessed time and again, the crucibles of Christian endeavor were to be found in the East: in the rival cities of Antioch, Alexandria, Constantinople, and many more besides. Rome, for all its later boisterousness, simply did not count for a great deal.

Those epic decisions at the Council of Nicaea were reached by the bishops of the eastern end of the Mediterranean. The sitting pope, the eminently forgettable Sylvester I, sent a brace of representatives, and a sprinkling of Western prelates (from Cordoba in Spain and Lyon in France) fetched up for the council's deliberations, but the decisions that would define the future of Christianity were made by those we would now describe as Greeks, Egyptians, and Turks. And also by North Africans: the inhabitants of a region, the home of Cyprian and Tertullian, that did as much as any other to determine Christianity's attitude toward heresy.

The early North African church endured some of the worst blasts of Roman persecution. At such times, its religious leaders faced a bleak choice. They could either run the risk of martyrdom or comply with the offensive demands made of them by the Roman authorities. Many chose the latter course, offering sacrifices to pagan gods and surrendering holy scriptures and holy vessels: such clerics came to be known as *traditors* — meaning "those who handed over," and the root of our word *traitor.* Once the persecution ended, Christians wondered how they should view these backsliding priests. The key issue was whether the sacraments they dispensed still had value or whether they were tarnished by the flawed character of the officiating cleric. A consensus quickly emerged, summed up in the phrase *ex opere operato* — "from the work done." The purpose of a sacrament was utterly independent of the person who celebrated it: if it were not, then human action would be capable of limiting God's agency, which, so the logic concluded, was unthinkable.

Many North African Christians — precisely those people who were unwilling to forgive the temporizing of their priests and bishops — were unconvinced by this line of reasoning. Perhaps, it was loudly averred, the craven cleric had lost the grace imparted by the Holy Spirit: perhaps, if you allowed him to dole out sacraments, then his sin would spread, infection-like, throughout the Christian community. Once again, and this is reminiscent of Montanism, there was a thirst for a more rigorous, uncompromising faith.

Matters reached a crescendo in the second decade of the fourth century, when some North African Christians pointed out that one of those who had consecrated Caecilian, the new bishop of Carthage, had been Felix, bishop of Apthungi, a *traditor.* There was also mention of the fact that Caecilian himself had been overly indulgent of the persecutory Roman authorities: he hadn't been the greatest supporter of incarcerated Christians and, so the story went, he had been complicit in the effort to stop Christian prisoners from receiving food. The fact that he had managed to offend an eminent local noblewoman, whose opinion counted for a great deal, did nothing to help his cause.

Those who believed that all these deeds and rumors invalidated Caecilian's ordination elected a rival bishop of Carthage, Majorinus, who was quickly succeeded, in 313, by Donatus, from whom the Donatist heresy derives its name. All of a sudden there were two North African churches, and the prospect of reconciliation between the camps was made that much more distant by the long-standing tensions that lay behind the dispute. Donatism was not simply about issues of theology: it also highlighted the rivalries between the urban Carthaginian church and the rural Christians who lived farther south, in the region of Numidia. They had specific reasons for resenting Caecilian's consecration (it had gone ahead without the involvement of their own senior bishop), and they took the opportunity to voice their disapproval of the way the Carthaginian priesthood had tended to kowtow to the Roman authorities, even during periods of persecution. In this sense the emergence of Donatism represented an expression of Berber distaste for the degree to which North African culture was in thrall to Roman overlords.

This, at any rate, is what we used to think. In recent years a valuable scholarly campaign serves to warn us against identifying Donatism as some sort of proto-nationalist movement. This has provided a necessary corrective. We are used to regions asserting their autonomy and demanding rights, but people in the fourth century might not have thought in such terms. Also, and this has been amply proven, the concept of neat divisions between rural Donatists and urban anti-Donatists is hard to justify. And yet there is still some validity in the fundamental notion that the schism that divided the North African church had something to do with those on the periphery standing up for themselves. This, at any rate, is how Constantine and his successors seem to have seen things.

Adjudication of the dispute between the rival churches was quickly sought and, in 313, a letter outlining the "crimes of Caecilian" was sent to Constantine. Unfortunately for the Donatists, a meeting in Rome found in favor of their opponents: a decision that, in spite of a series of appeals, was confirmed in 316 when Caecilian was declared innocent of any wrongdoing. Regardless of this setback, Donatism continued to flourish across North Africa and, by 336, one of its councils was attended by no fewer than 270 bishops (bishoprics tended to be much smaller back then).

Imperial policy over the following years veered between conciliation and obstinacy but, in some places, Donatists and their opponents — who now referred to themselves as Catholics — managed to carve out some measure of uneasy coexistence. In 345, however, the Donatists once again sought imperial approbation and asked the emperor, Constans, to decree that theirs was the only legitimate North African church. Constans dispatched two envoys, Paulus and Macarius, but since they were suspected of harboring anti-Donatist sympathies, they were harassed by threats of violence and met by riots throughout their mission. The response of the envoys was harsh.

When Macarius encountered ten Donatist bishops in the town of Vegesula he had them all flogged, and one of them, Marculus, endured scathing examinations and pitiless tortures, was paraded through the towns of North Africa, and finally, on the heights above Carthage, he was reputedly marched to a cliff top and thrown to his death. The emperor's ultimate decision was to order a reunification of the North African church, but under *Catholic* control.

Over the next decades, a succession of Donatist leaders (culminating in the highhanded bishop Primian) grew increasingly radicalized, first condoning and then actively encouraging anti-Roman activities. Donatists began to exhibit an unflinching exclusivist attitude. If a Catholic entered one of their churches, they would ritually cleanse the place where he had stood. An extreme Donatist group, the Circumcellions, began to roam the countryside, demanding social justice in the name of the Gospel. They took up the clubs used to coax olives from the trees at harvest time and set about menacing the great and the good. Masters were dragged from their carriages and forced to give up their seats to the slaves they held in bondage. If the Circumcellions ultimately failed, they did so with panache: leaping zealously from cliffs and city walls to attain a martyr's crown. As Augustine (354–430) lamented in a letter to the Spanish priest Victorianus, instead of barbarians North Africa was plagued by Circumcellions, and "perhaps the cruelties of barbarians would be light in comparison. For what barbarian could ever have devised what these have done, casting lime and vinegar into the eyes of our clergymen."[12]

The dangers of Donatism were obvious. The movement represented a challenge to the religious mandate of imperial authority and, at an ecclesiological level, it threatened to destroy the much-cherished notion of catholicity — that there should be one worldwide church. The Donatists, by contrast, would presumably have been perfectly content to prosper as a regional, self-determining institution. At first, orthodox leaders, including Augustine, sought to heal the schism through discussion. It quickly became clear, however, that the Donatists had no interest in any variety of compromise or reconciliation. By 412 Donatism had been declared heretical, its places of worship were handed over to the Catholics, and any Donatist bishop who refused to return to the bosom of the church was banished.

It was because of the Donatist schism, and mainly because it so enraged Augustine, that the church first systematically articulated the idea that, when confronted with heresy, it was entirely legitimate to employ coercion. This was a fateful moment, and one document, a letter written by Augustine to a North African nobleman, sums up this momentous shift in the Christian worldview.

AUGUSTINE

Augustine, while his name is now almost synonymous with a certain variant of Christian orthodoxy, epitomized the chaos of the early church. He was the son of a Christian mother and a pagan father and, though he was baptized in 387, he had spent the earlier part of his life exploring the possibilities of Manichaeism — another of those dualistic ideas that invoked multiple divinities and the evils of the material world. At first, he found the Christian scriptures simplistic and looked for a more sophisticated way of understanding the universe. However, courtesy of the more ingenious schools of biblical analysis that were gaining so much ground, he was won over to the cause. After an ascetical period, he took on ecclesiastical dignity as bishop of Hippo in 395. This placed him in the midst of the Donatist crisis, and it was a crisis he was determined to snuff out: which brings us to that letter.

Augustine, always a skilled polemicist, was sure to itemize the Donatists' own outrages. "Anyone who had shown contempt for their hard words was compelled by harder blows to do what they desired." The houses of innocent persons who had offended them were either razed or burned. Heads of families were carried away half dead, or bound to the mill "and compelled by blows to turn it round, after the fashion of the meanest beasts of burden." The bishops and clergy, Augustine alleged, had suffered the worst hardships of all: "Some of them had their eyes put out, and one bishop his hands and tongue cut off, while some were actually murdered."

This, Augustine suggested, made the Donatists' complaints about their own ill-treatment somewhat hypocritical, but the Donatists were missing an even larger point. They constantly claimed that "Christians ought not to demand any assistance from Chris-

tian emperors." First, Augustine suggested, this was a little disin-
genuous. Their own appeals to the emperors Constantine and Constans had inaugurated and hardened the whole schism. "They were
themselves the first to do what they censure in us." Second, the very
notion that the emperor ought to avoid entanglement with religion
was flatly absurd.

Here was the nub of the argument. There was simply nothing
wrong with employing force or the threat of force to secure unity
of belief. It all depended on the laws you enacted. If it was an un-
just law, then the person who opposed it was a hero. If it was a just
law, then to reject it was criminal. There was no question that the
laws seeking to lead Donatists back to conformity were just. They
were enacted out of love: "The rules which seemed to be opposed
to them are in reality their truest friends." They had already delivered many Donatists back to the church and forced them to jettison
their "ruinous madness." The Donatists ought to remember that the
raging madman complains about the very physician who is trying
to treat him, just as the errant son fails to see that the chastisements
of his father are aimed at his reformation. The horse and the mule
"resist with all the force of bites and kicks the efforts of the men who
treat their wounds in order to cure them." If Donatists held that,
in matters of faith, "no one can be justified in using violence," they
were deluded.

It was the duty of kings to serve the Lord "by preventing and
chastising with religious severity all those acts which are done in
opposition to the commandments of the Lord." Hezekiah had destroyed the temples of idols, Darius had cast the enemies of God
into the dens of lions, Nebuchadnezzar had brutally punished
blasphemers, so why shouldn't today's emperors follow such prec-
edents? If adultery was punishable, then why not heresy? "Is it a
lighter matter that a soul should not keep faith with God, than that
a woman should be faithless to her husband?"

Augustine conceded that it was "better that men should be led

to worship God by teaching, than be driven to it by fear of punishment or pain," but sometimes the Christian ruler was left with little
choice. The shepherd first tried to lead back errant sheep by tender
words, but sometimes he had to fall back on the pain of the whip.
And surely the Donatists, through their excesses, had demonstrated
that tender words would be of little use in their correction. These
were the people who had burst into a basilica and beaten the bishop
of Bagai with cudgels and the boards of a broken altar, stabbed his
groin with a dagger, and dragged him through the streets. The bishop's response had been straightforward. He had asked the emperor
to punish his assailants and the emperor had done precisely that.
And, Augustine opined, quite right too.[13]

∽

In an instant, a ferocious theological logic had been unleashed: it
would endure for more than a thousand years. Force could be employed against heretics: as the Gospel of Luke had explained, it was
legitimate to compel the wavering and the errant to come into the
fold. Of course, there was still much to debate: not least the question of whether compulsion could mean the infliction of torture
and death. It is often forgotten that this was an extreme that Augustine would have much rather avoided, and his restraint echoed
throughout the early church. At the Council of Constantinople of
381, the goal of winning heretics over, rather than killing them off,
was writ large. Some heretics, those who followed the ideas of Arius,
for instance, could be reclaimed relatively easily: they would have
to provide a written recantation, make a promise to reject all heresies, and be anointed with holy oil on the forehead, nostrils, eyes,
ears, and mouth. Others, who had gone to more radical heretical
extremes, were to be regarded not so much as lapsed Christians, but
as "heathens." Their road back would be more arduous. They would
have to be exorcised—a ritual that involved "breathing thrice in

their face and ears," be made to undergo religious instruction and attend church services, and then, assuming all went well, they could be rebaptized.

It was all about rehabilitation, and the church had a word that summed this up: *caritas*. This meant being kind, relying on reform and instruction, in order to save a person's eternal soul. There was another word, however: *potestas*. This meant having the power, through coercion, to impose the church's will. Luke's Gospel used the phrase *compelle intrare*. It referred to a man who had invited his friends to a great feast. When they refused to come, he sent out his servants into the highways and byways with the order to "compel the people to enter" and enjoy the toothsome foods available. It was a harrowing parable: the man was acting violently but, so he imagined, he was doing so for his guests' own good. It was a parable that lay at the heart of the logic that Augustine set in motion — a parable, in fact, that he gleefully deployed. Heretics were the reluctant guests who didn't want to attend the feast, and the challenge of striking a balance between *caritas* and *potestas* would define the remainder of Christian history.

Many would come to lament this new Christian world: a place in which coercion was acceptable and in which religious faith and political power were so closely intertwined. More than a thousand years later some Christians were still mumbling their dissent. In the middle of the seventeenth century the Massachusetts politician Henry Vane looked back affectionately on the pure times before Constantine and Augustine, the "wilderness state," as he called it. For Vane, it was regrettable that Christianity had become the religion of the Roman Empire and begun to deploy "the carnal weapons of worldly power" like a persecutory beast.[14] His contemporary Roger Williams (one of the stars of an upcoming chapter) was also much dismayed by "the great mystery of the Church's sleep," during which the garden of Christ's faith had decayed into "the wilderness of national religion and the world [under Constantine's dominion]." The result, Williams concluded, had been a "most unchristian Christendom."[15]

Others would point out that if the empire had not come to the rescue, and if persecution had not given way to political approbation and support, Christendom itself might never have come into being. Adjudicating the interventions of Constantine and his successors would prove to be one of the sorest points in Christian debate. The jury is still out.

WHENCE AND WHITHER?

The church's first four centuries had been chaotic. Perhaps the most troubling realization was that men denounced as heretics had often been pillars of the Christian community. Vincent of Lérins — yes, him again — could not help but notice that so many seemingly orthodox Christians had turned heretic or, as he put it, "metamorphosed from a sheep into a wolf." Think of Nestorius, Vincent suggested, the man who had been patriarch of Constantinople but, because of provocative speculations about the nature of Christ, had been cast out of the church. Could this really be the same man who had "been elected by the high choice of the emperor, held in the greatest esteem by the priesthood, greatly beloved by his holy brethren, and in high favour with the populace"? He had expounded the scriptures every day and "confuted the pestilent errors both of the Jews and heathens."

Or, Vincent continued, take the great North African theologian Tertullian, who, late in life, became enamored of the heretical Montanist movement. Vincent wondered how this could possibly have come to pass: before Tertullian's falling away, who had been more learned, "who more versed in knowledge whether divine or human? Was not his genius of such unrivalled strength and vehemence that there was scarcely any obstacle which he proposed to himself to overcome, that he did not penetrate by acuteness, or crush by weight?" Still more ironic, he had previously bombarded heretical thought "by the force of his many and ponderous volumes, as with so many thunderbolts."

Vincent's solution was that God intentionally allowed such men to lapse into heresy in order to test the resolve of the faithful. The temptation to believe the errors of such previously exemplary Christians was overwhelming, but it had to be resisted. If a false prophet arose, you should not hearken to his words, "because the Lord God makes trial of you, to see if you love him or not."[16]

For our purposes, however, such a convenient explanation of heresy is unconvincing. We might be more inclined to return to the idea that Christianity was an inherently confused religion that was destined to provoke competing schools of theological inquiry. Sorting the wheat from the chaff (assuming such categories are even relevant) was never easy.

Perhaps the most telling example of how difficult it was to draw convincing lines between heresy and orthodoxy is provided by Origen (185–254). We have already seen him defending the new faith against the strictures of Celsus and in many ways Origen was a respected star in the early Christian firmament. The son of a martyr, Origen did as much as any of the first Christian theologians to refine the art of biblical criticism, and his thinking would exert huge influence throughout the course of Christian history. Some did not like his embrace of Greek philosophical nostrums, however, and his enemies would even secure his banishment from Alexandria in 231.

Other aspects of his thought provoked even greater uproar. Given the paucity of extant texts written by Origen, it is very hard to distinguish between his actual beliefs, the slurs of his detractors, and the misuse of his name by later (certainly more radical) interpreters. After his death "Origenism" would be roundly condemned, but the links between the postures of this later movement and the man from which it took its name are not easy to descry. Suffice to say that supposedly Origenist theology represented a heady cocktail: everything from a belief that human souls exist before the birth of human forms, to speculation that Christ's sacrifice would be played out repeatedly in future worlds, to a Christology that insisted upon Christ the Son being subordinate to God the Father (a heretical theme we've already encountered).

Quite what Origen actually believed is lost to us, but the crucial point is that the name of such a crucial contributor to the early Christian cause could so easily be linked to heresy. Tertullian, Nestorius, Origen, and many, many others were keystones of the intellectual and ecclesiastical architecture of the fledgling church but, with extraordinary ease, they could be tarred with the heretical brush. The sandbars of orthodoxy, it seems, were constantly shifting.

⁓

Heresy was not just about confusion, however, and this presumably came as something of a relief. Time and again, it proposed alternative ideas about the nature of God, Christ, mankind, and the church. The articulation of such alternatives was what made heresy seem so dangerous, but it is also what provided heresy with its phenomenal creative potential. The deeds and musings of heretics were perceived as an outrage, but they also compelled the leaders of the earliest Christianity to clarify and enforce their vision — the sacraments, scriptures, rituals, and devotions that were to be followed by every acolyte, the world over. This was of small comfort to those who had been beaten down but, although the church was never likely to admit it, it also meant that Christianity needed its heretics every bit as much as it needed its saints and martyrs.

Remember Arius, without whom the Nicene Creed would never have been formulated, without whom a tenable (however flawed) analysis of Christ's identity would have taken far longer to emerge. Remember all those Montanists and Donatists and Gnostics who, through their opposition, helped to define the articles of Christian belief. Remember Marcion, whose musings forced the rest of Christianity to set about establishing its scriptural canon, which, it was loudly averred, very definitely included the Old Testament, all four Gospels, and much else besides.

There is barely time to mention Pelagius (350–425), the British monk — a "fat man stuffed with porridge" as his enemies uncharitably described him — who, at the start of the fifth century, also fetched up in Rome and began promulgating a profoundly optimistic analysis of human nature. There was no such thing as original sin, he declared: "Evil is not born with us, we are begotten without fault." To the guardians of emerging orthodoxies — Augustine preeminently — this seemed preposterous. If, simply through the exercise of his uncorrupted free will, a person could strive for perfectibility and achieve salvation, then one might wonder why Christ had taken the trouble to die on the cross. Pelagius's heretical theorizing seemed to rob Christ's sacrifice of all its salvific importance. Infuriated by what Pelagius had to say, Augustine set about devising ideas about original sin — ideas that made salvation an unmerited gift from God — that would echo through the Christian world down to the present day. Because "heresy" had forced the arm of "orthodoxy," a somber Christian mentality came into being. Many would challenge it, of course, but many others would find a curious kind of sustenance in Augustine's melancholy image of sinful, impotent mankind being pressed, as he memorably put it, in the olive press of the Lord.

This is what heresy could achieve. It could come up with ideas of its own, but it could also force its opponents to clarify their own theologies. Christianity had a text for such occasions. As a verse from First Corinthians put it, "It is needful that there should be heresies among you, so that those which are approved may be made manifest." Or, as Tertullian explained, "We ought not to be astonished at the heresies . . . by affording a trial to faith, they give it the opportunity to be approved."[17] Heretical errors, so the logic went, helped make orthodoxy more transparent.

This notion of theological development (the genuine Christian message gradually coming into focus) would still be finding favor as late as the nineteenth century in the thought of John Henry Newman. He pointed to the "remarkable manner in which Divine Providence makes use of error itself as a preparation for the truth."[18] This was savvy but, at best, only half convincing. Heresy certainly helped define orthodoxy, but it still required a bold leap to equate that orthodoxy with the only reputable version of Christianity. Heresy did not just exist in order to clarify the Christian vision because heresy was often simply a different version (a hundred different versions) of that vision. As the next thousand years would make very clear, it had no intention of losing any of its potency.

4
THE HERESY GAP

CHRISTIANITY HAS ALWAYS had an exceptionally good, if selective, memory. Many of the theological challenges and puzzles raised by the first heresies would continue to simmer, and the church fathers' disgruntled analyses cast a spell that would never quite be broken. The thirst for unity and the notion that intellectual pride, the machinations of Satan, or both things intermingled were responsible for heresy would hold good for centuries to come. More than that, whenever a new heresy arose in future years it always stood an excellent chance of being perceived as some new, regrettable outcrop of an old heterodox folly. Terms like *Arianism, Donatism,* and *Manichaeism* would continue to be flung around with abandon, even when the newer heresies they were directed against were quite obviously something very different.

Most important of all, Augustine's solution to the problem of heresy would continue to rule the theological roost. *Caritas* first, then coercion: this was to be the rubric. The balance between such approaches was always up for debate (that pesky issue of whether one should go so far as actually killing heretics was especially persistent), but few questioned the notion that this was the balance that, in one way or another, had to be struck. It is sometimes said (and with good reason) that Christianity had all of its worthwhile debates and squabbles during the first few centuries: everything else simply represented joining up the dots. So far as the church's encounter with heresy goes, this analysis isn't so far wide of the mark.

All that remained to be seen was how Christianity would carry forward this uncompromising agenda. Here, in the short term at least, we seem to come up against an obstacle. Historians often talk about a conspicuous gap in the history of heresy. The fourth and fifth centuries were teeming with allegedly heterodox ideas, but then everything seemed to become a little quieter.

This apparent silence of the heretics can be deceptive. The waters became calmer only in the western half of Christendom, and this is easily explained. During the fifth century Rome fell. All those famous invading tribes arrived; the reign of the last western emperor, Romulus Augustulus ("little" Augustus), ended in 476; and a central locus of authority—always a key ingredient in the work of unearthing and annihilating heresy—disappeared. It used to be fashionable to describe this period in western Europe's history as the Dark Ages. Thankfully, we have moved beyond such historical insults and have begun to appreciate that these supposedly dismal centuries (say, the sixth to the tenth) were actually illuminated by any number of dazzling cultural achievements. Still, despite the little that is reported about them, these were unusually fortuitous times for those who might be deemed heretics. There is no reason to doubt that just as many people as ever were conjuring up theological alternatives, but the political wherewithal to seek them out went into abeyance. Heresy (an important point, this) could exist only if people were eager to define and destroy it.

The occasional heretic's name crops up in the historical record, especially during the Carolingian period, when Charlemagne and his successors were working hard to rekindle dreams of imperial plenitude. There's Elipandus, the eighth-century archbishop of Toledo who hammered out the so-called adoptionist heresy: in a challenge to the notion that Christ was fully human and fully divine, Elipandus devised a convoluted formulation whereby Christ, in his divine self, was the true and natural son of God but, in his human self, was the son of Mary but only the *adopted* son of God. Though roundly condemned by four church councils — Regensburg, 792; Frankfurt, 794; Rome, 798; Aachen, 799 — it proved impossible to remove Elipandus from his see, since at the time Toledo, like much of Spain, was under Muslim rule. And *then* there's Gottschalk, the ninth-century theologian who was among the first thinkers to talk about double predestination. God had not only decided, before the dawn of human time, that some people were destined to enjoy eternal bliss in heaven (a cheery notion), but he had also arbitrarily determined that some people, regardless of how they conducted their lives, were headed straight to hell (a less than comforting suggestion, though, as Calvin would demonstrate several centuries later, one with a bright future ahead of it). Gottschalk was unable to avoid the reach of ecclesiastical justice, and he was imprisoned by the archbishop of Rheims at Hautvilliers, where he died in about 867.

Such figures aside, however, the surveillance and the prosecution of Western heresy fell into something approaching desuetude. It was a good time to be a heretic.

Farther east, by contrast, there was no such holiday for heretics. That great heresy hunter Constantine had set up his new Rome in Constantinople, and while the Byzantine Empire endured all manner of external threats and internal political idiocies during the early medieval period, it never lost the will to expose and, whenever possible, eradicate heresy.

Heresy Redivivus

All those old debates about Christ's true identity continued to fester. The mighty decrees of Nicaea and Chalcedon were unable to dampen down speculation. In the sixth century the so-called Julianists, named for a bishop of Halikarnassos (modern Bodrum), returned to the old Docetist idea that Christ's humanity had been an illusion. As for the Monophysites, they went from strength to strength. So much so, in fact, that various seventh-century emperors sponsored an attempt to bring them back into the orthodox fold. The Chalcedonian notion of Christ's two natures, entirely human and entirely divine, was in the ascendant, but some theologians had the bright idea of creating the concept of Monothelitism (I know, so many *isms*), which argued that, behind the mysteries of the hypostatic union (see page 66 in case you've forgotten), Christ's two natures were combined, at some level, in a single *will* or energy. The underlying thought, presumably, was that any theological term beginning with the prefix *mono-* would appeal to the Monophysites. And so it did, for a while. Ultimately, however, this new attempt to conceptualize Christ was condemned at the Third Council of Constantinople in 680–681.

Perhaps even more sensational, and certainly as disruptive, was the return of dualism: the idea of two gods, or at least one God and a mischievous demiurge, one of whom was responsible for creating the corrupt material world. Such ideas enjoyed something of an Indian summer, courtesy of the Paulician sect, which flourished and caused considerable havoc in the eastern reaches of the Byzantine Empire from the seventh through the ninth centuries. The origins of the movement are obscure. Later commentators would talk of a seventh-century man named Constantine who, after enjoying a lusty sexual liaison with a Manichaean woman of loose morals, was converted to the dualistic cause. He established his first congregation in Armenia in 660. Periods of sporadic persecution followed but, by the dawn of the ninth century, the movement had attracted an impressive number of acolytes and, under the leadership of Sergius (who led the Paulicians between 801 and 835) the sect embarked on major evangelical efforts across the empire. As Sergius is supposed to have boasted, "From the east to the west, to the north and to the south I have journeyed proclaiming the gospel of Christ, walking with my own knees."[1]

This was all troubling enough for the authorities in Constantinople but, as the ninth century progressed, the Paulicians transformed themselves into a significant political and military threat. They began to establish fortified towns, most notably at Tephrice (the present-day Turkish city of Divrigi), and to contribute to Arab raids on imperial territory. Under the leadership of their general, Chrysochir, Paulician armies attacked places as symbolic as the cities of Nicaea and Nicomedia (modern Izmit), and in 867 they even managed to sack Ephesus.

Constant military struggles required their share of diplomatic negotiation — arranging the exchange of prisoners, and so forth — and it was during one of these routine embassies that a certain Petrus Siculus was sent deep into Paulician territory. He stayed with his hosts for a full nine months and, although his account is unremittingly hostile, it still provides the best remaining evidence of the Paulicians' troubling heretical ideas. By Siculus's account, they were indeed old-fashioned dualists: "The Paulicians are also Manichaeans, who have added the foul heresy they discovered to the heresy of their predecessors, and have sunk in the same gulf of perdition." They insisted that Christ had never taken human form, they held Mary in contempt, and they hated the cross, the symbol of Christ's supposed bodily crucifixion: "They heap it down with a thousand insults." Siculus also noticed a quasi-Marcionite tendency within Paulicianism: they had no tolerance for the Old Testament — it was peopled and written by "deceivers and thieves," they said.

Petrus Siculus was clearly alarmed by the spread of Paulicianism and its efforts to "tear to pieces holy and divine doctrines." Members of the sect had reached as far as the imperial capital and Siculus offered stark warnings to any right-thinking Christians who might encounter them. "The best plan for the simple is this: to avoid these corrupt people and not . . . try to answer their inquiries, but be silent when they make inquiry and, if possible, run away from private audience with them, as if they were snakes." "It is difficult for the simple not to be swept away by them as they quote all the sayings of the Gospel and the apostles in conversation, and their craft is only recognised by those who are very familiar with Holy Scripture." Like so many heretics before them, Siculus warned, the Paulicians were highly skilled at exhibiting a pious façade and of being all things to all men: "Like an octopus or a chameleon they change both manner and appearance to suit the occasions, to catch some of the witless."

Look a little closer, Siculus warned, and you would find them to be "poisonous and full of all kinds of filth." "No one should doubt that they are demons." The movement's great heroes, like the leader Sergius, were a sham. Behind the artificial holiness he was an arrogant megalomaniac: "the lover of darkness who called himself the star of daybreak." He had been "the enemy of the cross of Christ, the voice of impurity, the insulter of the mother of God and all the saints . . . the arch-adversary of the apostles of Christ, who hated the prophets and turned his back on Holy Scripture, wandering away into lies and fairy tales . . . the one who trampled under foot the son of God." Such, Siculus averred, were the Paulicians.

Siculus can hardly have enjoyed his time among them, but he sustained a confidence that their heresy wouldn't endure: "The waves of the verbosity of heretics always dissolve into froth."[2] This proved to be a little overconfident. As a military threat the Paulicians were all but destroyed in the war of 871–872 and many of them were forcibly relocated to Thrace. In the long run, this was a singularly foolish move. At this very time, Bulgaria was just in the process of being Christianized, and shipping in headstrong dualists might not have been the wisest idea from the perspective of enforcing orthodoxy. It is perhaps no coincidence that, in the coming few centuries, dualistic Christianity did excellent business in the Balkans.

∽

There was certainly no shortage of heresy in the early medieval Byzantine Empire, and there is room to mention just one more. It went by the name of iconoclasm and, for a good two centuries, it ripped the empire apart.

Iconoclasm

Christianity has often exhibited an ambivalent attitude toward holy images. By some accounts, pictures of Christ, Mary, or the saints could serve as excellent guides for devotion — especially for the illiterate. Others remained conscious of the risks of idolatry (an inheritance from the Jewish past) and feared that it was all too easy to cross the line between venerating images as representations of the true sources of Christian adoration and worshipping them in their own right. Such misgivings were especially acute in the eastern half of Christendom, where holy images were frequently lavished with extravagant attention: people would genuflect and prostrate themselves before them, icons would be kissed, and they would be held to work any number of miracles, both major and minor. If we believe the hostile chroniclers, it wasn't unknown for scrapings of paint from icons to be added to the flour and water when baking sacramental bread.

There was also the continuing Christological squabble to consider. Although the great church councils were supposed to have resolved all the debates about Christ's nature, there were still many within the Eastern Church who remained dubious about over-stressing Christ's humanity. Such people were deeply mistrustful of images of Christ since, by definition, the *human* side of him was all they could hope to convey. You couldn't paint divinity. Those who were firmly committed to Chalcedonian orthodoxy, by contrast, suggested that there was absolutely nothing wrong with portraying Christ's incarnate, human form. Some even suggested that dislike of pictures of the human Christ might indicate allegiance to something akin to flesh-hating Manichaeism.

There were many arguments to be had and, in the third decade of the eighth century, everything boiled over. In 726 the emperor Leo III, an iconoclast to his bootstraps, ordered the destruction of an icon of Christ situated above the gates of the imperial palace. There was immediate protest. A woman reportedly overturned the ladder of the workman entrusted with removing the image, a riot ensued, and in its aftermath many of those who had voiced their opposition to the removal of the image were treated to lashings, exile, and mutilation. Leo embarked upon a wide-ranging assault on the empire's religious images. As one dismayed commentator remembered, "In every village and town one could witness the weeping and lamentation of the pious . . . sacred things [were] trodden upon, vessels turned to other use, churches scraped down and smeared with ashes."[3] "Wherever there were venerable images of Christ or the mother of God or the saints, these were consigned to the flames or were gouged out or smeared over." In their place came images of birds and senseless beasts, "preserved with honour and given greater lustre."[4]

Under Constantine V (r. 741–775) the attack continued. Monks who continued to produce holy images were exiled or blinded. One church, devoted to Mary and crowded with portrayals of Christ's life, was turned into a storehouse for fruit and its offending images were replaced with "swirls of ivy, crows, and peacocks." On one Constantinople street, an image that depicted the deeds of the earlier ecumenical councils (a fairly innocent picture, even from an iconoclast's perspective) was obliterated and, by one account, made way for a portrayal of a "satanic horse race and demon loving charioteer."[5]

The iconoclasts were unflinching in their determination to outlaw religious images. As they declared at a council in 754, the painter of icons was among the most offensive members of society: "From sordid love of gain" he pursued "the unattainable . . . to fashion with his impure hands things that are believed by the heart and confessed by the mouth." He had the audacity to try to delineate the "incomprehensible and uncircumscribable divine nature of Christ." Therefore, "let no man dare to pursue henceforth his impious and unholy practice. Anyone who presumes from now on to manufacture an icon, to worship it, or to set it up in a private house, or to hide it, if he be a bishop or a presbyter or a deacon he shall be deposed; if he be a monk or a layman he shall be anathematized and deemed guilty under imperial law as a foe of God's commands and an enemy of the doctrines of the fathers."[6]

All such mutterings received a furious response from Rome. Just as the iconoclasts had declared iconophiles heretics, so Gregory II, as early as 731, returned the favor. Iconoclasm was declared an appalling heresy. Gregory II sent several letters to Leo III. The authenticity of the extant versions has sometimes been questioned (a familiar stumbling block for interpretations of this period), but letters were definitely sent, and the versions that have come down to us undoubtedly capture the scale of papal irritation at the iconoclastic events unfolding in the Byzantine Empire.

In one of them, the pope admitted to being "deeply grieved that you should persist in your error, that you should refuse to recognize the things which are Christ's, and to accept the teaching and follow the example of the holy fathers, the saintly miracle-workers and learned doctors." Instead, Gregory informed Leo, "[you] have followed the guidance of your own wayward spirit and have allowed the exigencies of the political situation at your own court to lead you astray." Leo should remember the policies of his predecessors: they "ruled righteously; they held synods in harmony with the popes, they tried to establish true doctrines, they founded and adorned churches." By contrast, "wherever you found churches adorned and enriched with hangings you despoiled them."

Leo hated religious pictures, but "men and women make use of these pictures to instruct in the faith their little children and young men and maidens in bloom of youth and those from heathen nations; by means of these pictures the hearts and minds of men are directed to God. But you have ordered the people to abstain from the pictures, and have attempted to satisfy them with idle sermons, trivialities, music of pipe and zither, rattles and toys, turning them from the giving of thanks to the hearing of idle tales." The emperor was there to preserve order: it came down to the pope to determine doctrine. Leo had forgotten this; he had "transgressed and gone astray . . . and driven from [himself] the Holy Spirit." The pope was "unarmed and defenceless, possessing no earthly armies," so he called upon "the prince of all the armies of creation, Christ seated in the heavens, commanding all the hosts of celestial beings, to send a demon upon you." "Do you see now, emperor, to what a pitch of impudence and inhumanity you have gone? You have driven your soul headlong into the abyss, because you would not humble yourself and bend your stubborn neck."[7]

In time, the rulers in Constantinople came around to the papal side of the argument. Under Leo IV the destruction tailed off and in 787 the empress Irene reversed imperial policy: at the Second Council of Nicaea, she also denounced iconoclasm as a heresy. Unfortunately, Byzantine emperors were never known for their consistency. In 815, Leo V overthrew Irene's decision and under his successor, Theophilus (r. 829–842), a new, even more extensive program of iconoclasm was embarked upon. "All painters of sacred images," it was declared, "should be done away with." And if they managed to live, it would only be because they had been willing to spit upon their paintings, throw them to the ground, and tread on them. Those who refused to buckle under, like the painter Lazarus, endured the most horrific punishments. He faced "such severe tortures that his flesh melted away along with his blood." When he recovered and began painting once again, red-hot irons were placed on the palms of his hands.[8]

Whichever side one takes on the issue of holy images, the iconoclastic controversy was an utter disaster. Charges of heresy were tossed from camp to camp, and all manner of cruel and grotty deeds were done. It was presumably with great relief that the whole unwholesome episode came to an end in 843, when Theodora once more reversed imperial policy and made holy images legal. It took a long time for the scars to heal, however, both literally and figuratively. Theodora's new patriarch, Methodius, was a living reminder of the ugly recent past: "his lips mutilated by the iron of the iconoclasts, obliged at public functions to hold his jaw together with white bandages."[9]

၅

Iconoclasm touched the West too, although the consequences were not nearly so gruesome. A very poor translation of the edicts of the Second Council of Nicaea (which had denounced iconoclasm) found its way to Charlemagne's court in the late eighth century and it raised many eyebrows, mainly because the bungled translation seemed to suggest that the council defended the excessive *adoration* of idols — which, as the original text showed, it did not. This was an unusually touchy subject at the time, since many parts of the western continent had only recently been weaned off paganism and its penchant for idol worship. There was also the unfortunate fact that the empress behind the council, Irene, was rather unpopular in the West. Charlemagne certainly didn't side with the iconoclasts of the East, but he refused to accept the conclusions of the Nicaean council, and various entirely unnecessary refutations of it were penned by his bishops. It was a colossal misunderstanding, stemming from a single mistranslated sentence, and it helped further sour relations between the eastern and western halves of Christendom.

It did prove two things, however: heresy was still a battleground and, after centuries in the doldrums, the West was once more pricking up its ears to signs of waywardness in doctrine and practice. As we are about to discover, the trend was set to continue. Little more than a century after the iconoclastic controversy had finally fizzled out, and more than five since the fall of Rome, the West was entering what, for good reason, has often been called the golden age of heresy. It quickly made up for lost time.

5
MEDIEVAL HERESY I

A FEW DAYS after Christmas, 1022, a famous heresy trial was mounted in the French city of Orléans. A Norman nobleman called Aréfast had recently sent a member of his household, a cleric named Heribert, to study there. Aréfast was scandalized by the theological ideas being peddled by Heribert's teachers: it seemed entirely possible that they were the leaders of a heretical sect located at the heart of the Christian establishment — in this instance, the Cathedral of the Holy Cross at Orléans. Aréfast, with the backing of his feudal superior (the duke of Normandy), decided to infiltrate their ranks to learn for himself about their noxious heresies. He played a wily game, posing as a humble layman in order to soak up their teachings. On December 28, a synod, presided over by the king of France (Robert II, "the pious"), assembled in the town and the clerics suspected of heresy were dragged in chains into the royal presence. Aréfast, still undercover, was also chained up, and there are conflicting reports as to what happened next.

Either he simply revealed himself as a spy and began to denounce the heretics who had been instructing him, or (and it's hard not to prefer this version of events) he kept up the subterfuge for a little longer. He announced that, as a simple soul, he was unable to

accurately recount what he had been taught: could his teachers possibly provide a digest of their theological positions? It was a brilliant
tactic: the heretical clerics would damn themselves through their
own testimony and, if we are to trust some of the chroniclers, this is
precisely what they proceeded to do.

It became apparent that the clerics of Orléans had been incu-
bating some unusually provocative theological ideas. They apparently believed in a new kind of gnosis, a special knowledge that left
the initiated entirely free from sin. This allowed them to tease out
the true meaning of Christ's message and made them sneer at the
empty rituals of the established church. They refused to believe that
Christ had been born of the Virgin Mary or that he had taken on
human form. As for the resurrection, their response to the notion
was blunt: "We were not there, and we cannot believe that to be
true." As many as twenty local clerics had apparently been seduced
by the heresy, alongside members of the nobility and a man named
Stephen — former confessor to the king's wife, Constance.

Even more appalling, rumors began to circulate that, as well
as rejecting all of the church's sacraments, the heretics gained sustenance from consuming the ashes of dead babies: the progeny, so
it was said, of their lascivious nighttime orgies. Having no need
of "earthly wisdom" and scorning existing theologies — "fictions
of carnal men scribbled on animal skins," as they reputedly called
them — they had turned their backs on the church and were now in
thrall to Satan.

Judgment upon the men, made easier by their bizarre will-
ingness to admit to some of their errors, was swift and brutal. The
priests were stripped of their vestments and condemned as heretics. As the queen's old confessor, Stephen, left the synod, Constance struck out his eye with a staff. Those who refused to repent of
their errors were taken outside the city walls to be burned alive, and
the body of Deodatus the cantor, who had shared their beliefs but
died several years earlier, was exhumed and incinerated. His ashes

were scattered on waste ground. Aréfast, we can safely assume, was lauded as a bold, loyal son of the church who had risked his eternal soul in order to expose the sect. It was a case study in the obliteration of heresy.[1]

⁓

This, for lots of good reasons, is the story that routinely opens accounts of medieval heresy. There is no reason to buck the trend. It was an epochal moment: the first judicial, state-sponsored execution of heretics in the medieval West. It was also emblematic of an astonishing flowering of eleventh-century heresy. Pockets of aberrant belief began cropping up with alarming regularity across the continent. At Monforte, in 1028, a group of heretics were executed for their bizarre ascetical ideas. According to the chroniclers (always happy to oblige), they shared all goods in common, worshipped pagan idols, and became obsessed with preserving their virginity. They looked forward to the day when the grubby business of coition would vanish from the human experience: eventually, they are supposed to have said (and one can obviously forgive the wayward eleventh-century understanding of biology), we would all reproduce like the bees.

At Goslar, in northern Germany, in 1051, another handful of heretics went the way of all flesh because of their apparent hatred of the creaturely world — a telltale sign, it was supposed, of their commitment to the idea of a dualistic universe in which the material realm was the brainchild of a second, evil god. They refused to eat meat and the clinching proof of their guilt was their unwillingness to kill a chicken: the start of a long-standing medieval relationship between vegetarianism and suspicions of heresy.

At Arras, a few years earlier, the local bishop had unearthed a sect whose members rejected the notions of baptism and marriage and refused to regard the Old Testament as a legitimate part of holy writ. This time around, mercifully, the putative heretics were won back to the church by a ridiculously long sermon from the bishop and a three-day spell in the local clink.

The church's immediate response to such troubling developments was to assume that ancient heretical battles, long dormant, were being rejoined. As the twelfth-century abbot Wibald of Corvey explained, it was impossible for heretics to "say anything new."[2] Whenever heresies emerged it was convenient to fall back on the assumption that they merely represented old poisons in fresh bottles. Those people at Goslar looked like nothing so much as Gnostics for a new age. It also made obvious sense to suggest that the same mischievous force lay behind all these heretical outpourings. Satan was to blame.

The Orléans heretics were accused of snacking on the remains of babies and, presumably, it was the same devil who held dominion over a group of heretics in twelfth-century Soissons, in northern France. They would hold their conventicles in cellars and sacred places, the chronicler Guibert of Nogent reported, and indulge in all manner of orgiastic and incestuous excess. If children were born of such unholy unions, they would be burned alive and loaves of bread — the heretics' perverse inversion of the holy sacrament — would be made from their ashes.

Such stories had an obvious propagandist appeal, as the frequency with which they were applied to different heretical groups testifies. So it was that the dualist Bogomils of the medieval Balkans were also charged with the slaughter of infants, "cutting their tender flesh all over with sharp knives and catching the streams of blood in basins." And when the Englishman Walter Map set about exposing a sect of French heretics in his late-twelfth-century book *De nugis curialium* (*Courtiers' Trifles*), he immediately pounced on the tried and tested strategy of associating the heretics with diabolical activities. They would assemble in a darkened room, he explained, awaiting the arrival of a giant black cat, which would descend via a rope. After singing their satanic hymns, the heretics would set about kissing the cat on its genitals and, thus stimulated, indulge in their inevitable promiscuities.[3]

Such inventions (and we'd have to assume that is what they were) represented artful exercises in propaganda. It was an old trick, somewhat reminiscent of Clement of Alexandria's second-century suggestion that Gnostics ate embryos and made their Eucharist out of semen and menses.[4] Such outrages made it abundantly clear that heresy was part of Satan's insidious plan to bring about the ruination of mankind, but they also carried an erotic, salacious charge that made them eminently memorable. There was also considerable irony in the fact that two of the most frequently invoked examples of repulsive heretical behavior — incest and cannibalism — were precisely the same charges that had so often been leveled against Christians in the early church. Christianity learned that lesson and turned it to its own advantage.

The church's reaction to these supposed heresies was therefore deeply unimaginative, but events in Orléans, Goslar, Monforte, Soissons, and a dozen other places besides can easily give the impression that medieval Europe was in the grip of a panic. Heresy seemed to be everywhere, and talk of diabolical machinations permeated the age. Such concerns would captivate the European imagination for the next five centuries, all the way down to the Reformation.

How seriously we ought to take this panic is an entirely different matter. Whether medieval heresy was quite as widespread as the records seem to show is a subject for important debate. The absurd claims about the heretics' practices immediately give one pause, and this is an issue we'll revisit. What really matters, however, is that medieval Europe seems to have bought the hype — if hype is, in fact, what it really was.

∽

What can be said with certainty about the events of 1022, and many of those other eleventh- and twelfth-century stories, is that they helped plot the trajectory of the subsequent five hundred years of the history of heresy and how the church dealt with it. First, there was the nagging uncertainty. There is absolutely no way of being sure whether the men condemned at Orléans were guilty of everything of which they stood accused. We can hazard a guess that, while talk of their orgies and their baby eating was a clichéd fiction, they might very well have subscribed to aberrant theological beliefs. It will always be impossible to get to the truth since, in virtually every recorded case of medieval heresy, we derive most of our facts and figures from openly hostile, and not necessarily trustworthy, sources — inquisitors, chroniclers, and churchmen.

Second, as we have already mentioned, the notion that Satan was behind the perversions and posturing of heretics was also very much in evidence at Orléans, and in the writings of those who chronicled events. This powerful idea, that heresy was the fruit of the devil's fury and malice of the devil, was hardly novel, but it would gain a new prominence in medieval Europe. This was the age, after all, that claimed to witness the expansion of that most demonic strain of heresy: witchcraft.

Finally, there was the none-too-subtle intersection of accusations of heresy and the workings of political power. Though the details needn't long detain us, the events at Orléans were intimately bound up with simmering political and ecclesiastical rivalries. The man who oversaw the synod, the French king, Robert II, had more than his share of enemies in Orléans. He had imposed his own candidate for bishop on the diocese, much to local displeasure, and there is at least a suspicion that the whole heresy-hunting campaign had been launched by Robert's rivals in order to show what a pitiful job the king's choice of bishop had made of sustaining order and orthodoxy. Indeed, two of the men at the heart of the supposed heretical sect had close links to the king and queen. Faced with all this, Robert seems to have seen the synod as an opportunity to demonstrate his orthodoxy and commitment to preserving the faith. This, at least, would explain the severity of the punishments handed down; it transforms Queen Constance's brutal attack on her old confessor, Stephen, from a random gesture of violence into a calculated moment of high symbolism: there was no better way to distance oneself from heresy than to strike out a heretic's eye.

This interplay of faith and politics, so apparent at Orléans, would reach its zenith (or nadir) during the medieval era. Heresy was only sometimes about rarefied theological disagreement; just as often it represented an outlet for political one-upmanship and rivalry. As we'll see, trumping up charges of heresy against your enemies, or at the very least tarring them with suspicions of having sympathy for heretics or displaying lackluster orthodoxy, would become favored pastimes of medieval politicians. Heresy was a commodity to be abused, and spurious accusations of heretical leanings blighted many parts of medieval Europe.

There was something missing in Orléans, however. The greatest transformation wrought by medieval heresy seemed to be largely absent. Some of the chroniclers made mention of the mob baying for blood outside the synod door, there was even some hazy talk of a "rustic" from Périgord having something to do with the origins of the heresy, but by the time the synod met in the winter of 1022, most of the central heretical characters had turned out to be priests. Their misdemeanors were decidedly idiosyncratic, but they had at least one thing in common with most of the heretics of the early church: their clerical rank.

This priestly dominance of the heretical landscape would come under siege during the medieval period. Suddenly there would be a far wider cast of heretical characters. Laymen, of varying social rank, would begin to figure prominently, and this contributed to a sea change in the complexion of heresy and the steps that were taken to eradicate it.

POPULAR HERESY

As we have seen, early Christian heresy was, more often than not, an elite pursuit: the realm of presbyters, priests, and deacons like Arius, Donatus, Nestorius, and all the rest. Even Marcion the ship owner is reputed, by some accounts, to have had a highly placed cleric (a bishop, even) for a father. As we've also seen, the debates that raged were often rarefied: a head-spinning mixture of Greek terms and sophisticated theologizing. It is very easy to have some sympathy for the nameless layman outside the debating chambers of one of those early church councils who took the logic-chopping theologians to task. Did they not realize, he bellowed, "that Christ and his apostles did not teach us dialectics, art, nor vain subtleties, but straightforward thinking which is preserved by nothing more than faith and good works?"[5]

It is important to stress that intellectual heresies did not disappear during the medieval era. How could they, during a period that saw the emergence of the great European universities? The subject matter was often entirely different (there were precious few who now challenged the central conclusions of Nicaea and Chalcedon, for instance), but the protagonists were still often men of great learning at the very heart of the church. The taint of heresy had always touched seeming paragons of Christian learning and the trend would continue. Before getting down to the nitty-gritty of popular heresy, it's worth spending a few moments on this more rarefied terrain.

Overt accusations, or at least weighty suspicions, of heresy overshadowed people like Berengar of Tours (the eleventh-century cleric who had unorthodox things to say about the newly minted doctrine of transubstantiation) and Siger of Brabant (the thirteenth-century Belgian who reached some radical conclusions about the immortality of the soul and an everlasting world — this last notion representing something of a body blow to the concept of the Last Judgment and the world's demise). Most famous of all was Peter Abelard, affectionately remembered as the man who fell in love with Eloise and lost his manhood as a result, but who was also a daringly speculative thinker.

Abelard enjoyed an eminent academic career, but his theological meditations brought him no end of trouble. His enemies claimed that he was addicted to the exercise of reason, even when this carried perilous theological consequences. Perhaps his most famous work, *Sic et Non* (*Yes and No*), was made up of dozens of contradictory patristic quotations set side by side. Abelard was not trying to provoke disquiet or dissent: his hope was that his book would prompt scholars to satisfactorily explain away all these hermeneutic puzzles. For many contemporaries, however, exposing such potential fault lines was a singularly foolhardy enterprise. Worse yet was Abelard's attempt to apply his rigorous critical thinking to the doctrine of the Trinity. It was this that brought him into genuine strife. Condemned twice, at the councils of Soissons and Sens (in 1121 and 1141), he suffered the indignities of being made to burn his own writings and being ordered to keep a perpetual scholarly silence. To Bernard of Clairvaux (one of the medieval era's most devoted champions of orthodoxy), Abelard resembled the seven-headed beast of the book of Revelation: he was, for all his learning, a heretic, and Bernard always adopted a harsh attitude toward heresy: "Should not the mouth that speaks such things be shattered with cudgels rather than rebutted with reason?" he once asked.[6]

So, no, intellectual heresy certainly didn't disappear. Throughout the medieval era, a venue such as the University of Paris was a hotbed of abstruse debates about fine points of theology, and charges and countercharges of heresy flowed accordingly. Even some of the things that Thomas Aquinas had to say came under scrutiny, and when 219 theses were condemned in 1277, some of Aquinas's ideas were among them. Such moments are easy to forget, not least because of the towering theological figure that Aquinas, in posterity, became. If even someone like Aquinas — the great syn-thesizer of Christianity and the nostrums of Aristotelian thought, the thinker whose reputation, at least in some circles, continues to soar — was once placed under the heresy-seeking microscope, then we are reminded that the line between orthodoxy and heterodoxy was always very thin.

This climate was not always popular. William of Conches, who won his own share of criticism, suggested that "whenever they know that someone is engaging in research they shout that he is a heretic."[7] This was a little unfair. The attempt to determine pre-cisely what counted as a heresy was usually painstaking and subtle. There was rarely a rush to judgment and there was a colossal ef-fort to distinguish between varying kinds and degrees of heretical thought within the clerical and academic fraternity: some ideas were patently outlandish, others might simply hint at thoughts that, if carried through to their logical conclusions, might prove to be heterodox. Nor, for all Bernard of Clairvaux's bluster, was it a matter of cudgeling errant scholars. It was more a matter of telling thinkers to keep their thoughts to themselves, robbing them of their jobs and lecterns, or sentencing them to close confinement in a monastery: harsh, but not overly so.

At the time, when modern notions of academic freedom didn't yet exist, this struck most people as a perfectly legitimate exercise in self-regulation. Abelard, for example, was a victim of the system, but he hated heresies as much as anyone else. "It is not ignorance that makes a heretic," he once wrote, "but pride. It is when, for ex-ample, someone wants — for novelty's sake — to make a name for himself and he boasts in putting forward something unusual, which he then tries to defend against all comers in order to look superior to everyone."[8] The irony is that this is precisely what his enemies would have said about Abelard. To us, he is the great champion: the man who crafted a radically logical approach to theological study, who reveled in the contradictions of scripture, who — so the story goes — was a forerunner of scientific textual analysis. And so he was, but to contemporaries he was a thorn in the theological side, and the process that closed him down was a process of which, in theory, he would have approved. This is worth remembering.

Perhaps it is useful to think of all this as a creaky old trend continuing: curiosity was always a little suspect, and it was customary to put it down to overweening pride. True wisdom, true *sapientia*, came from humility, and highbrow theological mutterings, when they overstepped the line, could lead to accusations of heterodoxy.[9]

༄

To return to our main point, however, there was also something startlingly different about a great deal of medieval heresy. The heretic was now just as likely to be someone like Bernard Servel, the humble Cathar blacksmith of Tarascon who, robbed of his property and made to wear penitentiary crosses on his clothes, was forced to cross the Pyrenees to find work. The so-called heretic was now someone like Hans, the fourteenth-century beggar of Augsburg who took up residence in an abandoned chapel and, along with his fellow gout sufferers, set about praying for a cure — without bothering to seek the approval of the local ecclesiastical authorities. He was burned at the stake for his trouble. Suspicions of heresy now began to attach themselves, with much greater regularity, to the middling and lesser sort, like the French wine merchant who, in 1236, was selling his wares in England when, because he seems to have done or said something that raised the eyebrows of ecclesiastical authority, all his goods were seized.[10] The advocate of staggering cosmological visions was now an Italian furrier named Stradigotto who boldly declared in the early thirteenth century that "this world and all visible things were created by the devil; that human souls are spirits that fell from heaven."[11]

For every clerical or academic heretic there was now a lay heretic. There would still be heretical clerics and scholars, such as Hus and Wyclif, but there was also Valdes, founder of the Waldensians, and very much the star of the next section of the book: and Valdes was a cloth merchant from Lyon.

Along with this adjustment in heretical personnel came a tangible shift in their obsessions. Squabbles about arcane issues of dogma and doctrine often gave way to arguments about ecclesiology — the nature of the church — and the knotty issue of how the individual might expect to commune with and serve his maker. Many of those denounced as heretics would question whether the established Christian hierarchy was entirely satisfactory. They wondered whether they really needed priestly intermediaries in order to worship and strike up a relationship with God. They wondered whether the pious layman (or even the pious laywoman: a dread thought in the middle of the Middle Ages) was capable of pursuing the goal (or myth) of apostolic purity and playing a more central role in the world of Christian devotion. Heresy was now about issues that directly concerned every member of the Christian republic: issues of authority, organization, and self-determination. People began to think, in increasingly provocative ways, about who should be in charge of the very important business of getting to heaven. And even when disenchanted clerics were leading the charge, as they routinely did, they still managed to draw a popular crowd.

We are bound to ask why this all happened. It is a difficult question to answer: a good place to start, as ever, is the stories.

VALDES

The saints of the Christian church are a mixed bunch. These days, achieving canonization requires the prospective saint to jump through any number of posthumous hoops. Proofs of extreme piety and miraculous deeds are required. In earlier times, the church was sometimes less rigorous. All it really took to make a saint was a seductive legend and enough people who believed in it. Saint Alexius was one of the beneficiaries of this more indulgent approach. By the ninth century many Christians were telling tales about Alexius's magnificent endeavors. Five hundred years earlier, he had been born the son of a wealthy Roman senator but, with the prospect of an arranged marriage looming, he decided to flee the scene. He was determined to serve Christ through a life of humility and abnegation.

He traveled east and set himself up as a hermit close to the city of Edessa. This new lifestyle took its toll and, after years of holy deprivation, he returned home to Rome. No one recognized his wizened countenance — not even his parents who, being good Christians, allowed him to lodge in a cupboard underneath one of the staircases of their sumptuous palace. Alexius, humble, happy, and anonymous, lived out the remaining seventeen years of his life catechizing children and offering up prayers.

It was an excellent story and cultic followers of Alexius eagerly spread word of his sacrifices. By the twelfth century it was a familiar tale and so it was that, in 1173 or thereabouts, a minstrel sang about Alexius's deeds in the French town of Lyon. One of the passersby was a wealthy merchant named Valdes. As luck would have it, he had a great deal in common with the fabled saint. He was rich, he had a loving family, and the world was at his feet, but he also shared Alexius's thirst to cast all this aside and follow Christ in a much humbler way. Suitably inspired, Valdes determined to jettison the possessions and attachments of the workaday world. He gave up all his belongings, made generous financial provision for the wife he was about to abandon, and placed his daughters in a local nunnery. Like the apostles of old, he would now embrace a life of poverty and austerity, finding all the spiritual sustenance he required in the passages of scripture he had had translated into his native Provençal tongue.

Thus far Valdes posed no obvious threat. His choices were curious, but they were his own, and there was little room to query the charitable work that he undertook. No one could really object to someone setting up soup kitchens for the poor during times of famine. But Valdes now went further, and it was at this point that he embarked, so far as the syndics of orthodoxy were concerned, on the road toward heresy. He began to preach his message of abnegation and people began to listen. He soon attracted followers who styled themselves the Poor of Lyon. To the guardians of the faith this was intolerable. Preaching was supposed to be the preserve of the priestly caste, the only true intermediaries between God and humanity. It was not the business of charismatic laymen, however well intentioned. Valdes was striking directly at the special, privileged role of the established church: at the men whose wealth and worldliness Valdes seemed to be mocking and denouncing by adopting a humble mendicant lifestyle of his own.

When the local archbishop ordered Valdes and his followers to desist, Valdes set out for the church council being held in the city of Rome, hoping to gain papal permission to carry on his preaching ministry. There are conflicting reports as to how Valdes was treated. Some claim that he was received sympathetically; others suggest that the assembled bishops set about humiliating Valdes by exposing his embarrassing lack of theological learning. In any event, the upshot was that Valdes was informed that he could indeed preach, but only if he received the explicit permission of his local bishop. Since this was never likely to be granted, Valdes had effectively been gagged.

Undeterred, Valdes and his followers continued to preach and, while Valdes made strenuous efforts to demonstrate his doctrinal orthodoxy — exhibiting, for instance, a passionate hatred for the heresy of the Cathars — he was soon banished from the city of Lyon. As things fell out, however, exile only inspired and energized his growing legions of followers. Soon, communities of Waldensians — as their enemies now dubbed them — were springing up throughout southern France and across the Alps in northern Italy.

Valdes died in or around 1218, by which time his movement had begun to splinter into opposing factions. Some Waldensians (primarily those in Italy) abandoned the notion of itinerant ministry and began to establish settled communities, train their own ministers, and support themselves through manual labor. It was all unfeasibly radical and, at its councils, the church dutifully set about denouncing the Waldensians as heretics.

The Waldensians' crime was that, as a result of their unregulated enthusiasm, they seemed to undermine the power structures of the church by reaching their own conclusions and establishing their own hierarchies and forms of worship. It was a challenge that was always going to provoke a hostile response, and centuries of persecution ensued.

෩

The Waldensian heretics of northern Italy probably fared the worst. Carpeted with vineyards, with forests of chestnut and mulberry, their alpine valleys seemed to hold out the promise of rural calm and plenty. But this was a scarred landscape, a place of awful memories, a charnel house. For centuries, popes and inquisitors, kings of France and dukes of Savoy — armed with the church's doctrinal blessing — would hound the mountain heretics to their deaths.

It is hard to sort the facts from the fictions. The Waldensians suffered mightily, so it was only appropriate that they would produce harrowing narratives of their struggle. Even if these narratives sometimes err on the side of exaggeration, they undoubtedly record the contours of actual historical events: and they make for grim reading. Savoyard troops, intent on carnage, would shatter the devotional peace of Christmas Day in 1400. In fear for their lives, villagers scrambled high into the mountains and passed the night of Christ's nativity without food or shelter. Tradition holds that many lost limbs to the freezing cold; others, dozens of infants among them, gave up their lives. Two generations later, in 1487, an entire crusading army flooded into the valleys of Piedmont and once more the Waldensians sought refuge in the high places, singing psalms as they scaled the treacherous mountain paths. Their pursuers lit fires at the narrow entrances of the caves and grottos in which the heretics were huddled. Many were suffocated by the noxious smoke; many more rushed out, only to be cut down by the swords of Christian orthodoxy.

Sometimes Waldensians died alone. In the crucible of the Reformation, stories would be told of unspeakable cruelty and torture, of men whose entrails were ripped from their writhing bodies, of men's mouths being crammed with gunpowder and set alight, of men being tormented to death by feral cats. There had always been periods of respite, but it was through the communal suffering that the Waldensians forged their plaintive identity. The greatest calamity of all came in 1655. Catholic troops demanded quarter in the Waldensian villages. For two days they bantered happily with their hosts, sharing their family meals. Then, early in the morning of Easter Sunday, at a prearranged signal, the troops abandoned their jovial façade and set about the organized massacre of hundreds of men, women, and children.

∽

Valdes was exceptional in that, albeit unwittingly, he had created a movement that would endure. That movement went far beyond anything Valdes had intended but, for all the persecutions, it clung on. So far as his initial vision was concerned, however, Valdes was far from unusual. The twelfth and thirteenth centuries were replete with disenchanted clerics and, more important, laymen who challenged the theological and ecclesiastical status quo. Some were every bit as well intentioned as Valdes; others were quite obviously lunatics or demagogues. But many of them shared the same desire to return to the rigors and purity of the apostolic past.

There was the twelfth-century heretic Peter of Bruis, for instance, who traveled around southern France denouncing baptism, prayers for the dead, and the Eucharist, claiming that true Christians did not require church buildings, and encouraging his followers to build bonfires of crucifixes and drag monks out of monasteries. By his account, the church's great symbol, the cross, was an instrument of torture, so it was obscene that it had become an object of fetishistic devotion. He was thrown onto one of his own bonfires in 1131.

Then there was Henry of Lausanne who, in 1116, arrived outside the town of Le Mans, in northwest France, with tangled hair and ragged clothing. At first he was welcomed by the local bishop as one of the stable-cleaning wandering preachers who were currently appearing across the continent. Henry was even granted permission to sermonize to local crowds. The trouble was, his preaching was unapologetically censorious. Making his "home in doorways, his bed in the gutter," he set about excoriating the wealth and corruption of the local clergy, their "flashing jewels and glittering gold." There was no need for church buildings, he declared; no need to fear the pains of purgatory. The younger clergy, shamed by Henry's strictures, were said to sit weeping at the heretic's feet as he preached. The prostitutes of the city, moved by his pleas for moral reform, cast off their old polluted clothes and sought out husbands. The entire populace rose up, cast out the clergy, and for a few months in the summer of 1116 the town of Le Mans became a site of revolution.

Again, it is unsurprising that Henry was condemned as a heretical demagogue. He was duly banished from Le Mans but, over the coming decades, he kept popping up in the towns of France. He was nothing if not persistent. At the Council of Pisa he was denounced as a heretic and he dutifully abjured his beliefs, only to set off on his heterodox odyssey once more. The authorities caught up with him again in Pisa and he was ordered to sequester himself in a monastery, from behind the walls of which he would no longer be able to pollute the Christian commonwealth. Again, however, he made good his escape.

Henry's theology, by any standard, was extreme. He questioned the notion of infant baptism (a heretical position with a long past and a healthy future), he came up with fresh interpretations of the meaning of original sin, he wondered if the institution of marriage really required a church ceremony to legitimize it, and he blithely dismissed the role of priestly meditation: you didn't need a cleric in order to confess your sins, and Mass could be celebrated by anyone. As for prayers for the dead, they were an irrelevance at best. Once you had died you were either damned or saved, and no amount of posthumous interventions by those you'd left behind could influence your eternal fate. In the face of all this (and since its efforts to silence him had come to naught) the church only had one option remaining: to smear Peter's name with the usual allegations of depravity. It was scurrilously suggested that he was overly fond of women and young boys: they "caressed his feet, his buttocks, his groin, with tender hands."[12]

৩

Let us not romanticize things unduly, however. Not every heretical seeker after apostolic purity was a good egg. There were also some veritable monsters and some charismatic leaders who caused levels of social chaos that not even the most tolerant society could have accepted. Fra Dolcino and the Apostolici (the apostolic brethren) are a case in point. This was a movement founded, in around 1260, by Gerardo Segarelli, an unlettered layman of Parma. At first, there was more show than substance. Segarelli's followers would clothe themselves in white robes, shave their heads, live by alms, and insist that they were the new, prophesied order of monks who would usher in the final days during which Antichrist would appear. This was worrying enough, especially since the movement had begun to attract several thousand followers in northern Italy. In 1300 Segarelli was burned to death as a heretic.

The reins of the movement were eagerly seized by Fra Dolcino, the illegitimate son of a priest. He declared that all clerics and all members of the established religious orders were nothing more than the devil's ministers. The new mendicant orders that had appeared at the beginning of the thirteenth century — the Franciscans and Dominicans — had shown some initial promise, but they too had fallen by the wayside. Now, by the year 1300, Christendom was in an age of terminal decline. Enter the prophecies. Some day soon a new king would arrive (Ferdinand II of Sicily was the preferred candidate for a while) and he would set about wiping out all the corrupt priests and prelates, even the pope himself. A new millennial age would begin and Christianity would be reborn.

Needless to say, this didn't come to pass, but on the road toward their crushing millennial disappointment the Apostolici headed to the mountains between Vercelli and Novara and established a communitarian society in which all goods were held in common. They also proved to be rather violent. The tales told of their outrages were doubtless exaggerated and we'll never really know if they slaughtered orthodox Christians by the score, hanged Christian husbands in front of their wives, and cut off women's breasts. It seems likely that some of their more subdued tactics — attacking churches, defacing artworks, stealing altar tables, and smashing bells — were a historical reality.

In any event, the established church did not sit on its hands. A military battle raged for two years in the hills of northern Italy and, at its culmination, Fra Dolcino was executed at Vercelli in 1307. It proved, by some accounts, to be an unusually horrific death. One of Dolcino's followers was dismembered alive in front of him. Then his own arms were removed with heated pincers and, after he had breathed his last, his bones were burned. No trace of him, so the thinking went, should remain.

This was heresy at its most militant but, in those turbulent medieval years, it was not all that unusual. Still, there was some room for the church to be grateful that all such events could be put down to rural excess. At least the bastions of Christian power had survived unscathed. This all changed, for a few years at least, with the arrival of Arnold of Brescia. Arnold was a cleric but he also had the common touch. He started his heretical career in the Italian town of Brescia, leading a popular revolt against the local bishop and clergy on the grounds that they were terribly worldly and in need of reform. He was duly banished from Italy in 1139 and, when he started preaching across the border in France, he was roundly condemned at the Council of Sens in 1141 (the same council, you'll remember, that scolded Peter Abelard).

Arnold wasn't quite finished, however. For whatever reason, he was allowed to return to Italy in the mid-1140s and he immediately set his sights on the powerhouse of Christian orthodoxy, the city of Rome. He began to denounce the pope: "not what he professed to be — an apostolic man and shepherd of souls — but a man of blood who maintained his authority by fire and sword." The crowds seem to have loved him and, while this is a curiously forgotten episode in the history of the eternal city, Arnold engineered something of a medieval revolution. The pope was expelled and, for a little while, a commune under Arnold's leadership held sway on the banks of the Tiber. It soon came crashing down, of course. Imperial troops arrived, the pope was reinstalled, and in 1155 Arnold was captured and burned at the stake.[13]

It was still an impressive achievement, as were many of these medieval heretical fluorescences. Some of them were grotesque, some of them were quite admirable, but they all raise an obvious question. What on earth was going on? Popular heresy, able to re-

cruit thousands upon thousands of supporters, had seemingly arrived, and we are obliged to look for some sort of causation.

There is an important argument to be had about whether the
deeds and posturing of men as diverse as Valdes, Peter of Bruis, and
Fra Dolcino ought to be seen as representative of a general mood
of disenchantment and protest. Given the breadth of the European
continent, and bearing in mind all of the places which didn't witness these sorts of heretical events, it would be premature to regard
the apparent explosion of popular medieval heresy as, in any way,
typical. This is a counterargument to which we'll return but, in the
meantime, it would not be entirely disreputable to take this extraordinary landscape of heretical outburst at face value. So let's do precisely that.

POPULAR HERESY: REALITY

The conventional explanation (and in many ways it is compelling)
for this twist in the history of heresy goes something like this. The
period between 1000 and 1500 witnessed two dynamic, discomfit-
ing trends: just the sort of developments, in fact, that forced the
laity to analyze and, all too often, criticize the political and ecclesiastical world in which they found themselves.

First, it was a time of extreme social and economic readjustment. Towns were multiplying and becoming more crowded, new
educational institutions were emerging, prices were waxing and
waning in unusually mercurial ways, novel political mantras were
being whispered, and feudalism was beginning to look rather moribund. The list goes on and, of course, it is very easy to reduce five
hundred years of history — not to mention the diverse fortunes
of an entire continent — into a woefully simplistic and schematic
process. Sometimes, however, this straightforward socioeconomic
explanation of the emergence of popular heresy works rather well.

Flowerings of heresy do sometimes seem to have coincided with particularly turbulent periods.

As just one example, think of the middle of the fourteenth century, when all of these trends were in full flow and, to add an extra layer of anxiety, a wretched disease, the Black Death, was ravaging western Europe. In the midst of all this, in 1349, groups of laymen began parading through the towns and cities of Hungary, Bohemia, Germany, and the Low Countries. They would arrive at the local marketplace, strip to the waist, and begin whipping themselves with knotted ropes until the blood began to flow. It is no coincidence that these so-called flagellants, who would soon be denounced as heretics, appeared at the same moment as the plague. To the leaders of the church, the flagellants were utterly unacceptable, located entirely beyond the control of ecclesiastical authority, but to many people they caught the prevailing mood of fear and anxiety: urging their audiences to repent of the sins that had brought pandemic disaster down on their heads. Neat and tidy explanations of the emergence of popular heresy should always be treated with suspicion, but they oughtn't be dismissed out of hand. It was in the worst times that the laity were perhaps most likely to voice their dissent or seek out their own paths toward redemption.

The second part of the default explanation of the explosion of popular medieval heresy, and here we enter more contentious territory, is that the era was riddled by growing dissatisfaction with the established church. Just think of all those mean things the heretics we've just encountered had to say about their clerical masters and the rituals they oversaw. What follows is a caricature of this supposed climate of disgruntlement, but it is one that secured a loyal and receptive audience, both at the time and in the studies of historians over the subsequent centuries. It contains, at the very least, a germ of truth.

Not unreasonably, since their jobs depended upon it, priests continued to insist upon their unique role, claiming that salvation was well nigh impossible without their ministrations. But surely this proposition was destined to come under scrutiny when those very same priests were behaving in less than ideal ways. We might detect an echo here of the old Donatist contention that worthless priests could hardly be expected to hold the keys to eternal bliss. Perhaps the pious layman was better left to his own devices.

Naturally and admirably, the church sometimes tried to cleanse its own stables. During the eleventh century, for example, a great reform movement — the Gregorian Reform — had been embarked upon. Popes had barked about clerical celibacy and simony (the selling of clerical offices and services for money or other advantages), they had asserted their right to guide the moral and political future of Christendom, and they had even tidied up the process of papal election. The trouble was, when such initiatives ran out of steam they left a swathe of disappointed expectations in their wake. By being exposed but not quite eradicated, the church's flaws had been placed in only sharper relief. Some priests were still ill-educated buffoons who charged exorbitant prices for their services, and clerical concubines were still a conspicuous blot on the religious landscape. It was nice to see a pope like Innocent III calling the priests in his charge "dumb dogs" because they lacked the wherewithal to preach properly, but if the dumb dogs remained in situ, then nothing much had really been achieved.

Things might have been more tolerable if those who inhabited the higher reaches of the Christian establishment had behaved impeccably, or if they had managed to preserve at least the appearance of unity, but this was manifestly not the case. Medieval Europe was an era of ecclesiastical chaos. The notion of a united Christendom from the Pillars of Hercules to the Bosporus grew less convincing with every new quarrel.

By the middle of the medieval era the Eastern and Western Churches had gone their separate ways, and many of those places where the earliest orthodoxies had been carved out, and where so many of the early church fathers had lived and worked, had nothing much to do with Rome anymore. East and West had grumbled over any number of issues — icons, as we've seen, the dating of Easter, clerical celibacy, the *filioque* clause, whether communion bread should be leavened or unleavened, whether priests ought to have beards — but by the twelfth century the game was assuredly up: Christendom was cleft in twain.

Even within the western half of Christendom there was precious little concord. Many church leaders, disheartened by the excesses and ineptitude of various medieval popes, began to talk about something called Conciliarism: they proposed that it might be wiser to vest ultimate ecclesiastical and doctrinal authority in the church's great councils rather than rely on the unreliable abilities of a supreme pontiff. This became an increasingly attractive argument. There was no shortage of unwholesome medieval pontiffs and, even when relatively respectable ones were in charge, things could still fall apart. During the Great Schism of the late fourteenth and early fifteenth centuries, rival popes and antipopes competed for the papal tiara. Antipopes were nothing new in Christian history. It always comes as something of a surprise, but there were no less than thirty-nine of them between 217 and 1449. Nonetheless, the years between 1387 and 1417, when two, then three popes battled it out for the leadership of Christendom, were still particularly unedifying.

Even in more settled times, rival factions (which usually meant ambitious Italian noble families and the minions of kings and emperors) sought to have their creatures elected as pope. Popes themselves would be accused of doing away with their predecessors or bribing their way to the top.

It was easy to become frustrated with this state of affairs. In the mid-thirteenth century, the people of Viterbo took dramatic action. A papal conclave had been chewing the electoral fat in their town for far too many years: decades, actually. The sequestered cardinals and bishops had been quarreling among themselves, depleting the town's food and resources, and hadn't come close to a decision about who should follow in the footsteps of Peter. An obvious solution presented itself: the citizens of Viterbo ripped the roof off the building in which their leaders were sitting. Perhaps enough heavy rainfall would put a spring in the pope electors' step.

And if bickering within the ecclesiastical establishment wasn't bad enough, there was also a growing sense that the epochal Constantinian unification of secular and ecclesiastical power, which had looked extremely elegant back in the fourth century, was also under threat. Relations between popes and the secular rulers of Europe had a habit of descending into chaos. There were endless rows between Rome and the kings of western Europe over papal taxation and the rights to appoint bishops, and they were matched in intensity by squabbles about the papacy's claims to temporal, as opposed to purely spiritual, authority.

It was an old battle. Back in the eleventh century Pope Gregory VII and the German king and later Holy Roman emperor, Henry IV, had fallen out very badly over an issue known as lay investiture. There had been a long tradition by which the emperor chose candidates to fill the bishoprics within his territories. When they took up their sees the lucky bishops would provide explicit promises of fealty and homage to the emperor: an acknowledgment that they owed their lands and office to him. The papacy, not without reason, saw this as a gross secular intrusion into ecclesiastical affairs. Gregory forbade the practice, Henry refused to heed him, Gregory excommunicated Henry, and, for a decade or so, this corner of Christendom seemed to be falling into chaos. There were fleeting moments of reconciliation — Henry traveling to Canossa in 1077, falling to his knees as a snowstorm raged, and begging for absolution — but, such high drama aside, the arguments continued. By 1084 Henry was driving Gregory out of Rome and placing his own pope on Peter's throne.

Such unseemly squabbles between papal and secular power would continue and, for anyone who still wanted to believe in the dream of political and ecclesiastical power jointly carrying forward the Christian tradition, it must have been profoundly depressing. The very worst part of this process was that, when the fights re-kindled — as they did with astonishing regularity — the parties were only too happy to use the very notion of heresy (which is what they were supposed to be jointly guarding Christendom against) as one more weapon in their rhetorical arsenal. If the notion of heresy could be used so glibly, so self-servingly, so opportunistically, then perhaps it is small wonder that some denizens of Europe voiced their concerns.

⌒

Of all the pope-bating emperors, none was more strident than Frederick II. He fell out with a succession of popes over territorial and jurisdictional issues, and supreme pontiffs were not slow to launch extraordinarily venomous rhetoric (and repeated excommunications) in his direction. In 1239, Gregory IX warned Christendom about the power-hungry and, by papal calculation, heretical emperor: "A great beast has come out of the sea . . . this scorpion spewing passion from the sting in his tail . . . full of the names of blasphemy . . . raging with the claws of the bear and the mouth of the lion, and the limbs and the likeness of the leopard, opens its mouth to blaspheme the Holy Name . . . behold the head and tail and body of the beast, of this Frederick, this so-called emperor." Frederick's spin doctors were quick to respond, likening the pope to "a Pharisee who sits on the plague-stricken seat, anointed with the oil of wickedness." Matters came to a climax at the Council of Lyon in 1245, where the Christian world was witness to the extraordinary spectacle of a Holy Roman emperor being put on trial.

Frederick did not deign to attend, and he did a very good job of dissuading (a euphemism if ever there was one) his bishops from accepting the pope's invitation. Even in their absence, astonishing deeds were done. The papacy attempted to secure the high ground, insisting that it had tried to make peace with Frederick, but he, "following the hardness of Pharaoh and blocking his ears like an asp, with proud obstinacy and obstinate pride has despised such prayers and admonitions." "By proofs which are not light or doubtful, but clear and inescapable," Frederick was denounced as a false son of the church. He had failed to keep his promise to lead a crusade. He was guilty of sacrilege through his seizure of the clergy's "crosses, thuribles, chalices and other sacred treasures of theirs, and silk cloth . . . like one who sets at nought divine worship."

He constantly flouted ecclesiastical authority and dignity by bullying and arresting bishops and cardinals and putting clerics in the galleys. Worst of all, he was deeply suspected of heresy. He had allegedly "joined in odious friendship with the Saracens," becoming addicted to the rites of the Muslim faith, allowing the name of Muhammad to be uttered "day and night" in Christian places of worship. He even appointed eunuchs as his guards, "whom it is seriously said he had had castrated."

Innocent IV declared that the heretical emperor was once again excommunicated and deposed, "bound by his sins, an outcast and deprived by our Lord of every honour and dignity," and he set about devising ways to enforce the decree of deposition. None of them came to fruition and Frederick died peacefully five years later in Puglia — wearing, in a way that rather undermined the charges that had been leveled against him, the garb of a Cistercian monk. But the failure of Innocent IV to make good his commitment to destroy Frederick II hardly lessens the enormity of what had transpired at Lyon. Frederick was perhaps the most perplexing medieval ruler, the "wonder of the world" by some accounts. His Sicilian court, set amid the orange groves of Palermo, was a curious establishment: a place of eunuchs, scientists, and poets. And Frederick was, for his time, unashamedly freethinking. But he was no heretic. Not that this had stopped a pope from abusing the fear and loathing of heresy to strike directly at his greatest political opponent.

Holy Roman emperors were not the only rulers to get on the wrong side of the papacy. Philip IV of France was as orthodox and devout as they came, but he still saw advantage in abusing the whole notion of heresy, especially when he had the misfortune to live in a Europe dominated by one of the punchiest popes in Rome's history: Boniface VIII.

At the end of the thirteenth century Philip wanted to impose new taxes on the clergy within his realm. Boniface, who was determined to protect every papal privilege available, was outraged and, in his bull *Clericis Laicos,* he declaimed that lay rulers had no right to tax clerics without papal permission. This squabble fizzled out, but in 1301, Philip arrested the bishop of Pamiers on charges of heresy. He insisted that Boniface support his decision. Boniface demurred and, in response, promulgated perhaps the most truculent of all papal bulls, *Unam Sanctam* — a document jam-packed with claims of papal power in both the spiritual and temporal realms.

The subsequent months and years were, to say the least, a maelstrom. Philip and his minions hinted (and rather more) that Boniface was a heretic, a devil worshipper, and quite possibly the Antichrist himself. Specific heretical charges were drawn up against Boniface, chief among them that "he has a private demon whose advice he follows in all things," that he had "a soothsayer who consults divines and oracles," and that "he seeks not the salvation of souls but their perdition."[14]

The denouement came when French troops burst into the papal palace at Anagni with the intention of kidnapping the aged pope. Stories differ as to what happened next. Boniface certainly knew the troops were coming and, after donning his sacred robes of office, he mounted the papal throne and waited for events to unravel. Horrifying, but likely apocryphal, tales would be told about the intruders urinating on the pope. Other more credible accounts talk of Boniface being beaten, possibly by members or henchmen of the Colonna family, who — as the whirligig of medieval heresy dictated — had, in their turn, been charged with heretical leanings by Boniface himself. The pope was invited to resign but, by some accounts, he insisted that he would rather die than abandon his apostolic duty. "*E le col, e le cape,*" he is reported to have said: "Here is my neck, here is my head." Whatever really transpired — and we will simply never know — local crowds intervened and chased the troops away, but the shock of it all utterly traumatized Boniface, and he died three weeks later. Philip artfully held the threat of a posthumous trial of Boniface over the heads of the next popes.

Such conflicts were deeply unedifying but, in case Europe needed one more example of how the charge of heresy could be abused by their leaders, there was also the strange tale of the Knights Templar. Again, it was Philip IV of France who lit the touch-paper. In October 1307 many French members of the Templars — one of the military orders set up to protect pilgrims in the Holy Land — were arrested, as heretics, on Philip's instructions. The Templars have long been adored by any writer in search of a sensational tale about the more shadowy byways of Christian history. In fact, as a religious order, they were not especially objectionable. They gamely protected travelers and pilgrims in and around Jerusalem, they fought bravely in the Crusades, and they provided Europe's wealthier residents with impenetrable fortresses in which to stash their fortunes. Their only miscalculation was to amass considerable wealth in the process. It was the sort of wealth that Philip IV was determined to seize.

A month after Philip's decree, Pope Clement V issued orders to extend the arrests to the whole of Europe and, by March 1312, the order had been suppressed. At Paris, in May 1310, fifty-four

Templars had been burned at the stake. Others would follow. Many charges were leveled against the Templars; chief among them was that of heresy. It was claimed that new initiates were required to deny Christ three times and spit on a crucifix. Then, having stripped naked, they would be kissed on the mouth, the navel, and the spine by their superiors: a foretaste, it was suggested, of the life of sodomy and bestiality that awaited them. A life, so the accusations continued, that was punctuated by the despoiling of sacraments and the worshipping of idols — including jewel-encrusted human skulls.

Serious historians now agree that many of these charges were a concoction. Spitting on crucifixes, if it was indeed a part of the Templars' procedures, was most likely a training exercise: in the Middle East it was what undercover Templars would be expected to do to prove their bona fides to local rulers and officials. The Templars were destroyed for political and economic reasons because their wealth and legal privileges were envied and because they were held partly responsible for territorial losses in the Near East. The accusation of heresy was little more than a pretext: one that gained considerable credibility from the fact that some Templars made false confessions of their own heretical behavior under the pressure of horrendous tortures.

It all looks a lot like a mess. There were too many incompetent priests, the unity of Christendom was in jeopardy, and its very leaders were throwing around accusations of heresy like rhetorical confetti. With so much amiss, it might come as little surprise that some Christians — just the sorts of heretics we've already encountered — expressed their misgivings. If the whole Christian edifice was apparently falling into disrepute, then it must have been very tempting to start dreaming of a mythical apostolic era, when every-

thing was pure and unsullied, and to set about re-creating it outside
the framework, and without the supervision, of a corrupt church.

It is an attractive idea, but the denouncements of chaos and
corruption can easily be exaggerated. Fallings-out between popes
and emperors only rarely made much of an impact on the devotional lives of ordinary Christians. Similarly, a master narrative
of escalating anticlericalism, leading inexorably to the climacteric
of the Reformation, is much harder to sustain than it used to be.
Yes, there were bad popes and bad priests, but there were lots of
competent ones too. Many parishioners across the continent were
perfectly satisfied with the devotional, spiritual, and sacramental
worlds in which they found themselves. Also, lest we forget, the
medieval church hardly lacked its glories: this was something of a
golden age for Christian art, architecture, and scholarship. Cathedrals were being built, scientist-priests were inventing experimental
science, and decent monks were rising at dawn to sing lauds and
retiring at dusk after singing compline.

Any notion of general malaise or universal disenchantment is
thus suspect, but this doesn't mean that certain individuals — any
number of people who would be denounced as heretics — weren't
still brassed off.

Everything we've just seen was certainly grist to the mill of
those who wanted to criticize the established church. It provided
them with ammunition and receptive audiences. We might almost
expect a resurgence of heretical thinking, based more than ever on
issues of authority. And, as the record seems to show, this is precisely what happened.

But there is still room to wonder how representative these heretics were, and whether they constituted a coherent, even intercon-
nected, attack on the status quo. Given the evidence, and it is extensive, it is easy to conclude that there were simply more heretics
than there had ever been before. Better yet, we have some attrac-

tive explanations for this flowering of heresy. Some historians have wondered if matters were quite this simple and they too deserve their day in court.

POPULAR HERESY: MYTH

The clerical establishment, so this alternative argument goes, was certainly under siege. In this scheme, all the problems and conflicts I've just recounted remain fully operative. People were complaining about a lackluster, corrupt church and, even if the criticisms were often exaggerated, they still stung. The church needed a way to assert its authority, to prove that it was still needed. And what better way than to convince western Europe that it was under attack from legions of heretics? If you could persuade the European laity that it was in the midst of a vast diabolical conspiracy to subvert Christendom, then all the minor grumbles would suddenly seem much less important. The more heretics there were (or seemed to be), the more indispensable the established church would become. Crucially, different camps within the church could flex their anti-heretical muscles in order to win prestige and trump their ecclesiastical rivals.

Any notion of a centralized, coordinated strategy seems well beyond the realm of likelihood, but if this process was going on in even minor, localized ways, it was a brilliant strategy. Scurrilous, perhaps, but brilliant. And, to add another layer of intrigue, such a tactic worked just as well for secular rulers. All those medieval kings and potentates groping for increased power over their territories may well have seen some potential in convincing their subjects that there were heretics in every corner. If that was the case, then a dose of centralized authority was just what the body politic required.

It sounds outrageous, I know, and (with a few notable exceptions) it is probably safer to think in terms of political and ecclesiastical leaders *exaggerating* the threat of heresy rather than simply *inventing* heretical groups to destroy. But, given the nature of heresy, it isn't really so far-fetched. As our trawl through the early church revealed, heresy was often just a construct. It came into being only when someone *called* something a heresy. There was huge potential here. All you needed to do was make the accusation more frequently and establish efficient mechanisms to seek out heterodoxy: the more rocks you turned over, the more potential heretics would crawl out. And if you happened to find one, there was wisdom in suggesting that he was not an isolated individual but part of a broad and bewildering heretical campaign. Oddly enough, some of the facts from medieval Europe's encounter with heresy seem to fit this peculiar theory rather well.

လာ

There are a few extreme examples of the unfolding of this logic. In the thirteenth and fourteenth centuries, for example, church leaders made much propagandist hay out of the heresy of the Free Spirit. There was, so the story went, a Europe-wide movement that was assaulting all the norms and assumptions of traditional Christian worship and replacing them with dangerous talk of a private, individual encounter with God. As recent scholarship has all but proven, there was no such "movement." There were simply random individuals who were saying things along those lines. The trick, though, was to group them all together and concoct a heretical category. This, it seems, is precisely what some within the church set out to do. Perhaps they believed it, perhaps they didn't, but the consequences were much the same.

It is also impossible to ignore the other development that defined the medieval church's approach to heresy: endless legislation and increased bureaucratization. This was often an exercise in asserting power and demonstrating that you were working hard to hold back the heretical tide: both good ways to enhance authority and prestige. Beginning in the late twelfth century, there was an extraordinary outpouring of papal bulls and conciliar decrees that forced Europe to search for heretics as never before. Secular leaders were told that they now had an overriding duty to identify and snuff out heresy. If they didn't oblige they might be declared heretical themselves. As one such papal pronouncement put it, if a ruler "neglects to cleanse his territory of this heretical filth, he shall be bound with the bond of excommunication," and if he failed to comply within a year his vassals would be absolved from all promises of fealty and be entitled to seize his lands.[15] There was no greater threat, and where there was a stick, there was also a carrot. Those who sought out heresy in their dominions would secure the same indulgences as rulers who went on crusade to the Holy Land. The uncooperative cleric, meanwhile, was told in no uncertain terms that if he failed to pursue heresy with due diligence, he would be degraded from his clerical status.

Because they felt obliged to follow such instructions, or because they saw personal political advantage in joining the heresy hunt, all manner of medieval rulers launched their own inquiries and inquisitions — on an unprecedented scale — and the church itself did precisely the same thing. The thirteenth century saw the birth of what would come to be known as the Inquisition. At first it was an assemblage of local, temporary tribunals, but it was extraordinarily efficient. Detailed records were kept, intricate procedures were introduced, and from time to time, the methods of unearthing heresy could become brutal. The 1252 papal decree *Ad extirpanda* sanctioned the use of torture in inquisitorial proceedings.

It is vital not to subscribe to the old Black Legend of the Inquisition — even if, in some circles, the legend remains very popular. Yes, there were some unfortunate moments and some unusually vicious inquisitors but, for its time, the Inquisition was a relatively fair-minded institution: its procedures were certainly no more savage or vindictive than those deployed by secular legal tribunals. Some of its methods — not informing accused people of the specific nature of their supposed crimes, nor of the names of their accusers; the resort to physical threats and violence — strike us as unacceptable, as well they might. Most of the time, however, the local medieval inquisitions were far more interested in winning potential heretics back to the church than in slaughtering them.

In the typical course of events an inquisitor arrived in a locality and, after a little sermonizing, invited those of dubious beliefs to come forward during the next days and weeks in order to confess their sins and receive suitable penances. In addition, concerned citizens were granted the opportunity to approach the inquisitor and spill the beans on those they suspected of harboring heretical ideas. Again, the accused were quizzed, chastised, and punished suitably — made to publicly recant their errors, sent on penitentiary pilgrimages, or forced to wear penitential crosses on their clothes (the medieval equivalent of the scarlet letter). This is almost always how matters transpired. The number of people who were handed over to the secular authorities so that they could be killed (the church always took care to avoid getting blood on its own hands) was very small indeed.

It was only when someone refused utterly to recant, or when a previously identified heretic relapsed after promising to mend his or her ways, that the truly horrific punishments were deployed. In the context of its time this was not especially atrocious and, more often than not, efforts were made to correct rather than punish and to avoid unnecessary excesses.

Still, medieval heresy was undoubtedly being codified and sought out more rigorously than ever before. Files were now kept on potential heretics; inquisitors were now producing manuals that taught their colleagues how to go about their tasks. Some historians have seen this as part of the birth of the persecutory society, which, in one way or another, is still with us today.

There were certainly times when zeal bubbled over into reckless persecution. If we accept the idea that the church, for selfserving reasons, went out of its way to unearth heresy during the medieval period, then our mind will turn instantly to the Cathars: everybody's favorite medieval heretics. They felt the finger of the Inquisition on their collars but, for several thirteenth-century decades, they endured much, much worse.

THE CATHARS

Dualistic ideas, first glimpsed in the thought of Marcion and the Gnostics, were resilient. Whether by direct transmission or through independent meditation, similar notions had emerged among the Paulicians of the Byzantine Empire and, from there, proceeded to the so-called Bogomils of the tenth-century Balkans. Their westward journey was not yet over. Talk of a universe created by a malicious (or mischievous) second god (or demiurge) passed along trade routes and, we can safely assume, they were carried home in the kit bags of crusading armies. Just to make sure, Bogomil dignitaries made the journey themselves, entrancing western Europeans with their talk of a cosmos sharply divided between the luminous world of the spirit and the vile, creaturely world of flesh and matter.

By the late twelfth century, alarming reports of dualistic ideas were starting to come in from Flanders and the Rhineland, but they seem to have had a particular appeal in the south of France. This had always been an ideal place for heresy to flourish. There were many trade routes, so heretical ideas had a better than average chance of arriving; there was weak political and ecclesiastical control, so such ideas often managed to secure a foothold; and the topography was perfect — there were mountains and hills to which the Cathars (as these particular dualists came to be known) could retreat.

The Cathars of the Languedoc achieved a huge amount. First, their ideas were very popular, even managing to infiltrate local noble households. Second, the Cathars seem to have been exceptionally well organized. They established a full-fledged ecclesiastical structure of their own, led by their equivalent of priests — the *perfecti*. These leaders were renowned for their piety (always likely to impress a medieval crowd). They refused to eat meat, marry, or reproduce (for these were the marks of the foul, creaturely world) and they had a whole arsenal of sacraments at their disposal. Most Cathars did not aspire to the perfection of the *perfecti* (although vegetarianism seems to have been common, even lower down in the ranks), but they could still be confessed by them; when they encountered them they could offer a sacramental gesture of greeting and reverence in the hope of receiving a blessing (the *melioramentum*); and they also had access to the *consolamentum*, a ritual of spiritual metamorphosis usually dispensed close to death.

To call the Cathars a tangible threat would be an understatement. They utterly rejected the existing church and they exploded the foundational idea of Christian monotheism. At first, the measures taken were relatively gentle. Priests and friars (notably Dominicans and Cistercians) were sent to preach to them and engage them in debate. Dominic Guzman, the Dominicans' founder and the future Saint Dominic, was one of those employed in such efforts. They achieved little, however. Sterner measures were required and attention began to turn to one of the unluckiest leaders of the entire medieval era: Raymond, count of Toulouse.

There were suggestions that Raymond, whose territories were crawling with Cathars, wasn't doing nearly enough to eradicate this noxious heresy. Some critics even hinted that he might have some sympathy for the Cathar project. In 1208 a papal envoy, Peter of Castelnau, was dispatched to the region and, after drawing his conclusions, he determined that Raymond required chastisement. Raymond was excommunicated but, eager to improve his situation, he organized another meeting with Peter. Unfortunately, it didn't go well and, worse yet, as Peter was traveling home he was set upon by some of Raymond's supporters and assassinated. The jury is still out as to whether Raymond orchestrated the hit, but he certainly showed few signs of regret or remorse when news of Peter's demise reached him.

To an already impatient pope, Innocent III, this was the final straw. In March 1209 he declared a crusade against the Cathars. The nobility of northern France, eager to enhance its territorial portfolio, was delighted by the prospect. The pope had given carte blanche for the rest of France to seize Raymond's lands and wipe out the Cathars. As Innocent's invitation put it, "Since those who fight for liberty of the Church ought to be fostered by the protection of the Church, we, by our apostolic authority have decided that our beloved, who in obedience to Christ are signed or are about to be signed against the provincial heretics, from the time that they, according to the ordinance of our legates, place on their breasts the sign of the quickening cross, to fight against the heretics shall be under the protection of the apostolic seat and of ourselves."[16]

Raymond was no fool, however, and (whatever the critics suggested) he was no kind of Cathar, either. His first instinct was to construct a defensive alliance. This failed to materialize, so he took the only course of action available. He offered abject apologies to the papacy and, in June 1209, stripped to the waist, he did penance in front of the abbey of St. Gilles. He also asked if he could be allowed to join the upcoming crusade against the Cathars. Given the crusaders' likely targets, this sounds like an odd strategy but it was actually rather astute. Raymond imagined that, from within the crusaders' ranks, he might be able to divert the armies away from his own territories and push them toward those of his local enemies — most especially his hated nephew, Raymond-Roger, viscount of Trecavel and lord of Albi and Carcassonne.

At first, at least, the tactic worked, and the carnage began. The crusaders had a convenient list of more than two hundred Cathars resident in the town of Béziers (within Raymond-Roger's domains).

They demanded that the townsfolk hand them over. They refused and, after a surprisingly brief siege, the crusaders poured in. Tales (and they don't seem to be massively exaggerated) tell of thousands of people being massacred. When the terrified crowds sought refuge in the church of La Madeleine, the crusaders set it (and its occupants) alight.

Over the next few years the south of France endured many such horrors. Raymond's efforts to protect his patrimony became less and less successful, especially after the arrival of the northern noble Simon de Montfort. De Montfort's antics, which were directed toward taking over most of southern France, became so outrageous that even the pope began to grumble at his overweening ambition. After seizing the city of Lavaur, de Montfort ordered the burning of four hundred heretics (to which no one had much objection) but also decreed that the city's commander and eighty of his knights should be hanged (an unusually merciless act, according to the dictates of thirteenth-century chivalry).

The details of the subsequent military campaign need not detain us. Suffice it to say that, by 1219, Simon had lost his life trying to defend the city of Toulouse, and the coordinated military stage of the attack on the Cathars had all but petered out. Raymond, for the record, managed to survive but lost some territories and was strong-armed into allowing his daughter to marry the French king's brother. More important, the Cathar heresy, in spite of having suffered such brutal assaults, was not close to being eradicated.

Over the next three decades, religious and political leaders changed tack. There were still sporadic military assaults, but most orthodox energy was devoted to the process of Inquisition. Countless Cathars were hauled in for questioning and, in time, such intrusions provoked a backlash. In 1242 Cathars attacked and killed a group of inquisitors at Avignonet. In response, forces of the French king and the local bishops assaulted the Cathars' mountain stronghold at Montségur. Here, finally, a definitive moment in the eradication of Catharism was reached. In March 1244 a bonfire was lit in Montségur, and two hundred Cathar *perfecti* — the flower of the movement — perished in its flames. It was a blow from which Languedocian dualism would never fully recover. By the middle of the next century, after a few fleeting episodes of resurgence, Catharism had essentially vanished from the religious landscape.

∽

If ever there was an example of overreaction to the threat of heresy, it was surely the crusade against the Cathars. Lots of historians have argued in recent years that the movement was perhaps not nearly as unified and coherent as we used to think. It certainly had its share of internal divisions, notably between absolute dualists, who believed that the creator of the evil, creaturely world was a fully fledged god, and mitigated dualists, who opined that this creator was of less lofty rank. Catharism was real enough, however, and the church's response to it does seem to encapsulate a new, more rigorous way of dealing with heresy.

6

MEDIEVAL HERESY II

IT IS HARD to reach a firm conclusion. Was there really more heresy during the medieval era, or simply more attempts to seek it out and eradicate it? The second line of argument has a definite appeal and sometimes this is precisely what seems to have been going on. There was a suspiciously energetic attempt to convince Europe that all these explosions of popular heresy were related. In the midst of the military assault on Catharism, the papacy offered this ringing condemnation of the satanically inspired plot to subvert Christendom: "We excommunicate and anathematize every heresy raising itself up against this holy, orthodox and catholic faith . . . we condemn all heretics whatever names they may go under. They have different faces indeed, but their tails are tied together in as much as they are alike in their pride."[1]

This was a tried, tested, and woefully simplistic strategy, but it should not blind us to the fact that, however advantageous sounding the heretical alarm might have been, various medieval Europeans actually did voice opinions that were regarded as heterodox.

The key point is that, for contemporaries, it hardly mattered whether medieval heresy was, at least in part, a mirage. Western Europe was entirely convinced that it existed — that it was everywhere. The fear of heresy permeated medieval culture, in both its popular and elite variants, and in all the spaces in between. Heresy continued to be perceived as an especially noxious crime against society, comparable to incest, homicide, or treason. Heretics, like those who committed suicide, were not to be granted Christian burial. The flinty rhetoric of an earlier age continued: in Dante's *Divine Comedy*, heresiarchs were provided with their own circle of hell, in which they would suffer forever in burning sarcophagi.[2]

Everyone admitted that, in the here and now, they would be harder to spot. As one historian has recently noted, the well-defined pictorial portrayal of "the heretic" is strangely missing from medieval art, but this indeterminacy — the result, it was supposed, of heretics' ability to shift and disguise themselves — made them only more frightening.[3] The phantom is, by definition, spooky.

Heresy obsessed the church's councils from the twelfth century to the fifteenth. There were few serious medieval thinkers who did not address the issue and, most important of all, the attempt to expose and punish heretics was a part of the everyday landscape of medieval Europe. People would become familiar with inquisitors arriving in their towns and cities, launching into denunciations of heresy, and commanding that those with heretical sympathies step forward so that they might be corrected and reformed.

There was also a continued certainty that heresy, when exposed, sometimes warranted the most extreme punishments. Thomas Aquinas, one of the greatest medieval thinkers and, in many ways, a practitioner of expansive theological speculation, knew where to draw the line. In his hugely influential *Summa Theologiae* he examined the arguments in favor of tolerating heresy. It was sometimes suggested that, as the Bible insisted, "the servant of the Lord must not wrangle," so perhaps undue animosity was not to be welcomed. Some argued that punishing heresy robbed heretics of the chance to repent and still others relied on the idea that it was necessary to tolerate that which was necessary for the church — and as we've seen, heresy, even from a supremely orthodox perspective, was very useful in the work of codifying true doctrine. Aquinas did not object to postponing harsh punishment and believed that reform and admonishment had their place in the arsenal of ecclesiastical justice. Ultimately, however, when heretics did not repent of their sins they "deserved not only to be separated from the church by excommunication but also to be severed from the world by death." It was not uncommon for forgers to be killed for their crimes, so surely an equivalent fate ought to await those who dealt in the false coin of heterodoxy. Aquinas eagerly quoted Jerome: "Cut off the decayed flesh, expel the mangy sheep from the fold, lest the whole house . . . the whole body, the whole flock, burn, perish, rot, die."[4]

∾

So yes, real or imagined, heresy was part and parcel of medieval life. The only problem remaining was how, exactly, it ought to be defined. It was easy enough to call a Cathar a heretic: by most theological standards that is precisely what he was. Likewise, those as militant as Fra Dolcino and his Apostolici were a threat that simply had to be snuffed out. It was harder to adjudicate the deeds of someone like Valdes of Lyon, however. He was merely trying to return to the days of apostolic purity and he never harmed so much as a flea.

Sometimes people like Valdes were denounced as heretics; sometimes very similar people were lauded as pious harbingers of a new and better age. This only goes to show how hard it was to draw the line between heresy and challenging, but acceptable Christianity. There is no better proof of this than the story of Valdes's close contemporary, Francis of Assisi, who did many of the same things but, instead of being persecuted, ended up being venerated as a saint.

FRANCIS

Born in 1182, Francis, the son of an Assisi cloth merchant, was, by his own admission, something of a wastrel during his youth. After being taken prisoner during a war with nearby Perugia he began, just like Valdes, to reassess his life. He took to prayer, pilgrimage, and helping the poor. His father was not best pleased with these developments, especially when his son sold valuable cloth to fund pious enterprises. After father took son to court, Francis cast off his family and took up a life as a hermit among outcasts and lepers. Again, with the story of Valdes ringing in our ears, this all sounds very familiar.

By 1208 Francis had begun preaching about the apostolic ideal and he quickly attracted a small but loyal band of followers. He traveled to Rome to seek papal approval. This, clearly, was Valdes all over again. This time around, however, papal support was granted. A brand-new religious order came into being, and by 1221 there were as many as five thousand Franciscan friars. They became the darlings of the church, soon joined by a female branch (the Poor Clares) and a third, lay order. The Franciscans' life of poverty was applauded, they were granted full papal approval in 1223, and, after receiving his stigmata on Mount La Verna in 1224, Francis died in 1226. Within two years of his death he had been canonized.

With Valdes in mind, we have to ask what the difference was. The only sensible answer is that Francis simply happened to approach the right pope at a more fortuitous moment. It was precisely that arbitrary.

In time, the papacy began to wonder if it had made the right decision. Franciscans were keen to do the pope's bidding — they were especially useful because they stood outside the structures of episcopal authority — but some of them proved to be unusually disruptive. With some irony, heresies began to emerge within a group that spent much of its time confronting heresy.

Francis had been insistent on the absolute poverty of his followers: this, he argued, had been the hallmark of the apostles, so it was the perfect model to adopt. This vision became harder to sustain as the order became increasingly successful. Perhaps there was room to bend the rules: if Franciscans set up settled communities then, so the theory went, there was no real harm in storing wheat and wine in their granaries and cellars. Such adaptations were duly granted papal approval: Francis's rules on poverty could be modified.

This move infuriated many within the Franciscan order: they saw it as a betrayal of their founder's objectives. Such people came to be known as Spirituals, or Zelanti — as the term implies, they were unusually zealous and this caused the papacy an almighty headache. It split the Franciscan order in twain and, more important, it encouraged some Spiritual Franciscans to indulge in theorizing that bordered on, and often crossed over to, heresy.

Peter John Olivi began to see this struggle between the Spirituals and their foes as a sign that the end times were approaching. Francis was not merely an inspired religious leader, he was almost a second Christ, heralding a new age. Olivi set about recasting the whole of Christian history. The past had not lacked its glories. There had been a First Age, which coincided with the resurrection, the sending of the Holy Spirit, and "the founding of the primitive church, especially within Judaism under the apostles." Olivi's Second Age was important too: beginning with Nero's persecutions, it was the time of testing and confirmation through the martyrs, when Christianity was "set upon by the pagans throughout the world."

The Third Age, dating from the time of Constantine and Nicaea, was that of the doctrinal exposition of the faith: the age in which order and unity were pursued and heresy was refuted. The Fourth Age was that of the anchorites, who fled the world in "favor of extreme solitude and zealously disciplined their bodies, thus illuminating the whole church by their example, as if they were the sun and stars."

So far, so wonderful. Unfortunately, a Fifth Age had arrived. From the time of Charlemagne, corruption and worldliness had set in. Priests now thirsted after power and they were obsessed with their temporal possessions. Things had to be set aright and, for Olivi, this is where Francis began to weave his magic. He had set things in motion with his return to apostolic poverty and, before too long, a glorious Sixth Age was destined to unfold.

Evangelical life would be renovated, the sect of Antichrist would be driven out, the Jews would be converted, and the church would be rebuilt. This would usher in the seventh and final age: a time of "quiet and marvelous participation in future glory, as if the heavenly Jerusalem had descended to earth. Insofar as it applies to the other life, it is the general time of resurrection and glorification of the saints and final consummation of all things."[5]

Many of those who subscribed to Olivi's ideas talked in rather ferocious terms about the scale of change and reform that would be required. The whore of Babylon would have to be destroyed, and some identified this creature with the existing ecclesiastical hierarchy, even the pope himself. Popes and cardinals were likened, at best, to the Pharisees of Christ's acquaintance.

Members of Francis's order (men like Olivi) were openly flouting papal commandments by insisting upon absolute poverty and some of them were dreaming up theological fantasies that threatened to overturn the entire Christian commonwealth. Unsurprisingly, the papacy struck back. In 1318 four Spiritual Franciscans were burned at the stake in Marseille. The insistence that Christ and his apostles had lived in absolute poverty was now defined as heretical. This was undoubtedly one of the most conspicuous examples of a medieval heresy being manufactured in the interests of political convenience.

WHERE TO DRAW THE LINES?

This is all very confusing: it certainly puzzled contemporaries. It was hard to distinguish between two almost identical projects — those of Valdes and Francis. Moreover, even the sanctioned project, for all the successes it would continue to enjoy through the centuries, had itself endured an outbreak of internal heresy. The seemingly wayward Franciscan Olivi sums up this chaotic situation. He was always a brilliant thinker, but one who would oscillate between prestigious teaching appointments and moments of censure. At his death, no one could quite decide whether he was a saint or a villain.

This is very much a theme of heresy. The same sorts of thistly debates had surrounded figures as eminent as Origen and Abelard. Time and again it would be difficult to draw the lines between orthodoxy and heterodoxy. In the early church, those who indulged in self-abnegation and became hermits in the Syrian desert were showered with compliments. At the same time, there was a fear that some varieties of ascetical excess were perhaps beyond the theological pale. Contrariwise, sensible criticism of such excesses was deemed virtuous and acceptable but, if you went too far in your dissent, you ran the risk of garnering your own allegations of heresy. In the fourth century, for instance, Jovinian grew a little tired of the lionizing of celibate, fasting ascetics, and wondered if it was really fair to position them as "better" Christians than everyone else. He criticized a little too loudly, however, so Jerome set about destroying his reputation: he was "the Epicurus of Christianity . . . rutting in his garden among young men and women."[6] Just as Belloc wrote, heresy could be one of fifty things.

Who was a hero and who was a heretic? In the eleventh century Ramihrdus was burned as a heretic by the people of Cambrai after snatching the sacrament from priests he deemed to be unworthy; Pope Gregory VII later referred to him as a martyr. We have seen the fourteenth-century self-flagellants being denounced: but, in the right hands (famously those of Saint Peter Damian) self-flagellation was a mark of extreme piety. In 1184 the so-called Humiliati were condemned for their secret meetings and austere life in Lombardy; by 1201 they had secured papal approval.

As for the realm of Christian spiritualism and mysticism, some of its most outlandish inhabitants were bathed in praise. In earlier centuries, the church seemingly had no objection to Stylite monks abandoning all the trappings of organized religion in order to climb to the top of sixty-foot columns and spend the rest of their lives silently meditating on the divine majesty. In a later era, no one fell into paroxysms of anger when the medieval anchoress Julian of Norwich sequestered herself in order to indulge in ecstatic spiritual encounters with Christ. Others were not treated with such indulgence. The Dominican Meister Eckhart enjoyed an illustrious academic career, including a spell in the chair of theology at the University of Paris. When he moved on to Cologne, however, the local archbishop objected to Eckhart's unusual speculations about God's immanence: they smacked of pantheism. Subsequently, Eckhart's ideas were described as heretical. To this day, historians argue over whether this was the right decision.

The difference between acceptable and threatening idiosyncrasy often came down to whether the party in question had secured clerical approval or supervision. Francis got the papal nod; Valdes didn't. There was no more conspicuous example of medieval Christianity's inability to neatly define the borders between heresy and orthodoxy than the Beguines, who were welcomed, at first, by paeans of support and ended up being thrown into the flames.

The Beguines

From the late twelfth century, women across northern Europe began to gather together to live the holy life. They survived on alms and the small fees they earned from manual labor and their handiwork — whether wool carding, spinning and weaving, caring for the sick, or child care.

Initially, the Beguines (as they came to be known) were a long way from being a formal, well-organized movement, but they quickly won their share of plaudits. The French cleric Jacques de Vitry described their origins thusly: "Many holy maidens had gathered in different places . . . they scorned the temptations of the flesh, despised the riches of the world for the love of the heavenly bridegroom in poverty and humility, earning a sparse meal with their own hands. Although their families were wealthy, they preferred to endure hardship and poverty, leaving behind their family and their father's home rather than to abound in riches or remain in danger amidst the worldly pomp."[7]

Such seemingly pious women attracted many influential supporters, most notably two kings of France, Louis IX and our old friend Philip IV. Important clerics wrote biographies of Beguine notables and, thanks to de Vitry, the Beguines were granted unofficial papal approval to set up their establishments in France, Germany, and the Low Countries. The Beguines went from strength to strength. Their communities came in different forms: some larger than others; some isolated from city life, others in the urban cut and thrust. Many Beguines devoted themselves to a life of contemplation while others carved out careers working in hospitals and leper houses. There was occasionally some grumbling from the textile guilds, who didn't enjoy being undercut by the Beguines' very generous rates, but by and large the beguinage became a familiar sight in many of the towns and cities of northern Europe.[8] In places from Cologne and Frankfurt to Ghent and Louvain they were a new, welcome addition to the urban landscape.

Behind the successes, however, there had already been some mutterings of concern. The Beguines were not a formal religious order — they took no formal, public vows — but they still struck some observers as groups of women, gathered together, pursuing a religious life without any direct male supervision. They insisted that they were not a new religious order, but they often wore distinctive clothing and lived together in walled communities, sometimes under the leadership of someone who looked very much like a traditional abbess. Worse yet, it wasn't unknown for Beguines to indulge in sophisticated theological contemplation and this, so the prevailing culture insisted, could hardly be a good thing.

Criticism mounted and, for the unfortunate Beguines, the tide began to turn. Those who had indulged in spiritual and theological speculation earned the most opprobrium. Most famous of these was Marguerite Porete, who found herself in all sorts of trouble in early-fourteenth-century France. Her innovative spiritual work, *The Mirror of Simple Souls,* was deemed to be full of "errors and heresies" and she was burned at the stake in Paris's Place de Grève in June 1310.

Long before this, however, the Beguines had fallen out of theological fashion. They began to be associated with the Spiritual Franciscans we've already encountered and with the phantom heresy of the Free Spirit, also mentioned earlier. In 1312 at the Council of Vienne, the Beguines were denounced as a malignant sect of "faithless women." It was necessary to chide

> the women commonly known as Beguines, since they promise obedience to nobody, nor renounce possessions, nor profess any approved rule [and] are not religious at all, although they wear the special dress of Beguines and attach themselves to certain religious to whom they have a special attraction. We have heard from trustworthy sources that there are some Beguines who seem to be led by a particular insanity. They argue and preach on the holy Trinity and the divine essence, and express opinions contrary to the Catholic faith with regard to the articles of faith and the sacraments of the church. These Beguines thus ensnare many simple people, leading them into various errors. They generate numerous other dangers to souls under the cloak of sanctity. We have frequently received unfavorable reports of their teaching and justly regard them with suspicion. With the approval of the sacred council, we perpetually forbid their mode of life and remove it completely from the church of God.[9]

A good deal of persecution and many sordid tales of sexual excess and moral depravity followed — as they so often did.

This was not quite the end for the Beguines, however. The details of the council's condemnation were rather hazy, and in many places there was a determined effort to distinguish between "good" and "bad" Beguines. In France and the Low Countries beguinages would survive for several centuries. Still, the movement had been tarred with the name of heresy and this is surely one of the more extraordinary examples of initial enthusiasm giving way to doubt and criticism.

In Ghent in 1328, a routine investigation of the beguinage of St. Elizabeth was carried out. One contemporary was at pains to explain just how holy and harmless the institution was. The beguinage, he reported, was encircled by ditches and walls and had its own church, cemetery, and hospital. All of the houses inside the walls had their own small gardens and their residents spent their days in the most innocent of pursuits. They would rise early, attend Mass, then spend hours on end silently going about their work of washing wool and cloth. They had few possessions — the clothes on their back, a bed, and a chest — and some of their number welcomed even greater deprivations, sleeping on straw pallets and eating nothing more substantial than coarse bread and potage. The women had left behind all the vanities of the world: there were no hoods, nightcaps, gloves, or mittens within the beguinage of St. Elizabeth.[10]

The point was clear. If this was heresy, it was of a very unusual, entirely harmless kind.

ALL THE OTHERS

It has been a constant opinion amongst Christians from the beginning, that the devil is the author of all false religions; that

> he moves heretics to dogmatize, and inspires men with errors,
> superstitions, schisms, lewdness, avarice, and intemperance.
>
> — PIERRE BAYLE, *Dictionary*[11]

The identification of medieval heresy was a cumbersome and confusing pursuit. Nor was the heretical category monopolized by disruptive laymen and women who either retreated from the world or talked about returning to the brave old days of apostolic purity. Adding to the mayhem were singularly bizarre people like Cecco d'Ascoli, burned at the stake as a heretic at the age of seventy for using his recondite learning to reinterpret the nature of Christ's passion.

D'Ascoli was a fourteenth-century Bolognese astronomer with a place on the faculty of the city's university. Unfortunately, he was also an astrologer, entirely committed to the idea that everything (absolutely everything) that happened on earth was determined by the stars' positions. He decided to calculate Christ's horoscope and he concluded that all the social disadvantages (being lowly born in a stable) and all the sufferings (up to and including the crucifixion) were the result of Jesus's astrological bad luck. Such musings came to the attention of the local inquisitor who, understandably, dragged d'Ascoli in for questioning. He was accused of heresy, he was robbed of his lectureship, he was forced to pay some hefty fines and, most important, he was told to abandon the astrological profession.

D'Ascoli refused to listen. He headed to Florence and was soon up to his old tricks. Another local inquisitor was obliged to intervene and, since the reach and resources of the Inquisition were now extensive, he sent a colleague over to Bologna to see if d'Ascoli had been caught by the ecclesiastical radar in the past. The files showed that he had and this was terrible news for d'Ascoli. The relapsed heretic — the person who had erred before and not learned his lesson — was a doomed heretic. D'Ascoli was brought to trial at Santa Croce and, after being convicted of pertinacity, he was taken outside to the adjoining piazza and, on September 16, 1327, burned alive.[12]

Heretics like D'Ascoli made the already crowded religious landscape even more bewildering: and then, just to augment the chaos, there were the witches.

ᔐ

The skull of a decapitated thief doubtless made for an ideal witch's cauldron. And so far as the people of Kilkenny, in southern Ireland, were concerned, it was in just such a vessel that Alice Kyteler mixed her odious potions. The eyes of ravens, the brains of unbaptized infants, and the fingernails of the deceased were all rumored to be mainstays of Alice's diabolical storeroom. It was with such materials that she apparently did away with her husbands — and, by common consent, Alice had married and survived an alarming number of men. William Outlawe, a wealthy resident of Coal Market Street, had been the first victim, back in 1299. Twenty-five years and three more spouses later, it was decided that Alice — by now an extremely wealthy woman — was in league with the devil. She offered him sacrifices, enjoyed sexual relations with a demonic incubus, and had established a heretical devil-worshipping sect that had infected even the highest social echelons of Anglo-Irish society.

There was the key word: *heresy.* The devil had always been thought to lie behind some heretical infractions. From the days of the early church he had been portrayed as using and abusing mankind's pride and curiosity in order to subvert Christendom. Priscillian, the first heretic ever to suffer state-sponsored capital punishment, was killed in 386 on the back of charges of sorcery. The medieval era took this notion to its logical extreme. Satan was no longer simply meddling: he was actively recruiting wayward souls like Alice Kyteler in order to carry through his mischievous stratagems. Those who played along were the very worst heretics of all.

The charges against Alice had been manufactured by the disgruntled children of Alice's dead husbands, who had lost out on their inheritances. But the charges were believed, most passionately by Richard de Ledrede, the bishop of Ossory. In 1324 he launched legal proceedings against Alice and her presumed accomplices: they "practised all kinds of sorceries" and were "well-versed in all kinds of heresies." Being a woman of some influence, Alice managed to flee the scene. Others in her social circle were not so lucky. Some were whipped through the streets of Kilkenny; some were burned at the stake.[13]

It was a watershed moment, replicated in many of the countries of western Europe. There had always been a dozen ways to explain heresy — lunacy, vainglory, political agitation — but from now on there was a new, especially noxious species of heretic: the practitioner of demonic magic.

The division between faith and magic had often been blurry. It was not uncommon for medieval Europeans to utilize Christian objects (images, the sacrament, and so forth) in magical endeavors: their power was not to be underestimated. *Magic* and *the occult* had not always been dirty words, especially when associated with kindly, disease-curing village mavens or the alchemists and necromancers who had been the darlings of European courts and universities. A veil of suspicion now fell over such practices. This had telling consequences for the future of Western science — an enterprise that, in its medieval incarnation, often mingled with the darker arts — but the real victims were not the wealthy and the learned. For the next three centuries hundreds of innocent people (with women in a sizable majority) would be persecuted as demonic heretics, or witches.

In 1320 John XXII declared that the frequenting of demons was a heresy. In a bull of 1326 he announced that those who "make or have made images, rings, mirrors, phials, or other things for magic purposes and bind themselves to demons" were among the most wretched residents of Christendom. Popes and kings became convinced that practitioners of black magic were plotting their destruction; charges of witchcraft and wizardry were used to blacken the names of rivals in love, economic competitors, and political adversaries; and the European witch-craze engulfed the continent.[14]

The association between heresy and witchcraft was soon well established: a fact that Joan of Arc discovered when she was tried and executed in the 1430s. By 1484 there was nothing exceptional about Innocent VIII's describing witchcraft as the worst of "heretical depravities" and something that had to be "put far from the territories of the faithful."[15] News had recently arrived from Germany of witches deploying their malevolent skills in order to kill children and livestock and ruin grape and fruit harvests. This, Innocent declared, certainly entitled local officers of the Inquisition to pursue such villains with all possible fervor. Two years later the famous *Malleus Maleficarum (The Hammer of Witches)* was produced by two Dominicans and in its pages the linkage between heresy and witchcraft was plain for all to see. Witches were heretical traitors to the faith: they had been given the opportunity to embrace Christian truth but, instead, they had cackled their way down the road of apostasy. They made pacts with Christ's greatest enemy, Satan, and they mocked the church's rituals at every opportunity. As the authors reported, witches would abuse sacred objects in their spells, using altar cloths to cover waxen images and, in one instance, smuggling their wafer of sacramental bread out of church in a handkerchief in order to place it in a jar alongside a toad. Witchcraft was now deemed to be a heresy of a very special, peerlessly noxious kind.

෴

Medieval heresy, it is safe to say, was many things. Deciding who was a heretic was sometimes hard; sometimes it was easy. Amid all the turmoil, there was possibly a sense of relief when one of the more well established threats of heresy (its ability to send a corner of Christendom into political turmoil) raised its head. In theory, at least, this was easier to anatomize and contain. Jan Hus, our final medieval heretic and the man who leads us nicely to the greatest heretical event of them all — the Protestant Reformation — was more than happy to oblige.

HUS

> And if any person within the said realms and dominions, upon the said wicked preachings, doctrines, opinions, schools, and heretical and erroneous informations . . . do refuse duly to abjure . . . [he will] before the people in an high place cause to be burnt, that such punishment may strike fear into the minds of others, whereby no such wicked doctrine and heretical and erroneous opinions, nor their authors and factors, in the said realm and dominions, against the Catholic faith, Christian law, and determination of the Holy Church, which God prohibit, be sustained or in any way suffered.
>
> — DE HÆRETICO COMBURENDO, 1401 (an
> English statute against the Lollards)

In 1412 a student dressed himself up as a prostitute and, with a mock papal bull hanging from his mock bare breasts, he marched through the streets of Prague. He was lodging his scurrilous protest against the hawking of indulgences — those amenable commodities that, purchased for a fee, were held to reduce the time a person might expect to languish in purgatory. Others shared his theological distaste. Indulgence-preaching sermons were disrupted, indulgence-carrying chests were smeared with excrement, and those Franciscan friars who were foolish enough to defend the notion of buying oneself out of posthumous suffering were slapped unceremoniously across the face. It was only the most recent outburst of religious disaffection in Prague.

Bohemia, the land with Prague as its cosmopolitan capital, was heartily tired of German dominance. There were 1.1 million Czech speakers in Bohemia and only 100,000 Germans, but the Germans had long monopolized the choicest positions in the church, the universities, and the government. Czechs were determined to assert what we might now term their cultural independence: and what better way of achieving this goal than to stress their novel, reformist religious ideas? The morality of the clergy was pilloried, regrettable doctrines were denounced, and it was suggested that perhaps the mighty church of Rome did not possess the lofty status it had always claimed. Perhaps there was some merit in the idea of independent local churches.

Of all the Czechs who espoused such ideas, none became more famous than the academic-cum-preacher Jan Hus. Born in around 1369 to a peasant family in the south of the country, Hus had won an enviable reputation at Prague's recently founded Charles University: accumulating degrees, rising through the academic ranks, and, by 1400, after his recent ordination, enjoying a teaching position in the theology faculty. He drew impressive crowds at his lectures and they were soon matched at Bethlehem Chapel, where he began preaching in 1402.

As well as providing spiritual advice to the great and the good of Prague society, Hus became increasingly critical of clerical abuses within the church, and at the top of his list of complaints was simony: the sin of buying or selling religious offices, services, and objects. Hus was also much attracted to some of the provocative theologizing of the English thinker John Wyclif.

Wyclif had many disturbing things to say. He insisted upon the centrality of the Bible in Christian worship (by preference, a vernacular Bible) and he drew some controversial conclusions from his own scriptural readings: among them a denial of the doctrines of transubstantiation and purgatory. He was also attracted to the idea that it was the duty of the secular ruler to impose reform on his or her own local church. There was a catch, however. Any who claimed dominion in such matters were legitimate only if they were in a state of grace (the sinning ruler had no real right to rule) but, assuming this condition was met, Wyclif looked forward to a Christendom made up of distinctive territorial churches, curated by local leaders. Needless to say, the pope in Rome did not figure very prominently in this scheme of things.

Not everything Wyclif suggested went down well in Prague (his denial of transubstantiation, for instance) but many of his ideas — the need for reform and the notion of local self-determination — struck an obvious chord among the disenfranchised Czech-speaking community. In England Wyclif's project would never come to full fruition. His followers, known as the Lollards, would endure considerable persecution and, after the second decade of the fifteenth century, noble support for the Wyclifite cause began to slip away. In Bohemia, by contrast, Wyclif's ideas, as interpreted and adjusted by men such as Jan Hus, would fare rather better.

The dominant German speakers immediately noticed the burgeoning reformist agenda and they set about itemizing and condemning Wyclifite doctrines. Purges of the university were carried out but, because they tended to concentrate on older men, they succeeded only in bringing young Turks like Hus to greater eminence. The reformist party made good progress, even winning some support from Bohemia's ruler, Wenceslas IV, who was in the midst of a contest with his rival to the imperial throne — a man supported by the majority of German speakers. In short measure, the reformers won a majority on Prague's council and secured more voting power within the university. Hus himself became rector in 1409.

There was a predictable reaction from those of more conservative tastes, and the Hussites were ordered to stop their radical preaching in Prague's churches. On July 16, 1410, there was a mass burning of suspicious books. This only fueled the fires of dissent, however. Hus and his colleagues continued to preach (almost always in Czech) and Prague became used to popular demonstrations mounted in the name of reform.

In February 1411, Hus (correctly identified as one of the ringleaders of all this righteous rabble-rousing) was excommunicated by the papacy. He was called to the papal court to answer the charges leveled against him, but instead he retreated to various noble castles in the countryside around Prague and devoted his time to writing and scholarship. He probably hoped that the controversy would die down.

It did not. Everything became increasingly radical. People (such as the transvestite student with whom we began) protested the sale of indulgences, started denouncing the pope as Antichrist, and began promoting theological ideas that went far beyond Hus's original agenda. To his credit, and in the interest of unity, Hus refused to condemn these excesses. As ever, there was strength in union.

The theological temperature ran high. Hus had been excommunicated and the whole city of Prague was under interdict for continuing to shelter him. Finally, Hus was summoned to the church council currently being held in the Swiss city of Constance to argue his case. A showdown was looming.

❧

It was an unfortunate moment to be a heretic. Over the past few decades, the church had been rocked by schism. Rival popes had battled for primacy, and at the Council of Constance no fewer than three supreme pontiffs presumed to rule over the Christian world. The council's great task would be to bring such a ludicrous state of affairs to an end (leveling more of those internal accusations of heresy in the process), but along the way there was an especially urgent need to stamp out any other challenges to the tranquillity of Christendom. Hus represented precisely that kind of threat.

He had been lured to Constance with the promise of safe conduct, but when he set about preaching his dangerous message all the guarantees evaporated. Hus was thrown into the grimmest jail the city could provide. He was then dragged before the council, witnesses were called, his writings were examined, and he was invited to recant his errors.

Hus had hoped for a serious debate. It was not forthcoming. The Parisian theologians in charge, men like Pierre d'Ailly and Jean Gerson, were already convinced that Hus was a heretic. Hus was presented with a list of thirty accusations. Most of them, he insisted, were irrelevant: he had never said many of the things with which he was charged. He refused to abjure what he had never taught. As for the ideas he *had* espoused, he stood by them and he would not offend his conscience by betraying his spiritual vision. The Christian church was in no mood for such bombast.

Hus was formally declared a heretic on July 6, 1415. He was stripped of his ecclesiastical vestments, his writings were cast on bonfires, and the newly minted heresiarch was taken outside the city walls of Constance and burned at the stake, his ashes scattered in the river Rhine.

His death appalled then galvanized his countrymen. As early as September 1415 a formal protest was sent to Constance and, fearing what was coming next, 452 Bohemian nobles with Hussite sympathies formed a protective alliance. The events at Constance also helped radicalize many within the Hussite camp — they now had a martyr. Older devotions gave way to simple services in Czech, during which priests wore humble garments instead of ornate vestments, and wooden or tin liturgical vessels replaced those made from silver and gold. Images of saints were removed and the laity were offered both bread and wine at communion.

Not all Hussites were pleased with these developments: some of the new departures certainly went beyond what Hus had intended. Still more alarming were the events in the countryside around Prague. The faithful on Mount Tabor inaugurated a communitarian republic where, so the story went, even eggs and crusts of bread were shared out equally. They anticipated the apocalypse, warning that all the cities of the world would soon burn to ashes.

One thing could still bring the Hussite fraternity together, however. In July 1419 a demonstration in Prague led to anti-Hussite councilors being thrown from the windows of the town hall. They survived, but only long enough to be killed by the people in the street below. The shock of hearing the news of this outrage apparently killed King Wenceslas, but his successor, Sigismund, was determined to eradicate (or at least curtail) the mounting Hussite menace. He launched a decade-long anti-Hussite crusade. It claimed many victims. At Kutna Hora, Hussites were cast down mineshafts in the hundreds and left to starve. There were also stunning victories, however. In 1421, on the slopes of Vitkov, Bohemian forces defeated a crusading army of eighteen thousand troops.

The Hussite rebellion had managed to provoke consternation across Europe. It is even suggested that Joan of Arc, who would herself shortly endure politically motivated accusations of heresy, took time out from her battles with the English to scold the Christians of Bohemia: "It has come to my ears, to me, Joan the Maid, that you have become heretical Christians, like blind people and Saracens. You have extinguished true belief [with] a revolting superstition that you defend by blood and fire . . . you destroy holy images and reduce churches to rubble. You are completely mad! What insane fury possesses you? You want to persecute, destroy, and extirpate the true faith."[16]

Finally, however, the revolt crumbled. At Lipany, in 1434, Sigismund secured his victory and the radical days of Hussitism all but came to an end. A compromise was carved out to allow the Utraquist Church, a rather watered down version of Hussite practice, to survive. And so it would, for many years to come.

The radical fringe did not vanish entirely. A man named Peter Chelchicky had long hated any entanglement with the secular powers. From the early 1420s he began elucidating his vision in print. True religion, he opined, was about brotherly love. The true Christian would want nothing to do with the political world of power and, at every opportunity, he would retreat into private contemplation and immediate divine encounter. He would quietly go about his spiritual business in the midst of the noisy, corrupt world. By the 1450s the Unity of Brethren had emerged: they would later be known as the Moravians (quite the nicest heretics you could ever hope to meet) and they are still with us today.

Chelchicky was the man who tamed the impulses of Tabor, and it is a shame that he is not better remembered. As for Hussitism as a whole, it certainly seemed to point the way forward to the schisms of the sixteenth century: battles in which ideas of local self-determination and the questioning of established doctrines and rituals would loom large. It would even be called the Morning Star of Reformation, although, as we will shortly see, the appellation was perhaps not as fitting as it might seem.

THE FABLED ROAD TO THE REFORMATION

It is more than a little tempting to suggest that all this medieval heresy blazed the trail for the coming turbulence of the Reformation era. Disenchantment, anticlericalism, and (witness Hussitism) local grievances had been stewing and fermenting for centuries and, thanks to the great protests of Luther and Calvin, they finally burst the already crumbling banks.

This is an old, bold idea, but not an especially useful one. At first blush, the evidence seems to support it. In 1498, Jean Vitrier preached in the city of Tournai and, as reward for his audacity, he was called before the theology faculty of the University of Paris because of what he had said: namely, that it was better to cut the throat of your child than place him in an unreformed monastery; that if you knew a priest who kept a woman in his house then you should go and drag her out; and that indulgences came straight from hell.[17]

There would seem to be the straightest of arrows pointing to someone like Luther who said similarly nasty things about monks, priestly concubines, and the practice of selling indulgences.

The trouble is, a desire for reform was not quite the same as a thirst for the Reformation. In 1512, even closer on the heels of Protestantism's arrival, John Colet, dean of St. Paul's Cathedral in London, gave a famous sermon to his clerical colleagues. He began in the most uncompromising terms: "Never was there more necessity and never did the state of the church more need your endeavors ... The church, the spouse of Christ, which he wished to be without spot or wrinkle, is become foul and deformed." The bride of Christ had "committed fornication with many lovers whereby she has conceived many seeds of iniquity and daily bringeth forth the foulest offspring."

Priests were now men of the world, carnal not spiritual, and defined by covetousness: "All things in the church are either the lust of the flesh, lust of the eye, or the pride of life." Just look at the endless competition to secure bigger and better clerical jobs: "a breathless race from benefice to benefice." Just look at all the "feasting and banqueting . . . vain babbling . . . hunting and hawking" to which priests were addicted: they were "drowned in the delights of the world."

Was this not, in its way, heresy of a sort? Colet invoked Bernard of Clairvaux, who, four centuries earlier, had itemized "two kinds of heretical depravity — one of perverse doctrine, the other of perverse living," and this second species of heresy "reigns in the church." The first sort of heretics was still much in evidence, of course. There were still "men mad with strange folly," "but this heresy of theirs is not so pestilential and pernicious to us and the people as the vicious and depraved lives of the clergy." And if "the priests and bishops, the very lights, are in the dark ways of the world, how dark must the lay people be?"

If such words could emerge from within the heart of the church, then a crisis must have been imminent. It is crucial to realize, however, that Colet was deliberately exaggerating the sins and shortcomings of his peers in order to prod them toward reform. He demanded a purgation of immorality, but he was confident that this could be easily accomplished: "the diseases which are now in the church were the same in former ages, and there is no evil for which the holy fathers did not provide excellent remedies." Colet even used the word *reformation,* but he meant it in a very particular sense: "Bend your whole minds to reformation," he insisted, but all he meant was reform and improvement, not, for a moment, revolution.[18]

This, in fact, was the dominant intellectual and theological culture at the dawn of the sixteenth century. There was grumbling about the papacy — and in these decades there was more to grumble about than usual — but this was nothing new. Conceptualizing the late medieval church as a moribund institution that was on the high road to collapse has long been dismissed as a historiographical fiction. There was no shortage of criticism but, at the level of popular devotion and affection, many aspects of Christian life were in rude health.

The end of the fifteenth century saw many new ideas emerge: they are usually grouped together under the umbrella term *humanism.* And, make no mistake, someone like Erasmus devoted his eminent literary career to castigating the empty formalism and wretched superstitions that, to his mind, had despoiled the Christian commonwealth for far too long. What he neither desired nor envisaged (and the same could be said of Colet) was the destruction of a united Christendom.

There is a danger, then, in thinking of the Reformation as an inevitable climacteric. In fact, hardly anyone saw it coming, so it can hardly have been all that inevitable. Once it was underway, it took many people a great deal of time to choose sides, and the border between those who carried forward the humanist project and those who desired more radical change was often hard to spot. Far from being the culmination of medieval heretical trends, the Reformation was one of the oddest, most inexplicable events in Western history.

Of course, hindsight has intervened (we know what the Reformation led to) and, historically, this has joined forces with confessional pride. For Lutherans or Calvinists there was always huge solace in remembering how they had cast off the Roman yoke and made the theological world anew. It was only a short step to bold, teleological narratives in which everything that transpired had been bound to happen — it had all been coming for a long time and, better yet, it was divinely inspired. Contrariwise, for those of Catholic sensibilities, the Reformation could be glibly dismissed as just the latest heretical excrescence.

As we're about to see, the Reformation was far more complicated than that.

7
REFORMATIONS

THE REVOLUTION

> We that live now at this time, gentle reader, do both see and feel
> that very evil and troublesome are our days by means of certain
> questions that within these fifty years Luther and his followers
> have moved in religion.
>
> — RICHARD BRISTOW, *A briefe treatise of diverse plaine and
> sure wayes to finde out the truthe in this time of heresie* (1599)

> For the Church was born by the word of promise through faith,
> and by the same word is nourished and preserved. That is to
> say, it is the promises of God that make the church, and not the
> church that makes the promise of God. For the Word of God is
> incomparably superior to the church, and in the Word the church,
> being a creature, has nothing to decree, ordain, or make, but
> only to be decreed, ordained, and made. For who begets his own
> parents?
>
> — MARTIN LUTHER, *The Babylonian Captivity of the Church* (1520)

THERE HAS BEEN much talk of the great church councils in earlier chapters. Whenever heresy raised its head, councils had gal-
loped to the rescue, identifying error and pointing the way toward
the annihilation of heterodox musings. This constitutes an impressive catalogue of anti-heretical strategizing and, for the historian of

heresy, it is very useful. It tells us precisely which threats the church took seriously at any given time.

Most of these exercises in enforcing orthodoxy were entirely reactive and largely retrospective. It was less about nipping heresy in the bud and more about confronting glaring threats that were already in full bloom. There is, therefore, room to feel a little sorry for the eminences who fetched up at the Fifth Lateran Council, held in Rome between 1512 and 1517. They have sometimes received an unkind press from historians. Given what came next, they might easily be accused of neglect. Did they really not see the Reformation coming? Much necessary, workaday business was undertaken. There were the usual, well-intentioned fulminations about clerical misbehavior and attempts to scold the French church for resisting papal authority, but one could pore over the decrees and diktats of the council for a very long time without gaining any tangible sense of the extraordinary events that, courtesy of Luther et al., were about to unfold. No one seems to have anticipated the revolution. And perhaps that is because, whatever it subsequently turned into, and whatever unfolded in its wake, it was not — at least at first — intended as any kind of revolution at all.

This is an odd kind of thought. It flies in the face of the traditional narrative of Reformation with which we are all very familiar. The Reformation was surely the very model of religious insurrection. Before tweaking this entrenched analysis it might be wise to revisit it. Aspects of it stand up to scrutiny, although others could benefit from a nudge in a slightly different interpretative direction.

〰

The Reformation, according to the familiar tale, was the place where heresy finally triumphed, where men denounced as heresiarchs by the established church turned out to be the founding fathers of religious denominations that spread out across western Europe and,

in the fullness of time, much of the globe. Over the previous millennium and a half, groups of frowned-upon Christians had sometimes managed to survive prosecution and persecution and even
succeeded in setting up alternative church structures of their own.
Many withered on the ecclesiological vine, but others are still with
us today, and we've encountered some of them already. For all their
woes, the Waldensians battled on: they can still be found in parts
of Italy (although, these days, they are partners in a curious marriage of convenience with Italian Methodism). If you travel widely
enough, you might even encounter the Copts of the Middle East or
the Nestorians of Asia.

For all that, the churches that emerged from the sixteenth
century were of an entirely different caliber. They truly turned the
Christian world upside down. Just look at what had happened to
Europe by the year 1600. Old certainties had been punctured, traditional devotions had been discarded by large swathes of the European population, and, behind all these disruptions, new theologies
(heresies turned would-be orthodoxies) had emerged.

At the dawn of western Europe's sixteenth Christian century,
Rome was still dominant. There were still pockets of Lollardy in
England and other challenges to orthodoxy here and there but,
while irritating, they were comfortingly localized. There were certainly no pan-European challenges to Rome's primacy in the West.
Within a few decades, however, thousands of Calvinists across the
continent were turning to Geneva for guidance, and Lutherans were
looking to Wittenberg.

Still more extraordinary were the theological breakthroughs
that the religious leaders of such cities had managed to engineer.
Luther had talked about a priesthood of all believers, which seemed
to imply that every Christian should be entitled to cleave to God in
his or her own way. He had insisted that scripture was all that really
counted: *sola scriptura*. All the mechanisms of worship and all the
deposits of tradition counted for nought when stacked up against

the greatest source of Christian truth — the Bible. And when he'd looked at the Bible closely, Luther had fastened upon another explosive idea.

The whole point of being a Christian was to achieve salvation, to take advantage of Christ's supreme sacrifice on the cross. The lineaments of this salvific economy caused the young Luther any number of theological nightmares. He had been gripped by existential agonies. He thought of himself as a puny, sinning individual and he could not quite discern how he merited salvation. Why would God bother with a wretched soul like his? Then he stumbled upon a startling revelation.

The frequency with which the name of the apostle Paul crops up in the history of heresy is surprising. There is surely an irony in the fact that a person who devoted himself to cultivating Christian unity inspired so many heretics: he was the hero of Marcion, the man after whom the Paulicians were probably named, and he certainly saved the day for Luther. Courtesy of a couple of Pauline paragraphs, Luther latched on to the idea that his puniness and sinfulness did not necessarily leave him utterly adrift. The key phrase was justification by faith alone — *sola fide.*

Of course we are all wretches, none of us really deserve a place in heaven, but God, through the exercise of his inscrutable grace, just happens to offer some people the gift of salvation. All that was required was faith, and faith alone. It was the most emancipating of ideas and it did wonders for Luther. The old uncertainties evaporated. In darker days, Luther had been overwhelmed by the very concept of celebrating the Eucharist: first time out, he apparently fainted because of a sense of his unworthiness in the intimate presence of God. Now, suddenly, he was set free. He did not warrant salvation — no one did — but he might be saved anyway, because that was simply how God had organized things.

This was excellent news for Luther — as reports from his later years reveal, he became rather jovial: a wonderful conversationalist who was equally fond of a good tune or a scatological joke — but it was very troubling news for the cause of Christian orthodoxy. Luther had talked about some powerfully disruptive notions: a priesthood of all believers, an utter dependence on scripture, and a brand-new way of negotiating the path to eternal joy.

Down the road in Geneva, a few years later, equally provocative theologies began to surface. John Calvin loved the apostle Paul too. In his more hubristic moments (and he had more than his share) he even liked to think of himself as Paul's latter-day equivalent. Calvin was also interested in the crux of Christianity, the business of achieving salvation, but he went even further than Luther. The notion of predestination was certainly not a new arrival on the theological scene: it had provided the bedrock for Augustine's thought more than a millennium earlier. But Calvin took the notion to its devastating extreme.

God had decreed which human beings were destined for heaven and which were destined for hell. It had been an entirely arbitrary process. A few, the elect, would be saved: most of humanity would not. And there was absolutely nothing that feeble human beings could do to influence this course of events. If grace arrived, it was God's random gift. It was entirely undeserved, which made the gift especially beneficent, but its dispensation had nothing whatsoever to do with the exercise of human free will. You could behave as morally as you chose, you could go to church every day of the week, but if you were on the losing side of the salvific lottery, such gestures would not bring you one step closer to eternal bliss.

In an instant, a venerable Christian idea — that behaving in the right ways and doing good works could have an impact on your eternal prospects — was exploded. The decisions had already been made and you could only hope that the cards had fallen in your favor. Not for nothing did Calvinism become a religion of the anxious.

Admittedly, there were efforts (from within the Calvinist fraternity) to dampen down the bleakness. There were attempts, for instance, to suggest that apparent signs of piety and devotion might at least provide *hints* that you were among the elect. This was a perilous thesis, of course, and few claimed that it should lead to a sense of salvific assurance (after all, dissemblers and hypocrites could look, for all the world, like upstanding Christians), but perhaps it stood to reason that God's chosen few would be decent, upstanding people.

It was also suggested that a genuine conversion experience was a reasonably reliable indicator of elect status and, as a very neat crowning theological glory, the notion of "perseverance" was mooted. If you did happen to be numbered among the lucky minority, God would almost certainly test you, but never beyond your limits. Ultimately, if you were born of the elect you would live, die, and reign as one of the elect. You could never be sure of your fate, but you could be assured that the godly (whoever they happened to be) would remain the godly.

Such stratagems (many of which provoked heated squabbles within Calvinism — we'll encounter one of them when we get to New England Puritanism in a few chapters' time) go a long way toward explaining the appeal of a seemingly unappealing religious worldview. They were always grist to the mill of controversy, however, and they did not alter the theological bottom line: a person's actions in no way influenced his or her prospects of salvation. The deck was stacked. Human agency was a dead letter.

Calvin's speculations on such issues (along with his commitment to returning the church to its apostolic origins and placing scripture at the heart of the Christian enterprise) inspired him to pour a tremendous amount of scorn on the existing architecture of Christian worship. His acolytes, in tandem with the followers of Luther and other Reformation luminaries, set about questioning more or less every aspect of traditional Christian practice and devotion.

Some were more extreme than others, but the notion that theological certitude and age-old habits ought to be interrogated won over a staggering number of supporters. If you thought about salvation in these novel ways, and if you interpreted scripture afresh, then all sorts of assumptions could come under assault.

Where, as some at the more radical edges of Protestantism wondered, was the biblical sanction for an elevated priestly caste? Where, in holy writ, was purgatory mentioned, or most of the sacraments that Christianity had long been inflicting on its adepts? People were obsessed with saints, but if their heavenly intercessions on your part were a colossal waste of time, then surely it was absurd for people to spend their time adoring their relics or embarking upon pilgrimages to their shrines. In Calvin's Geneva, even naming your child after a saint became a perilous enterprise.

There was a need for new liturgies and new prayer books. Many of the fixtures of the Christian commonwealth — exaggerated devotion to the Virgin Mary, monks chanting in their monasteries — had to be abandoned. Old superstitions and the dregs of popery, such as kneeling at the altar or making the sign of the cross, descended into disrepute. As for transubstantiation, those of a Calvinistic stamp determined that this was an appalling medieval theological invention. The Eucharist was an opportunity to remember and feel grateful for Christ's sacrifice. It was a memorial, not a magical transformation from bread to flesh and wine to blood. *Hoc est corpus meum,* and here we might locate the origin of the famous phrase, was hocus-pocus. Corpus Christi processions, those high points of medieval urban life, were to be outlawed. Altars, the seat of the whole obnoxious deception, the place where corrupt priests elevated the host, were to be pushed to the side in church: the pulpit, where the words of scripture could be declaimed, took center stage.

Those within the developing Protestant community disagreed violently about many of these issues. Luther, for instance, was reluctant to entirely abandon the old interpretation of the Eucharist and

he came up with a compromise — the doctrine of consubstantiation. Some Protestants took the rejection of a special priestly estate
to extremes: Presbyterians insisted that self-determining individual
congregations ought to make up any legitimate ecclesiastical structure. Bishops, in their book, were an abomination. Others were less
militant, and the Protestant pastors — stymied in many ways, bereft
of their lavish vestments, but still influential — entered the religious
landscape. Similarly, some Protestants, from the iconoclasts of Ulrich Zwingli's Zurich onward, tore down the religious images and
whitewashed the walls. Others were less keen to abandon the sump-
tuousness of Christian worship and fought a rearguard action to
keep a little color and glamour in Protestant churches.

For all these internal schisms and squabbles Europe, by the
year 1600, was a place transformed. It was a continent where traditional Christian holidays had disappeared in many locales; a place
of bare ruined choirs; a place where people were thinking in new
ways about grace and salvation. Crucially, it was also a continent
where Christians were confronting Christ in the vernacular.

The early reformers were often obsessed with translating scripture into local tongues. It was obviously hard for, say, a German to
benefit fully from the Bible unless he was able to understand the
words he was reading or (more often in an illiterate age) to which
he was listening. There is an assumption that this was an innovative
idea. It wasn't, but it took flight in the sixteenth century and, understandably, it proved very popular. And it added to the chaos.

As for the political transformation, this was plain for all to
see. By the end of the sixteenth century Christendom was divided
as never before. Different polities had charted their idiosyncratic
Reformation trajectories, but from England to Hungary, from the
Baltic to the cantons of Switzerland, it made sense to talk about
a Protestant Europe. Places where the people now referred to as
Catholics had once ruled supreme had changed utterly. In Amsterdam, Catholics now had to assemble in covert house churches. In

England, Catholics had to conform to the new environment and attend Protestant services or face hefty recusant fines. The little solace
available was to be found in installing priest holes in their houses
to make life easier for the newly illegal Romish missionaries, who
ducked and dived their way through the English countryside.

Ancient and medieval Western Christianity could always cling
to the fiction of unity; later Christians (however hard they tried)
could never ignore the fact that their faith had been rent asunder.
There were now two churches—or more like twenty. They described one another in the most unflattering heretical terms and,
from time to time, fell into military conflict. As contemporaries put
it, Europe now faced a struggle between Christ and Antichrist, the
lamb and the beast, the whore and the virgin.

The struggle tore families apart. The Catholic Mr. Hamerstan
enjoyed eleven years in prison during the reign of Elizabeth I but,
when his father finally managed to secure his freedom, Hamerstan
wasn't remotely interested in returning home. His jailer told the
missionary priest William Weston that Hamerstan "preferred to die
gloriously in prison for the faith, in the midst of all those evils . . .
than to live with a heretic, even a parent." To do so would be to risk
"his salvation, an unavoidable danger among heretics, whose crafty
persuasions, blandishments and other noxious arts, should he enter
their midst, he would be unable to avoid."[1]

It also caught God's attention. It sometimes seemed as though
a mighty cosmic battle was raging and that God was directly in-
tervening. The Catholic polemicist Miles Hogarde told of a Saxon
woman giving birth to a child with feet like an ox's; a mouth, nose,
eyes, and ears like a calf's; and "a lump of flesh upon his head like
a priest's crown." So far as Hogarde was concerned, this was God's
none too subtle way of telling the world that Luther and his doctrines were monstrous.[2] From the other side of the confessional di-
vide, the martyrologist John Foxe treated his readers to countless
examples of how God was punishing the persecutors of the new,

true faith. For example, Dr. Foxford had been "a common butcher of the good saints of God," and one unhappy day, he found himself "suddenly sitting in his chair, his belly burst and his entrails falling out before him."[3] This (just cast your mind back) was Arius for a new age.

The Catholics were the heretics now, and God was striking them down. Or, depending upon whom you asked, the Protestants were the most odious heretics ever to pollute Christianity. There were battles to be fought, there were sides to be taken, and, if you exhibited cowardice or dared to associate yourself with your religious enemies, then you could expect God to send perils your way. When the Catholic Richard White went to a Protestant service, divine providence ensured that a flock of kites and crows pursued him to his home, "putting in him great fear for his life." Given some of the warnings and punishments that God supposedly dispensed, White got off rather lightly.[4]

Quite the revolution, then. It was Catholic versus Protestant, heretic versus heretic, and there was no room for compromise. Well, yes and no.

THE REFORMATION MUDDLE

I would hate to spoil a good story, and this is an excellent one, but there is some cause for caution and lots of room for nuance. No one could suggest that the Reformation did anything less than change Europe, utterly and forever. What is rather less obvious is whether it all happened quite so quickly, quite so straightforwardly, and quite as elegantly as historians used to suppose.

The Reformation turned out to be the heretical event par excellence but, for those who had to live through it, it was deeply confusing. The trick is to abandon hindsight. This is impossible, of course, but on balance it is well worth the vain attempt. There was nothing inevitable about the course of sixteenth-century Christian history.

First, what we now call Protestantism took an awfully long time to codify itself. By century's end there were confessions of faith, rules, and rubrics, and there was no going back. This did not happen overnight, however. When thinking about the early decades of the century it makes little sense to talk about Protestantism as a coherent religious category: just another neat and tidy *ism* in the long history of heretical *ism*s. When talking about the first half of the sixteenth century I'll sometimes use (and already have used) the term *Protestantism* (this is simply easier than groping for one of the alternatives, none of which are any more satisfactory) but the lines between reform-minded Catholics and more adventurous so-called Protestants often vanish in the sand as soon as we try to descry them.

Both camps (not that either of them formed any sort of cohesive group) shared agendas — eliminating corruption, encouraging vernacular translations of scripture, banishing unnecessary formalism and empty ritual, and more besides. In somewhere like 1520s France or 1530s England it was often hard to tell the difference between pushy humanists and those who were committed to a more radical cause. Many people fell between these stools.

Second, although *we* can see that a mighty schism was in the process of opening up, contemporaries were not nearly so certain. There were colloquies in which the rival camps sat down together, polite theological letters were sometimes sent between the protagonists, and, at least until the 1540s, there was some hope that the Reformation, as we now call it, could be put back in its box.

Third, and this is by far the most important point, we see the Reformation in black and white terms: protests launched, new churches emerging, adamantine theological shibboleths setting down roots. For some people, someone like Calvin or his theologically well informed counterpart in the Roman Catholic Church, it may well have been this straightforward. They could see the consequences and perhaps they knew that all the urbane correspondence and abortive colloquies would come to nothing. They could see the writing on the wall, and from very early on: but what about everyone else?

The notion of Europe being instantly and irrevocably divided between Protestantism and Catholicism does a huge disservice to the lived reality of the Reformation era. There was an astonishing amount of theological certitude circulating during the sixteenth century and it usually involved a learned, splenetic tract insisting that followers of a particular interpretation of Christianity should have nothing whatsoever to do with the heretical demons who clung to a different agenda. The trouble was, this imposition of theological correctness (while a tried and tested way of conducting Christian business) proved to be rather unwieldy in the new Europe.

An awful lot of people were more interested in carving out a tolerable, uncomplicated life in unsettled times. There was more sense in floating with the drift, reserving judgment, temporizing for a while rather than rushing headlong toward the martyrs' pyres. Even if you disliked your neighbor's theological stance, this didn't necessarily mean that you ought to turn her in to the authorities. Not, to reiterate an already well iterated point, because you believed in modern ideas of religious freedom and pluralism, but because it simply made life easier.

A few were bewitched, many more were bothered, but the majority was bewildered. And bewilderment does not a seamless revolution make.

THE OTHER REFORMATION

This was the other Reformation, the one that had nothing much to do with the confident proclamations of Calvin or the Council of Trent. It represented a befuddled, wishy-washy, but eminently sensible middle ground, which, as historians are beginning to realize, was the territory that many Europeans chose to inhabit. It is crucially important because it offers a glimpse of how a heresy (which is what, at first, the Reformation was) actually unfolds. This time around — and this is the joy of sixteenth-century history — we actually have a wealth of anecdotal evidence to interrogate, but one has a sneaking suspicion that this was how heresy often played out, down at the parish level.

The pronouncements about how a Christian ought to behave were always clear. The invitations to take one side or the other were always insistent. There was heresy and there was orthodoxy: full stop. But many people were presumably confused. Just remember all those Christological debates of the early church: is it really feasible that more than one out of a hundred people had a coherent grasp of the issues involved? For all we know, there was a Marcionite or a Gnostic baker in ancient Rome who happily sold bread to his more orthodox customers. Not because he shared his patrons' views, but because getting into a theological argument was more trouble than it was worth, because it would dent his profits, and, ultimately, because both baker and client were not nearly as certain of their theological opinions as deeply learned theologians were.

The pronouncements from on high always trickled down eventually and, as I've already argued, there was nothing necessarily disreputable about this. If you are running a church, you require rules. This is simply what Christianity demanded for fifteen hundred years. As we'll soon see, this is precisely what happened during the Reformation too. All of those extraordinary speculations of Luther and Calvin hardened into new orthodoxies. Catholics soon felt duty bound to hate Protestants; one sort of Protestant felt obliged to hate all the other varieties. This was the familiar story, a crucial component of the history of sixteenth-century heresy. It was business as usual. But ahead of all that, it behooves us to spend a little time among the head scratchers.

Let's take England as an example. England enjoyed one of the most bizarre Reformations in western Europe. Imagine, if you will, being a hundred-year-old Englishman in 1600. First you would remember Henry VIII. He was never any kind of Protestant but, out of marital necessity, he had cast off papal authority: a familiar tale that doesn't require retelling. While it was never safe to be a vocal advocate of Lutheran, still less Swiss Reformed, ideas, in Henry's England, those of evangelical sympathies (including two of his wives — Anne Boleyn and Catherine Parr, his archbishop — Thomas Cranmer, and his chief minister during the 1530s — Thomas Cromwell) did all they could to push the nation in the direction of reform: not, at this early stage, Reformation, but reform certainly.

At the same time, those of more conservative tastes did every-thing they could to rein in such efforts. The result was chaos: moves in one theological direction, followed by rearguard actions mounted in defense of rival theologies. The historical record and the statute book demonstrate just how muddled everything was: one set of ar-ticles of faith was apt to be replaced by another; one royal proclama-tion about who should be allowed to read a vernacular Bible would be trumped by a contradictory one. The monasteries were dissolved (largely in the pursuit of profit) but, in a dozen other ways, England still looked very much like a Catholic country — simply Catholi-cism without the pope, as the hackneyed phrase puts it.

If ever there was a time for puzzlement this was surely it. Cath-olics found guilty of treason and evangelicals who had voiced their distaste for the Catholic Mass could be executed on a single day. As the chronicler Edward Hall reported of the year 1540,

> the thirtieth day of July, were drawn on hurdles out of the Tower to Smithfield, Robert Barnes, Doctor in Divinity, Thomas Gar-ret, and William Jerome Bachelors in Divinity, Powell, Fether-stone and Abel. The first three were drawn to a stake, there before set up, and were hanged, headed, and quartered. Here ye must note, that the first three, were men that professed the

Gospel of Jesus Christ, and were preachers thereof . . . The last
three . . . were put to death for Treason, and in their attainder,
is special mention made of their offences, which was for the denying of the king's supremacy, and affirming that his Marriage
with the Lady Katherine was good: These with other were the
treasons, that they were attainted of, and suffered death for.[5]

Things became much clearer under Henry's son, Edward VI.
Though very young, Edward seems to have been a rather precocious
individual who held genuine sympathy for the reformist cause: a result, perhaps, of being educated by some decidedly forward-think-
ing individuals (one more indication of just how crazy Henrician
England had been). Between 1547 and 1553 England became something of a Protestant hotbed: and, by now, it made sense to talk of a
coherent entity by the name of English Protestantism. Increasingly
radical prayer books flowed from the presses, and the realm became
the favored sanctuary of continental Protestants who were enduring a tough time at home. Men as eminent as the Strasbourg-based
reformer Martin Bucer and the German biblical scholar Paul Fagius
made England their refuge. As Sir Richard Morison opined, "The
greater change was never wrought in so short space in any country
sith the world was."[6]

Had all this continued, had Edward lived, it seems likely that
England would have become one of the more radical Protestant
countries in Europe. It wasn't to be, however. In 1553 Mary I ascended to the throne, and she was as Catholic as they came. Mary
has endured a bad press down the years, mainly because of all the
Protestants she burned — almost three hundred of them. People
like Bucer and Fagius were no longer welcome: in fact, Mary's com-
missioners at the University of Cambridge took the time to disinter
the corpses of these two Protestant luminaries and condemn them,
posthumously, as heretics.

There was more to Mary's reign than savagery, however. As recent scholarship has rightly insisted, she actually did a decent job

of revitalizing English Catholicism and, crucially, her efforts were well received by her subjects. Protestantism, regardless of Edward's initiatives, had lacked sufficient time to win broad support among the hoi polloi. Once again, if Mary had survived, it is reasonable to speculate that England would have become a bastion of the Counter Reformation.

Mary died in 1558, so it was left to her half sister, Elizabeth I, to carry England's puzzling Reformation experience forward. Here, things became even more bizarre. Protestantism was once more in the ascendant, but no one could quite decide which sort of Protestantism was best. The Elizabethan church became, at least in theory, quite radical, from a theological perspective. Calvin, albeit in a diluted form, was the guiding light (though very sensible policy discouraged overly impassioned discussions of controversial issues such as double predestination). For all that, more radical Protestants (usually, though not always helpfully, grouped together and referred to as Puritans) couldn't help but notice that there were many reminders of the Catholic past. There were still bishops, there were still overly lavish vestments, and there were still all sorts of papist-looking ceremonies in the country's churches: making the sign of the cross, kneeling at the communion rail, and so forth.

Such "dregs of popery" infuriated a sizable section of the Protestant community and some people grew increasingly tired of "tarrying with the magistrate." To them, the English church looked like a church "half-reformed" and, come the first decades of the next century, they would decide to strike out on their own in the new colonies across the Atlantic.

෴

This has been a whistle-stop tour, admittedly, but surely we would all feel rather sorry for our notional hundred-year-old who had had to live through it all. There is also room to sympathize with the actual people who had to endure at least some of the story's twists and turns. Older histories of the Reformation were always fixated with the martyrs and brave souls who, despite all the uncertainty, took a firm stance. Newer histories rightly focus on the people who could never quite work out what was going on. They were legion.

In 1554, just as Mary Tudor's reign was gathering steam, the Venetian ambassador to England observed that the constant shifts in the nation's religious affiliation had brought some people "to such a state as well nigh not to know what to believe nor on what to base their faith."[7] There were many such observations during the sixteenth century, although most of them were highly censorious. There were many confused people and this annoyed those with theological learning at their fingertips. In 1547 Stephen Gardiner (a man of conservative sympathies) complained to Thomas Cranmer (whose reformist leanings were becoming increasingly apparent) about all the nitwits in the pews: "For the most number of them . . . when they have heard words spoken in the pulpit, they report they were good, and very good, and wondrous good, and they were better to hear them: but what they were, they use to profess they cannot tell."[8]

A fictional minister in a dialogue by the Elizabethan writer Nicholas Breton was even harsher: "For my parishioners, they are a kind of people that love a pot of ale better than a pulpit, and a [corn rig] better than a church door; who coming to divine service more for fashion than devotion are contented after a little capping and kneeling, coughing and spitting, to help me sing out a psalm and sleep at the second lesson."[9] Did such people not realize what was at stake in the grand Reformation battle? George Gifford, also writing in Elizabeth's reign, launched a savage assault on the "simple sort" with no "skill of doctrine," who "speak of the merry world when there was less preaching, and when all things were so cheap that they might have twenty eggs for a penny."[10]

But perhaps it wasn't quite so preposterous to long for the good old days before all this Reformation madness had arrived. There is a colossal amount of evidence pointing toward the fact that people in sixteenth-century England, despite all the bickering and all the calls to arms, were far more interested in keeping life going along its comfortable tracks than launching into ferocious theological debate. If this was the heretical battle royal, many people opted to stay on the sidelines.

Walter Staplehill was mayor of Exeter between 1556 and 1557, and a devout Catholic to boot, but he still had Protestant friends, and even when they refused to conform to Queen Mary's settlement of religion, he opted to "lovingly bear with them and wink at them" rather than haul them over the coals of ecclesiastical justice.[11] In 1585, when the theological tables had turned yet again, a constable at Cawthorne in Yorkshire "openly refused to undertake to bring in his neighbours, saying that he would not trouble" them for refusing to turn up at the prescribed services in the local parish church. In the very same year, one minister admitted that "he himself knew some who had not received the communion since 1558 but for friendship's sake he had borne with them."[12]

Such admissions had a tendency to land their perpetrators into trouble, but they were far from unusual. There was simply common sense in looking the other way in the interests of community solidarity and, ultimately, the Elizabethan regime had little right to complain about such pragmatic gestures. There were times when Elizabeth's Royal Chapel was home to Catholic clerks: let off the hook because they could sing so well. In areas where Puritanism seemed to be getting out of hand, that same regime had a habit of rather enjoying the fact that Catholic-minded justices of the peace kept their seats on the bench.

Sometimes, in the Reformation stew, a refusal to abide by the prevailing theological wisdom — the commandment to hate your supposed religious enemies — was good policy.

In the 1570s, the Catholic Henry Chaderton spent a little while in his brother's house. Being a Catholic during the 1570s was a hazardous pursuit. The pope had recently excommunicated Elizabeth I and all sorts of anti-Catholic legislation had found its way into the statute book. It caught many priests in its grasp but, down at the local level, things did not always have to be quite so decisive or risky. As Chaderton reported, he openly read forbidden books, said Latin prayers, and steadfastly refused to attend Protestant services. For all this, members of the local yeomanry "used to come and play games with me," and two JPs, both Protestants, "exchanged visits almost daily with [him] and his brother." Perhaps they were keeping tabs; more likely they were indulging in idle pastimes. Only when a nosy Puritanical parson reported Chaderton's misdeeds did this happy state of affairs come to an end.[13]

And even when the game was up, when you had been caught and imprisoned, common courtesy did not always vanish. Being a religious prisoner in Elizabethan England could be very tough indeed. Aside from the risk of being tortured, the diet could be truly awful. John Finch complained about being fed on "sodden beans only, and on other days with pieces of beasts' livers."[14] Just sometimes, however, life was slightly less onerous. The priest George Napper was arrested early in the reign of James I, but the man charged with Napper's confinement, Sir Francis Evers, insisted that he should have a decent bed to sleep in and good broth for his supper. The next morning, Lady Evers brought him milk laced with cinnamon and sugar: hardly enough to stop Napper contemplating his likely fate, but a gesture that puts a hole in the notion that every resident of the sixteenth century had nothing but contempt to throw at religious dissidents. They sometimes provided a scrumptious breakfast.[15]

More than anything else, it is the sense of frustration and confusion that comes through from the tales of this other Reformation. Thomas Nashe complained that "our divines in these days . . . contend about standing and sitting, about forms and substances, about prescription and confusion of prayers," but this made them into mere "geometricians." "As preachers they labour not to speak properly but intricately," and this surely "chokes the Word of God with false controversies and frivolous questions."[16]

One of the best summations of how that stock figure from so many histories — the ordinary person — confronted the Reformation is provided by an obscure tract from 1589. In it, a fictional doctor called Balthasar attends a parliament where every man could "speak truly his mind, without any interruption, for the proof of his religion." Balthasar reports the results to his friend, Benion, and poor old Benion is baffled.

Balthasar tells him what the Catholic delegate had to say, and Benion is suitably impressed: "If this were his talk, and if this be true what he hath said, then this . . . Catholic religion [is] laid on such a ground or foundation, bringing also with it such antiquity, that I know not presently to the contrary." Unfortunately, Balthasar's account of the Protestant delegate's ideas sounds rather attractive too: "He must needs go away with the victory, otherwise I am much deceived," Benion admits. There was still the Puritan case to consider and, so far as Benion is concerned, this had its merits as well. His conclusion must surely have been shared by many of his real-life contemporaries: "O Lord what shall I say? Or upon what religion shall I now stay me, whereby I might now find out the truth . . . Lord have mercy on us, what shall we say that are unlearned in this troublesome time of so many religions and opinions, or whom shall we believe?"[17] Wise words, indeed.

∽

Most people who had to live through the Reformation did not fully understand its theological quarrels, and even when they did, some of them worked inordinately hard to constrain the excesses the quarrels inspired. In this sense, at least, the Reformation — along with

Catholicism's response, the so-called Counter Reformation — was a very clumsy and not very popular revolution.

This is a crucial corrective, but ultimately a corrective is all that it is. It would be nice to stop here, bask in all the common sense, and posit the sixteenth century as the moment when the age-old heretical Punch and Judy show finally lost its audience. It isn't quite that simple. The fumbling, temporizing, even charitable antics add nuance to the picture and they should always be borne in mind. They do not alter the fact that, for all the attempts to contain and deflect religious hatred during the sixteenth century, that hatred often held sway. Many were confused, but others were possessed of certainty, and they were the ones who usually had the thrones, pulpits, and printing presses at their disposal. They also had fifteen hundred years' worth of Christian history at their backs, encouraging them to carve out a specific version of Christian truth and sneer at those who dissented from it.

We have visited the people who were not entirely convinced that all the spleen and bloodshed was necessary: not (and I can't stress this enough) because they were pioneers of pluralism and religious freedom, but because they sensed that all the acrimony was unhelpful. They are terribly important, and I dare say they had their equivalents in every era of Christian history. They tell us a great deal about the workaday response to heresy, but their pragmatism was often trumped. It is time to return to the people who rather relished the conflict: the people who, for both good and bad reasons, kept the same old anti-heretical bandwagon rolling. They ensured that, come what may, the Reformation turned out to be a revolution after all.

The brilliantly brutal Tudor writer John Bale, who dedicated his pen to demolishing the case for getting along with one's religious rivals, had this to say: people were constantly criticizing him for saying noxious things about his Catholic opponents but, so he insisted, they ought to realize what was at stake. "Gentle and soft

wits are oft times offended that we are nowadays so vehement in re-
bukes," he once wrote, but he wondered "what modesty they would
use if they were compelled to fight with dragons, hydras and other
odible monsters." If you were trying to change the world, and if you
had to do battle with the "puffed up porklings of the pope," then
harsh words and harsher deeds were necessary. His fight, he said,
was against "the proud church of hypocrites, the rose-coloured
whore, the paramour of Antichrist, and the synagogue of Satan,"
and Bale's opponents were more than capable of coming up with
equally combative talk.[18]

It was the logic that, on all sides of the ever-widening Reformation chasm, was adopted at least as often as its more peaceable
alternatives. It has recently been calculated that, across Europe in
the sixteenth century, as many as five thousand people were legally
executed for their supposedly heterodox religious beliefs. As we'll
see, the whirligig of history brought in its revenges, and the kinds of
common sense and pragmatism we have just witnessed would one
day secure a perilous kind of victory: they laid the foundations for
the ideas of religious tolerance we now enjoy. In the interim, however, the old certainties remained regnant. If there was heresy then
it had to be pummeled. The troubling shift was that there were now
two very powerful, state-supported camps of Christians who were
more than willing to charge their enemies with heresy. The results,
which add up to the more familiar tale of Reformation, were often
bloody.

REFORMATION CERTAINTY

The England we have just explored (peopled by kindly neighbors,
indulgent officials, and generous captors) was also the country
where, one day in 1543, the Windsor musician Robert Testwood was
spat upon in the street because of his reformist religious credentials;
the country where the future Catholic priest John Armstrong was

beaten horribly as a child simply because he refused to attend Protestant services; and where, in 1583, recusant Catholics were whipped through the streets of Winchester.[19]

From the very start, some people did indeed take sides. Protestants, albeit of a radical variety (the poor old Anabaptists, to whom we'll return), were being burned alive in the Low Countries as early as 1523. The carnage would continue, and highlighting moments of inter-confessional strife during the sixteenth century is the easiest parlor game in the world. In the England of Mary Tudor something approaching three hundred Protestants would be executed. If you were unfortunate enough to be the deceased wife of a reformer like Peter Martyr Vermigli, your bones would be disinterred and cast on a dunghill.

During the same reign, Richard Woodman ended up "wearing one while bolts, otherwise shackles, otherwise lying on the bare ground; sometimes sitting in the stocks, sometimes bound with cords, that all my body hath been swollen . . . sometimes called dog, sometimes devil, heretic, whoremonger, traitor, thief, deceiver."[20] A few years later, when something resembling Protestantism was once more dominating the statute book, Elizabeth I's minions would expose Catholic priests to similarly unspeakable tortures.

Almost every country in Europe endured such traumas. Holland would have its so-called Wonder Year of 1566, during which the frenzied populace set about desecrating churches with abandon. France would have its decades-long wars of religion punctuated by events like the Saint Bartholomew's Day Massacre of 1572, when Catholics slaughtered Calvinists to such a degree that the Seine supposedly ran red with blood. France became a place where attentive Catholics kept watch over local graveyards to make sure no Calvinists were interred in holy ground. If any managed to slip through the net, it wasn't unknown for such heretical corpses to be dug up, dragged through the streets, or even urinated upon. For all the attempts to calm the waters, they routinely boiled over. Heresy, and the bullish response it provoked, still counted for something.

ↄ

For at least one participant in this overheated process, the established church in Rome, the official response to the evangelical challenge was relatively straightforward. Only a few years after Luther launched his Wittenberg protest, the papacy issued a condemnatory bull. It was a ferociously angry document and one that sought to dismiss Luther as the latest incarnation of the age-old heretical menace. The same old battle was being fought yet again.

"Foxes," it began, "have arisen seeking to destroy the vineyard . . . The wild boar from the forest seeks to destroy it and every wild beast feeds upon it." Once more, as through all Christian history, "lying teachers are rising, introducing ruinous sects, and drawing upon themselves speedy doom. Their tongues are fire, a restless evil, full of deadly poison. They have bitter zeal, contention in their hearts, and boast and lie against the truth." Just like the heretics of old, these new enemies twisted scripture to their own advantage and were "inspired only by their own sense of ambition, and for the sake of popular acclaim."

The solution was simple. Christ had advised "that there must be heresies to test the faithful . . . still they must be destroyed at their very birth . . . so they do not grow or wax strong like . . . wolves." Therefore, "let all this holy Church of God, I say, arise, and with the blessed apostles intercede with almighty God to purge the errors of His sheep, to banish all heresies from the lands of the faithful, and be pleased to maintain the peace and unity of His holy Church."

There was still hope that Luther might see the error of his ways:

Therefore let Martin himself and all those adhering to him, and those who shelter and support him, through the merciful

heart of our God and the sprinkling of the blood of our Lord
Jesus Christ by which and through whom the redemption of
the human race and the upbuilding of holy mother Church was
accomplished, know that from our heart we exhort and beseech
that he cease to disturb the peace, unity, and truth of the Church
for which the Savior prayed so earnestly to the Father. Let him
abstain from his pernicious errors that he may come back to us.

If such admonitions fell on deaf ears, however, the task was clear: to
"cut off the advance of this plague and cancerous disease so it will
not spread any further in the Lord's field as harmful thornbushes."[21]

This was fighting talk but, although steps were taken to debate
with, chastise, and silence Luther in the early part of the 1520s, the
church's broader response to the evangelical threat was decidedly
sluggish during the first few years of Reformation. It took a further
two decades for a church council — the place where heresies had
always traditionally been exposed and assaulted — to finally assemble. There were many reasons behind this cautious approach.

In recent times, popes had become increasingly wary of councils. They had helped Christianity define itself, but they also represented an alternative font of influence, threatening to detract from
the ultimate authority of the papal curia. For critics of Rome's hegemony, the church council had always been the place where a wider
Christian constituency could have its say. Popes had learned to distrust such assemblies — they invited far too much scrutiny, far too
many opportunities for the pope's enemies to vent their anger. Sixteenth-century popes, even with Luther threatening to revolutionize the entire Christian commonwealth, knew this only too well.

The church's response to the arrival of Protestantism was also
delayed by the fact that two of the most influential Catholic monarchs — the Holy Roman Emperor Charles V and the French king
Francis I — were at loggerheads, and frequently at war, throughout
the period. For both men, and for long stretches of time, Luther
was not their most pressing concern. He was just another heretic.

This was a boon for fledgling Protestantism: it gave it, so to speak, a twenty-year head start. Eventually, however, perhaps the greatest of all the church councils assembled in the city of Trent.

It was a ramshackle affair from the outset. The first scheduled meeting in November 1542 simply evaporated when Charles and Francis forbade their bishops to attend — a mere thirty-one delegates took the trouble to make the journey to Italy. Given the stakes, this was deeply embarrassing but, by 1545, momentum began to build, and in three distinct phases (1545–1548, 1551–1552, and 1562–1563) the church set about not only denouncing the Protestant menace but, with every bit as much verve — as a direct counterblast — reforming and refining its own doctrines, personnel, and institutions. Heresy was continuing to play the oddly constructive role in which it had always excelled.

The council suffered from interminable delays. Years would sometimes go by between sessions while the church waited either for favorable political circumstances to arise or for a pope to be elected who actually believed that convening a council was the best way to combat Protestantism. And when proceedings finally recommenced there were all the predictable rivalries and animosities. Debates were regularly disrupted by disgruntled priests shouting out abuse or launching into feigned coughing fits.

For all that, a huge amount was achieved. Trent inaugurated the most dynamic period of reform and refashioning in Catholic history. The Protestant challenge was faced head-on. Tradition, so the council barked, counted as much as scripture. Good works, not just arbitrary grace, helped a person toward salvation. All seven sacraments had legitimacy. Everything, from priestly conduct to education to the nature of saints and their relics, was redefined.

The Council of Trent should not simply be seen as a counterblast to Reformation: it was as much an exercise in internal reform as an urgent response to a new theological rival. Nonetheless, it remains the most well documented, most virtuosic example of how

the church reacted to the threat of a perceived heresy — *and* of how
it matured because of a heretical threat.

⸎

A simple logic had begun to emerge in some Catholic circles almost from the outset of the Reformation, and Trent only served to
articulate and refine it. Protestantism was heretical and it had to be
denounced as such. Forget the hopes of reconciliation, forget all the
colloquies: Protestantism had to be confronted. There were many
ways to achieve this. Sometimes the censures were gentle, though
no less insistent for that.

In 1534 Edward London wrote some unfortunate words against
the pope. His study at New College, Oxford, was ransacked and
the offending papers were found. London was dragged before the
college warden, who just happened to be his uncle. The warden
decided to deploy the notion of familial duty in order to snap his
nephew out of his heretical mischief. Edward was told to mend his
ways, "partly for your own shame, partly for mine, and thirdly for
your poor mother." What was he thinking! "After that she shall hear
what an abominable heretic she hath to her son I am well certain
she will never eat more bread that shall do her good."[22]

Humiliation was another favorite mechanism for nudging heretics toward conformity, as one sermon-goer in 1556 Cambridge
reported. "On Sunday, frost and cold wind . . . my lord of Chester
preached in Trinity parish at nine, where a poor fellow stood with a
pair of beads in his hand all the sermon time in the mid-pass before
the choir door." During the sermon, the bishop of Chester "called
him heretic, and at the bead time the curate read unto him an ab-
juration." The "poor fellow" was obliged to read out a statement in
which he declared his "detestation of all his heresies" and to take an
oath to be a good Catholic henceforward.[23]

The punitive measures were often a good deal more drastic.

Sometimes, as the French king Francis I explained, brutal action was required. Francis had been a relatively indulgent monarch. The line between heresy and Catholic reform was unusually hard to draw in 1520s and 1530s France — Francis's own sister was a member of the latter constituency, which presumably made treading lightly even more advisable. In 1534, however, some especially provocative proto-Protestants plastered the capital with explicit denunciations of the Catholic Mass — the so-called Affair of the Placards. Francis immediately adopted a more aggressive stance. In January 1535 he led a procession through the streets of Paris in the company of his courtiers, guildsmen, priests, and university luminaries. Francis walked bareheaded, dressed in black, carrying a solitary candle, and then announced to the crowds that he was determined to eradicate heresy "in such manner that if one of the arms of my body was infected with this corruption, I would cut it off, and if my children were tainted with it I would myself offer them in sacrifice."[24] The burnings began and this was a familiar story all across Europe. Sooner or later there was almost always a turning point.

We would expect a bullish response from Catholicism. This was always how Rome was ultimately going to react to the Protestant challenge as soon as all hope of reconciliation had evaporated. Events within the Protestant fraternity were rather less predictable. Here we enter a strange new chapter in the history of heresy. Luther, Calvin, and the rest started out as heresiarchs but, once they began to win power and influence, they began to see the wisdom in elucidating strict orthodoxies of their own. As well as pouring vitriol on Rome, there was a need to identify dissenters within their own ranks.

In one of the more notable *plus ça change* moments of European history, the persecuted quickly became the persecutors. Influence brought new responsibilities and a host of new "heresies" were born.

THE NEW HERESIES

Early Protestantism (and again, this catchall term is deployed only for the sake of convenience) faced two urgent challenges. Its response had momentous consequences for how heresy was conceptualized and attacked.

First, the Catholic Church asked a profoundly irritating (and rather brilliant) question of its upstart adversaries. Where was your church before Luther? It seemed odd that, if Protestantism was so wonderful and so necessary, God would have allowed fifteen Christian centuries to sail by before introducing the Protestants' much-touted "truth" into the world. The Catholic Church was playing to its strengths here. It had its much-cherished apostolic succession and generation after generation of sacrament-dispensing priests. It had its soaring cathedrals and it could invoke all those church fathers and church councils and luxuriate in fifteen hundred years of tradition. What, by contrast, did Protestantism have? An upstart Augustinian monk (Luther), an icon-smashing Switzer who died on the battlefield (Zwingli), and a demagogic émigré French lawyer turned theologian (Calvin), was the bruising Catholic answer.

The Protestant riposte was ingenious. There had been a true church all along, and Protestantism was simply its latest incarnation. The established church of Rome had been the impostor. Protestantism was simply trying to put things back on track. Its project wasn't about making things new; it was about returning to the Christian origins that had been defiled and clouded by centuries of papal nonsense, superstition, and brutality.

Most of the sixteenth-century reformers who busied themselves with turning the Christian world upside down adamantly stated that they were not trying to break fresh theological ground.

As Calvin insisted in a letter of 1539, his whole purpose was to emulate "the ancient form of the Church," which "the Apostles instituted." This was "the only model of a true Church, and whosoever deviates from it in the smallest degree is in error."[25] However accurate or inaccurate such a claim might have been, it made excellent propagandist sense. At a stroke, it provided Protestantism with a much-needed pedigree. It allowed for the erection of a historical counter-narrative. In a sense, it said, the true church had always existed: it had lived and breathed in the deeds and musings of the apostles and the early church and, subsequently, in those people who, because they had exposed fraudulence and corruption, had been struck down.

It wasn't necessary to throw out the whole of the Christian tradition. That would be absurd. The writings of those early church fathers and the decisions of those early church councils were part of Protestantism's birthright. Such people and events represented the first installments of the genuine Christian story. The texts of scripture, the deeds of the apostles, and the martyrs who had died under Trajan, Decius, and Diocletian were more venerable still. Protestants claimed them as their own. Look a little harder, they said, and a much wider cast of earlier Christians could be recruited by the Protestant cause, including some people who had been denounced by the official church as heretics: not the truly wayward, of course, but an impressive band of pioneers who had been dedicated to exposing the worldly, avaricious, plenitude-seeking antics of Rome.

As Luther memorably put it: "These 'heretics' have done nothing wrong against God, indeed they committed a much more serious crime: they desired to possess the Holy Scriptures and God's word and — poor sinners that they were — insisted that the pope live a moral life and preach the word of God honestly and forthrightly, not threaten people with papal bulls with the gay abandon of a drunken sailor."[26]

As polemic goes, this was impressive stuff, and it contributed to a grand vision. It was conveniently (and conspicuously) silent about all the fissures that instantly began to open up within the reformed camp — not, after all, the most promising sign of the fulfillment of the true Christian message. It sometimes bowdlerized and bastardized the writings and wishes of people like Wyclif and Hus in order to fit them into a neat teleological scheme. But it was also a vision that, for the most part, was heartfelt and very effective.

No one articulated this Protestant mytho-history with more skill and verve than John Foxe, one of the first, and perhaps the greatest, of Protestantism's martyrologists.

⤷

In Foxe's scheme, Christian history had begun with a period of suffering: the three hundred years of imperial persecution. There had been horrors, but it was in this crucible of persecution that the dream of Christian truth and unity had been born. You will recall Ignatius of Antioch: to Foxe he was the Christian champion who "strengthened and confirmed the parishes through all the cities as he went," urging them to "cleave and stick fast to the tradition of the apostles." Next had come the "flourishing time": another three hundred years under the protection and auspices of Constantine and his successors. This had been a wonderful era: "coming out of this Red Sea of bloody persecution . . . after long and tedious afflictions . . . [God] hath sent this meek Moses (Gentle Constantine, I mean) . . . to turn their mourning into joy, to magnify the Church of his Son, to destroy the idols of all the world." For England, it had meant the arrival of Christianity and the conversion of the Saxons.

Unfortunately, the "declining time" had been next to arrive: the period during which the pope, who was Antichrist, had risen to dizzying political heights and placed Christianity in a Babylonian captivity. The last three hundred years, which, by Foxe's math, brought us to the eve of the Reformation, had shown some signs of improvement. All manner of people had begun to criticize the papacy and its corrupt establishment. As sure as eggs is eggs, the papacy had worked to strike such heroes down, but there was no reason to be deceived by its savage actions. There was always a battle between the visible church and the true, invisible church, made up of the authentic confessors — even if those confessors were routinely labeled as heretics.

"The proud and misordered reign of Antichrist" had endured and popes had continued to be stuffed with "ambition, stoutness, and pride" in their attempts to secure "all the riches and power of the whole world." There had been good men too, and Foxe set about claiming them as precursors of the Protestant cause. They included many of the heretics we've already encountered. The Waldensians had identified the "the pride and hypocrisy" of the so-called church. They had seen "some spark of the true and clear light of the Gospel," but, inevitably, "the more diligent [Valdes] was in setting forth the true doctrine of Christ against the errors of Antichrist, the more maliciously their fierceness increased."

Foxe's recruitment policy was surprisingly inclusive. He happily poured praise on Berengar of Tours; Catherine of Siena was applauded because she was "wont much to complain of the corrupt state of the Church"; even the Cathars earned a mention because they "began to smell the pope."

One thing was clear. By the early thirteenth century there was no mistaking the "iniquity and raging pride of the popish Church," but God stepped into the breach. He began to "resist and withstand the corruption of that whorish church, by stirring up certain faithful teachers in sundry countries." It was no coincidence that "heresy (as [the pope] calleth the truth of God, or the doctrine that rebuketh sin) began to rise up very high, and to spread forth its branches abroad."

The pivotal year was 1360: the thousandth anniversary (give or take) of the end of imperial persecution. First there had come

Wyclif, whom God had decided to "raise up here in England, to detect more fully and amply the poison of the pope's doctrine, and false religion set up by the friars." He was much needed: "The poor Christians, as ye see, like to the silly Israelites under the tyranny of Pharaoh, were infected and oppressed in every place but especially here in England." Then there had been Hus and finally, of course, the great reformers of the sixteenth century.[27]

It was a bravura performance, full of convenient parallels and often entirely bereft of historical accuracy, but in a place like England, which had endured such a curious Reformation journey, it proved inordinately popular. It threw Catholicism's question — where was your church before Luther? — back in its face. Heresy had never looked so good. Unfortunately, Protestantism's riposte to Catholicism's other annoying challenge would have less happy results for those of heretical inclinations.

‿

Catholics were quick to point out the divisions that almost immediately sprang up within the Protestant camp. One famous woodcut of 1529 shows a seven-headed Luther giving birth to all kinds of rebellion, murder, and catastrophe. As Miles Hogarde, the polemicist of Queen Mary's reign, sniped, "If these good fellows will needs be of Christ's Church, as arrogantly they presume by their own confessions; they must needs have one unity of doctrine as the church hath, which surely they have not."[28] This was a charge that Protestantism took very seriously and it set about dampening it down. With a vengeance.

At the outset, Martin Luther appeared to be largely untroubled by the theological free-for-all that his ideas — vernacular Bibles, a priesthood of all believers — threatened to unleash. Here he is in 1523 in his *On Secular Authority:* "Each must decide at his own peril what he is to believe, and must see to it that he believes rightly.

Other people cannot go to heaven or hell on my behalf or open or close the gates to either for me." Therefore every person's religious stance "is a matter for each individual's conscience." Bolder yet, the secular authorities "must use no coercion in this matter against anyone."[29]

How quickly things were to change. Only a few years later, Luther was spouting very different sentiments and working hard to outlaw unnecessary speculation and dissent. One event above all others inspired this shift in theological gear: the great revolt of the German peasantry.

꙯

The women of Frankenhausen pleaded for clemency. They had seen most of their sons and husbands — as many as five thousand souls — perish in battle. A few men had survived and they had sought refuge in the drainage canals of the town's salt works. Legend tells that the besieging army promised to let these random survivors live, on condition that the women of Frankenhausen punished two of their rebellious leaders — beating them to death with cudgels for a full half-hour. That might be myth, that might be truth, but one fact is clear. The 1525 battle of Frankenhausen had begun with optimism, with massed troops of peasants and urban artisans gathered under rainbow-bedecked banners. It had ended in slaughter and with it the German Peasants' Revolt had all but petered out.

At first the German peasantry had not sought conflict — merely the redress of grievances. Surely it was wrong for a local noble to ask his vassals to collect seashells (a key component in the business of yarn-winding) when these vassals were already busy gathering in the harvest with which they supported their families through the winter months. It was a typical abuse of feudalism: masters expected the peasantry to fulfill age-old obligations but rarely provided the reciprocal care and protection envisaged by the feudal contract. In

1524 groups of peasants began marching across southern Germany, gathering support and itemizing their complaints. Without the slightest qualm, the peasants revealed, landlords had been seizing the peasantry's ancient streams and leasing them to fishermen; they had begun to forbid the selling of salt, geese, and ducks and the carrying of crossbows; they had started to inflate the punishments of feudal justice — striking another man in the face used to carry a penalty of five shillings, but it was now deemed a felony.

The aim of these wandering peasant bands was negotiation, but none (of any meaningful kind) was forthcoming. And then, as nothing more than a historical accident, heresy entered the equation. These were no ordinary years in the patchwork territories of Germany. Martin Luther had recently lodged his protest against the doctrines and hierarchies of Rome and the Reformation had begun. This Reformation contained messages that fed the disaffection of the German peasantry. Luther talked of a priesthood of all believers, of the Bible being the only true religious authority, of the rights of the laity to elect their own preachers. It smacked of democratization, and many within the German peasantry seized upon its message. Perhaps Lutheranism could legitimize the peasants' protests; perhaps the Gospel (and here was an idea with a long future ahead of it) could be a tool of social justice. As one of the peasants' manifestos boldly suggested, the nobility should act "as true and genuine Christians" and either "gladly release us from serfdom or else show us from the Gospel that we are serfs."[30]

Over the coming months the rebellion fanned out across Germany — along Lake Constance, into Swabia, Alsace, and the Rhineland, and as far as Saxony and Salzburg. Others — urban workers, the miners of Upper Austria — were recruited to the cause, and as the movement's radicalism grew, so the religious element of the protest blossomed. If the old order had to be criticized or even dismantled, then there was no more conspicuous element of the old order than the established church. Blesy Krieg, from a village near Freiburg, entered a convent and with his blacksmith's hammer smashed the pyx containing the holy sacrament. He and his friends grabbed the communion wafers and, in an act of daring sacrilege, stuffed them irreverently into their mouths. They donned priestly vestments and mockingly enacted the elevation of the host, stole church furnishings, ripped up devotional books, and beat with sticks the statues of saints.

Confronted with such outrages, the religious and political authorities of Germany struck back and, in routs like the battle of Frankenhausen, quelled the peasantry's rebellion. In the town of Kitzingen the public executioner — known locally as "Master Ouch" — did excellent business. He was paid piecemeal and, with eighty beheadings and several dozen eye pluckings to his credit, he presented the municipal government with his bill for 114½ florins.

The German Peasants' Revolt sent shockwaves across Europe. Martin Luther, for all his theological daring, had little patience for social revolt, and he began to rue the democratizing words he had written as recently as 1523.

ოჳ

What Luther could not abide was the way in which the rebels had abused religion: "They cloak this terrible and horrible sin with the Gospel," he thundered. Earlier optimism was to be abandoned. "The powers that be, are ordained of God," Luther wrote, and "whosoever resisteth power, resisteth the ordinance of God. And they that resist, shall receive to themselves damnation." Might was right and it was perfectly acceptable to "smite, slay and stab, secretly or openly, remembering that nothing can be more poisonous, hurtful or devilish than a rebel. It is just as when one must kill a mad dog."[31]

From now on there was a need to take control. The Reformation would have to be a magisterial affair, in the sense of being overseen by magistrates and legitimate rulers. Not, absolutely not, the playground of rebellious peasants. The relationship between clerics and politicians would never be easy within the reformed camp. There was often a keen sense, for instance, that doctrinal matters should be left to the theologians and ministers who knew best, but the notion that someone had to guide the ship became, within the mainstream at least, normative. The corollary was that dissent and heresy, before the people once again descended into rebellion, would have to be expunged.

The answer to the Catholic charge that Protestantism meant chaos and rebellion (familiar tools in the devil's bag of subversive tricks) — and made so manifest by the events of the Peasants' Revolt — was quick and to the point. Protestantism could put its own house in order.

The Protestant revolution, if we choose to describe it as such, is often seen as one of the taproots of modernity. It is seen as democratizing the realm of faith. Insofar as it opened up new vistas of inquiry, this is an accurate assessment, but it is well to remember that its leaders quickly recognized the risks inherent in allowing too much space for speculation. Heresy, once it took on the mantle of the new orthodoxy, began to batten down the hermeneutic hatches.

The ill-fated Anabaptists would be among the first victims of this new stricter attitude. Revolting peasants were bad enough; people coming up with theological ideas that leaders of the reform found utterly repugnant were even worse.

DROWNED WITHOUT MERCY: ANABAPTISTS

> Whereas our Lords the Burgomaster, Council, and Great Council have for sometime past earnestly endeavoured to turn the misguided and erring Anabaptists from their errors and yet several . . . to the injury of the public authority and the magistrates as well as to the ruin of the common welfare and of right Christian living, have proved disobedient; and several of them, men, women and girls, have been by our Lords sharply punished and put into

prison: Now therefore, by the earnest commandment, edict and warning of our lords aforesaid, it is ordered that no one in our town, country or domains, whether man, woman or girl, shall baptise another; and if any hereafter shall baptise another, he will be seized by our Lords and, according to the decree now set forth, will be drowned without mercy.

— DECREE OF THE ZURICH COUNCIL, March 1526[32]

It is often forgotten (perhaps because theological amnesia is sometimes very useful), but adult baptism had been extremely popular in the early church. As appealing and logical as it might have been, adult baptism gradually fell from favor, becoming an errant (indeed, heretical) practice. It never died away entirely, of course, and it would always have its advocates, many of them suggesting that the baptism of a consenting, fully informed adult was of an entirely different (and patently superior) caliber than the baptism of a bewildered child. It was not until the Reformation of the sixteenth century, however, that support for adult baptism enjoyed a truly significant recrudescence.

Beginning in the Zurich of Ulrich Zwingli and spreading out across much of northern and central Europe, what came to be known as the Anabaptist movement began to fill the caretakers of orthodoxy, both Catholic and Protestant, with horror. Their response was extraordinarily energetic, and Anabaptism won martyrs at an astonishing rate. One thinks of Michael Sattler, tortured in the marketplace of Rothenburg in 1527, his tongue cut out and his mangled body lowered onto a martyr's pyre, or Balthasar Hubmaier, meeting an equally miserable fate in Vienna as his wife was drowned in the Danube, with stones hung around her neck.

The justification for such tactics was that Anabaptism not only challenged one of Christianity's sacramental certainties, but that it was led by fanatics who inspired social and political turmoil. This was, by any reasonable standard, unfair. Many Anabaptists were anything but revolutionaries: they could just as easily be portrayed as the inheritors of a lapsed but authentic Christian practice, which would, over the coming centuries, secure a newfound respectability among Baptist, Amish, and Mennonite congregations.

A measured, balanced analysis of Anabaptism did not matter one jot to the leaders of the established church or, more important for our present purposes, to the leaders of what would come to be known as Protestantism. Belief in the virtues of adult baptism represented a heresy, and when explaining it to the faithful the only sensible approach was to fill them with horror and stoke their paranoia. Happily for mainstream Protestantism — and catastrophically for the Anabaptist movement — an unrepresentative band of Anabaptists in the German city of Münster made this very easy to accomplish.[33]

Up until the early 1530s Münster had been the venue for moderate Lutheran reform. From 1533, more radical elements began to accrue influence in the city. Led by the Haarlem baker Jan Mathijs, extremist Anabaptists began preaching the immediate return of Jesus Christ, claiming that while most of the rest of the world would soon crumble away, the city of Münster would serve as Christ's New Jerusalem. In early 1534 Mathijs offered the residents of the city a stark choice: they could either conform to his doctrines and be re-baptized or be put to the sword. Mercifully, cooler heads prevailed and most of those who did not share Mathijs's millennial vision or his passionate belief in adult baptism were allowed to leave the city unharmed.

With the rump of Münster's population under his sway, Mathijs established himself as the city's dictator, taking the radical step of outlawing the holding of private property: it was decreed that every door in the city should be left open, by both day and night. With such a revolution unfolding in their midst, local Catholic authorities laid siege to the city. When Mathijs perished in a skirmish with Catholic troops, the reins of power were taken up by Jan Beukels, as deranged a figure as the history of heresy would produce. With

Münster under siege he ruled the population with arbitrary justice, introduced the practice of polygamy, and played the role of a latter-day biblical prophet — King David of all the world, as he styled himself — while the besieged Münsterites began dying of starvation all around him.

New laws were enacted, courtesy of which a swathe of sins (everything from blasphemy and adultery to the simple act of scolding one's parents) were to be punished with the death penalty. The forty-nine citizens who openly opposed the introduction of polygamy were all executed, and when one of Beukels's own wives dared to voice dissent, Beukels beheaded her and trampled on her body in the city's main marketplace. His bizarre reign of terror came to an end only when the Catholic troops finally gained entry to the city. In January 1536, the revolution's leaders were tortured with red-hot tongs and their corpses left to rot in cages above St. Lambert's Church.

This all spelled disaster for Anabaptism. Its more levelheaded advocates were easily ignored and, by some calculations, as many as two and a half thousand Anabaptists were killed during the sixteenth century — something like half of all those who perished during the period because of their religious beliefs.

For mainstream Protestantism, there were advantages. The task of defeating internal heresy had come into even sharper relief. Steps had to be taken to prevent their being any more Münsters. This was not the only Protestant response to dissent. Many Protestant leaders pleaded for a more irenic approach: Martin Bucer, the leader of the relatively easygoing city of Strasbourg, being the prime example. But not even the irenicists had much time for the Anabaptists. Some heretics were simply beyond the pale because a newly fledged orthodoxy, even though it started out in life as a heresy, decided that it could not tolerate heresies of its own.

The most infamous example of this logic playing itself out was the execution of Michael Servetus.

SERVETUS

Shortly after midday on October 27, 1553, Michael Servetus was marched through the city gates of Geneva, headed for Champel Hill. His heretical meditations on the Trinity had been denounced as "impious blasphemies and insane errors, wholly foreign to the word of God." A guard of mounted archers, robed clergymen and magistrates, and much of Geneva's citizenry accompanied the forty-two-year-old Spaniard. They would soon witness one of the sixteenth century's most notorious executions. Servetus was bound to a stake with iron chains, a crown of twigs and sulfur was placed on his head, and sticks of green wood — intended to burn more slowly and thus prolong his suffering — were lit. By some accounts, Servetus let out a cry: "*Misericordia, misericordia.* Jesus have compassion upon me." A copy of his infamous book — *Christianismi Restitutio* — burned beneath his feet.

For more than two decades Michael Servetus had been artfully evading those who sought his downfall. At only twenty years of age he had published a book that launched a theologically confused but full-throated assault on the cherished Christian doctrine of the Trinity: the belief in one God as three persons — Father, Son, and Holy Ghost — joined in mystical union, and all three responsible for our salvation. Puzzlingly, Servetus had boldly put his name to this most controversial of tracts (his printer had sensibly remained anonymous), but when inquisitorial proceedings were launched against him, Servetus did not hesitate to adopt a pseudonym. In his new guise as Michel de Villeneuve, he fled to Paris to study mathematics and medicine. A second, and third, career ensued, in which he served time as a proofreader in Lyon and, with some audacity, worked as the personal physician to the princes of the church (including the archbishop of Vienne) he had so offended.

He remained the theological maverick, however, and, in 1545 he made the fateful decision to strike up a correspondence with the

great reformer of Geneva, John Calvin. As we've seen, Calvin's theology was itself unfeasibly radical — it exploded centuries of Christian thought about salvation, grace, and predestination — but Calvin was never anything other than a devoted believer in the Trinity.
As such, he despised Michael Servetus, and when occasion arose
he set out to destroy him. When Servetus's *Christianismi Restitutio*
(a more mature anti-Trinitarian work) was published in 1553, the
French authorities arrested him and declared him a heretic. It is
likely that it was Calvin who informed his Catholic enemies that
they had a covert Unitarian in their midst: a curious, some would
say disreputable, moment of cross-confessional cooperation in a
century of religious strife. Again, however, Servetus made good his
escape. Early one morning he scaled the wall of the prison garden
in Vienne and headed off to Italy: all that was left to the infuriated
French authorities was to burn Servetus in effigy.

Bizarrely, and catastrophically, Servetus decided to stop off at
Geneva en route. Since he had arrived on a Sunday, he even took
the risky step of going to see John Calvin preach in one of the city's
churches. Calvin, out of theological distaste and in order to reassert
his waning political influence, engineered Servetus's arrest and trial.
A boisterous examination of Servetus's opinions followed, in which
the heretic was charged with spreading "endless blasphemies," calling the baptism of children "an invention of the devil," and even
studying the detested Koran "in order to controvert and disprove
the doctrine and religion that the Christian Churches hold." Worst
of all, he had allegedly described the Trinity as a "three-headed
devil, like to Cerberus, whom the ancient poets have called the dog
of hell, a monster."

Servetus's guilt was established to the satisfaction of the city's
Lesser Council and, while Geneva sought the advice of other Swiss
cities about how best to proceed, Servetus languished in prison. He
complained endlessly about his plight. "The lice eat me alive," he informed the city's magistrates, "my clothes are torn, and I have noth-

ing for a change, neither a jacket nor a shirt"; realizing that his prospects were bleak, he pleaded that he might be killed in as humane a way as possible. It was commonly supposed that the true martyr would endure his final agonies with unworldly serenity. Servetus feared that, if the flames began to lick, he would respond with a distinct lack of courage. As we have seen, his requests fell on deaf ears.[34]

~

The context of Servetus's execution is all important. By 1553, the rigors of John Calvin's regime were already well known. Nowhere was the concept of a controlled, magisterial Reformation more in evidence. During the 1540s and 1550s, as much as 7 percent of Geneva's population (a startlingly high proportion) was brought before its ecclesiastical tribunal, the Consistory: Protestantism's very own Inquisition. Some offenders had done nothing more heinous than play cards or don extravagant clothing. Others were adulterers, blasphemers, and religious dissidents, many of whom received punishments — ranging from excommunication, to banishment, to execution — that even by the standards of the sixteenth century were unusually severe. It was all part of John Calvin's plan to reform the morality of the city he hoped to turn into a Protestant paradise. Pierre Ameaux criticized Calvin's penchant for employing French preachers in Geneva's churches. As punishment, he was made to parade through the city's streets in a hair shirt, begging for forgiveness. Valentin Gentilis held theological views that Calvin found unappetizing, and was made to undergo the humiliation of publicly burning his own books. And yet, even in this oppressive climate, the particularly gruesome death of Michael Servetus stands out.

One contemporary, the French theologian Sebastian Castellio (1515–1563), found the whole episode deeply shameful. For Castellio, the execution was an unforgivable act of tyranny. He began to wonder if the very notion of persecuting heretics was not a betrayal of the entire Christian cause. Just what *were* heretics, Castellio asked: simply "those with whom we disagree." And while you might detest the people with whom you quarreled, it really wasn't appropriate to torture and kill them. Force and violence had no role to play in the arena of religious belief because the truth could not be hammered into people's minds. Persuasion was endlessly more efficient than coercion.

Castellio asked his Christ a rhetorical question. "I beg you in the name of your Father, do you now command that those who do not understand your precepts be drowned in water, cut with lashes to the entrails, dismembered by the sword, or burned at a slow fire?" Did Christ approve of these things being done in his name? "Are they your vicars who make these sacrifices?" Of course not. "O blasphemous and shameful audacity of men, who dare to attribute to Christ that which they do by the command and the instigation of Satan."[35]

The subsequent adjudication has been ferocious too. Servetus's execution is an event that has continued to haunt the people of Geneva. In 1909 an expiatory monument was erected on the site of Servetus's execution. It can still be visited today, where the Avenue de la Rosarie meets the Avenue de Beau-Sejour. Its inscription dutifully pays tribute to John Calvin — "our great reformer" and the man who, after all, made Geneva into one of the most influential cities in Europe — but it also apologizes for the death of Servetus as an odious crime against liberty of conscience. In fact, this was only the most recent outpouring of sympathy for Michael Servetus. Throughout the nineteenth century — when notions of religious freedom were very much in vogue — there had been a frenzied competition to see who could erect the most elaborate monument in his memory, or write the most adoring account of his deeds. It became fashionable to refer to Champel Hill, were Servetus was broiled alive, as a second Golgotha.

ᔐ

The truth is that someone like Castellio was very unusual. His condemnation of the Servetus affair won a wide readership and there was a good deal of grumbling about going so far as killing a fellow, if idiosyncratic, Protestant. That, so it was averred, was what Catholics did. Nonetheless, most contemporaries, if they complained at all, only worried about the specific circumstances of Servetus's treatment. Killing him was perhaps a little harsh, and killing him in such a savage way was a public relations disaster (and, for the record, Calvin himself suggested that Servetus be beheaded — a much less excruciating way to meet your maker). The execution was seen as a scandal across Protestant Europe. Hardly anyone doubted that he had to be silenced and punished, however. The events in Geneva in 1553 have grabbed the headlines for five centuries. Thanks to Castellio's reaction, they are routinely invoked as one of the steps on the road to religious toleration, but in the context of the sixteenth century Servetus's execution only represented the most extreme articulation of a prevailing logic. Protestantism, in places like Calvin's Geneva, had won the day. It was in charge and, in the interests of social order and theological respectability, it felt obliged to hammer out its orthodoxies and strike down its heretical enemies.

PLUS ÇA CHANGE?

> For did not Arius first, Socinus now
> The Son's eternal Godhead disavow?
> And did not these by Gospel texts alone
> Condemn our doctrine and maintain their own?
> Have not all heretics the same pretence,
> To plead the Scriptures in their own defence?
>
> — DRYDEN, *The Hind and the Panther*[36]

A parallel (clumsy but thought-provoking) might be drawn between developments in the early church and in the Reformation. In each case, a persecuted group managed to secure political influence: back in the fourth century, this change occurred thanks to Constantine; this time around it was down to German territorial rulers, the (albeit reluctant) citizenry of Geneva, and various European monarchs. As soon as this transformation had occurred, sustaining order became a vital priority. Just like leaders in the early church, the reformers found themselves with a great deal of criticism to fend off. Earlier, Celsus had bleated about how divisions in the church signaled a lack of authenticity; now Protestants had to contend with similar complaints lodged by Catholics. There was even the attempt to draw a line between ideas that were merely questionable and those that were flatly unacceptable (for Servetus and the Anabaptists, substitute the Gnostics or the Donatists).

Another common thread: none of these efforts had the slightest hope of containing all the divisions. The major difference is that the early church usually made good headway in wiping out heretical alternatives; sixteenth-century (and subsequent) Protestantism never came close to matching its success. The results are all around us today. It was easy to call the Baptists "Donatists new dipped," as one seventeenth-century commentator chose to do, but there was a major difference.[37] The Baptists survived: flourished, even. And so did the Quakers, the Methodists, and even the heirs of the once-pilloried Anabaptists.

We are bound to ask why this happened. There are two things to explain. First, why was mainstream Reformation not snuffed out, like so many earlier heresies? Second, why were the divisions within Protestantism's own ranks not closed down, despite the best efforts of leaders such as Calvin and Luther? The first of these puzzles is by far the harder to solve.

Conceptualizing the Reformation as the culmination of medieval heretical dissent and anticlerical sentiment is overly simplistic. However, once the process was underway, hackneyed complaints and criticisms could still prove very useful. All those old stories of papal corruption and lackluster priests offered Protestantism a wealth of ammunition, and Protestant leaders were certainly not shy about exploiting it. It was no accident that groups like the Waldensians and the Lollards jumped on board the Reformation bandwagon at the first opportunity. And once this bandwagon started to roll, there is little doubt that some were won over to the cause because of memories of the stale, redundant old church. The memories were usually false, but in the business of Reformation this did not necessarily matter: after all, it isn't very often that a polemical argument is won or lost on the grounds of truth or historical accuracy.

There was also the small matter of the print revolution. This factor cannot be overestimated, as historians have long recognized. The huge difference between the Reformation and all previous heretical movements was that it spread so fast and so wide. This was largely down to the fact that reformist tracts, reproduced far beyond duplicate or triplicate, could make their way from Wittenberg or Geneva to the far-flung reaches of the continent within days or weeks. This is not especially speedy in our terms, but as far as the sixteenth century was concerned, this was lightning fast. Within a few years of Luther's initial protest as many as 600,000 copies of his tracts were in circulation.

We should also give some credit to the reformers themselves. Their theological innovations sometimes struck a chord, and even an idea as seemingly bleak as Calvinism possessed a certain theological appeal: it made the puzzling question of salvation a great deal simpler, albeit in a stark, uncompromising way. Just as important, leaders such as Luther and Calvin were quick to contain the possible consequences of their theorizing, but this did not prevent many people (or at least enough people to turn a protest into a movement) from being seduced by all this talk of a priesthood of all believers, or returning to the Bible and seeing exactly what it had to say. And if you harbored such sympathies, how much easier everything became when you could pore over scriptures that had been translated into your own language.

The commitment to vernacular scripture is sometimes identified as a Reformation innovation. It was no such thing, but its role
in assisting Protestantism's spread was key. One of the more curious
events in Reformation history was the moment, in mid-Tudor England, when the people of Cornwall rose in revolt. One of their grievances was the recent arrival of English Bibles and prayer books. One
might imagine that they would have been quite pleased with such
a development. The trouble was, they were Cornish speakers, and
even if the Latin they were used to hearing in their churches was
incomprehensible, it was at least familiar. The newfangled English
services they now had to sit through struck them as the worst sort
of gobbledygook — an imposition dreamed up by their overlords in
London.

This was an aberrant occurrence. As one historian has recently
argued, vernacular scripture didn't always make the encounter with
Christian theology any easier — suddenly, all the Bible's contradictions and puzzling ideas were laid bare in a language that everyone
could understand.[38] By and large, however, people were pleased
with the arrival of the vernacular. It was certainly one of Protestantism's more popular ideas.

All of these factors were important (indeed, one of them, the
arrival of movable type at just the right moment, was unfeasibly
lucky), but they would presumably have counted for nothing if the
political stars had not been aligned in the Reformation's favor. Look
where Luther launched his protest: in the territories of Frederick
III of Saxony, who despised papal interventions and just happened
to be very proud of his new university in Wittenberg. He had little
sympathy with Luther's theological posturing. In fact, he was the
least likely sponsor of Reformation imaginable. Back in 1493, he had
purchased a thumb that had reputedly belonged to Saint Anne and,
over the next two decades, he amassed a dazzling assortment of relics. Nineteen thousand of them, all told, and when people visited
the yearly display of his relics at Wittenberg Castle, they received

very good value for their money: no less than 1.9 million years cut off their potential sentence in purgatory.[39] This was everything Luther stood against, but Frederick still defended him; he was not going to countenance one of his subjects being snatched up by external authorities. In a ham-fisted sort of way he protected Luther and gave him (albeit in the faux-incarceration of Wartburg Castle) breathing room; as a result, the Lutheran message stood a much better chance of reaching the wider world.

Likewise, Calvin. The people of Geneva grew very cross with the regime Calvin finally managed to inflict upon them, but it was their particular political situation that had allowed the whole enterprise to gather momentum in the first place. They were heartily tired of the interventions of the local political bigwig, the duke of Savoy, so they gave Calvin's quest for political and theological independence half a chance.

Who knows what might have happened if an earlier heresy had enjoyed the good political fortune with which Protestantism was blessed? There was print, there were lofty rulers willing to protect you, and, into the bargain, the very people who were supposed to oppose you were busy with their own concerns. Rome, as we've seen, was slow to mount a coherent defense against the Protestant threat. Charles V, the ruler who was gifted the task of dealing with Luther, was busy fighting his political rivals.

✍

Infuriatingly, as soon as you start to construct a list of reasons for Protestantism's survival, someone else can conjure up an alternative list that turns all your arguments against you. There is a compelling counter-case for most of the theories I have just floated. The print revolution could be deployed by the enemies of Reformation just as easily as it was utilized by its advocates. There were places where the Reformation succeeded because of political backing, but there

were also towns and territories where it triumphed in spite of political opposition. As for the inherent appeal of Protestant ideas, this
was sometimes a crucial factor but just as often (more frequently,
on balance), it took an awfully long time for Protestant nostrums to
win over hearts and minds.

All told, the continentwide success of the Protestant Reformation remains something of a mystery. This is one of the reasons why
professional historians spend most of their time anatomizing what
happened in a specific corner of Reformation Europe. This is what
economists, sociologists, and the practitioners of other soft sciences
call the low-hanging-fruit syndrome. It is much easier, and much
more sensible, to grab for the attainable objective: to anatomize why
Lutheranism or Calvinism managed to establish itself in a particular time and place. An overarching explanation of the Reformation's
overall success has always been, and will probably always remain,
out of reach.

⁓

Happily, our other task — to explain why Protestantism's own heresies emerged — is much easier to accomplish: a walk in the interpretative park. Fragmentation was in Protestantism's very bones.
It is often said that, from the perspective of building a church,
Protestantism suffered from an inherent flaw. It bruited the idea of
individual access to and interpretation of scripture, it talked of a
priesthood of all believers, and this could only end in chaos, however hard the leaders of the magisterial Reformation tried to put the
genie back in the bottle.

That original point about the mutability of the Christian message, which had been lurking in the background all along, finally
came home to roost, and there was precious little that Protestantism
could do about the consequences.

First, Protestantism lacked any central locus of authority. Catholicism had Rome and its church councils; Protestantism had Geneva, Wittenberg, and countless other local fonts of orthodoxy. From the outset, the notion of a unified Protestant church was a contradiction in terms. Second, Protestantism just happened to dwell on issues about which few people were ever likely to agree. The divisions were there from the start. Luther fell out with Zwingli over the meaning of the Eucharist, Calvin quarreled with almost everyone despite his attempts (which always rang rather hollow) to sponsor pan-European Protestant unity. Many of the issues that Christianity had been trying to brush under the theological carpet over the past millennium and a half were reenergized in the wake of the Reformation: precisely *because* of the Reformation's central suggestion that it was legitimate to reexamine scripture and Christian tradition.

More than that, many of Protestantism's own theological fixations were ripe for endless analysis and reanalysis. Take Calvin's concept of predestination, for instance. Many wondered how such a vision was to be interpreted. Some took the ruthless route. There was double predestination: people were either damned or saved and, given this fact, it made excellent sense to stake out the difference between the Visible Church (anyone who deigned to sit in a pew) and the Invisible Church (the short list of those who were actually saved). Some Protestants tried to impose this division in the here and now. Churches should open their doors only to those who could come up with some convincing proof of their elect status. Other Protestants thought this mad: how could such adjudications possibly be made? they asked. And wasn't their imposition bound to cause social dislocation and turmoil? Some Protestants even questioned the basis of Calvin's predestinarian theology and suggested that robbing human beings of any substantive role in achieving salvation was a colossal mistake: hence the Arminians of seventeenth-century Holland, who had at least a nodding acquaintance with concepts of free will and human agency.

The list could easily be extended: the obliteration of a clerical estate versus a sneaking feeling that priests (even bishops) might still have a role to play; a commitment to paring down worship to its whitewashed simplicity versus the idea that it wasn't entirely disreputable to retain some glints of glamour and beauty in the parish church; the troubling suggestion that personal encounter with the Godhead was all that counted versus an insistence that such wayward notions would lead to devotional mischief.

The divisions of Protestantism were all but inevitable, but this explains only one (albeit very important) phenomenon: why it shattered into so many competing denominations. The much tougher question is how such denominations managed to prosper. How on earth did the modern Christian landscape (self-consciously easygoing and inclusive for the most part, despite the recurrent moments of biliousness) spring into existence? How did the most turbulent of Christian centuries (a time, for all the local, levelheaded pragmatism, of bitter reproaches and cross-confessional strife) manage to set the scene for the more generous future?

Some other historical accident, something even odder than the Reformation, had to intervene. The idea of toleration had to claw its way into Christian minds. It was time for a new myth.

8

THE DEATH OF HERESY?

JUDGING BY THE first few decades of the seventeenth century, religious enmity was still inspiring many Europeans, and the campaign to locate and eradicate heresy was in rude health. After all, these years produced some of the most famous heresy-related contretemps in Western history: Galileo being brought to task and sentenced to house arrest for his astronomical speculations; Giordano Bruno being burned alive in 1600 Rome; the ill-fated Tommaso Campanella feigning madness in order to avoid the anti-heretical punishments of ecclesiastical justice. I won't dwell on such tribulations, since they are well known, but they make the point.

Paradoxically, these decades also provided the seedbed for a whole new approach to issues of religious faith and diversity of opinion. It was here that the march to modern-day toleration and pluralism — concepts that undermined the very notion of heresy — began. The trajectory was less direct than is sometimes supposed, however.

CAUTION

Caution is always advisable when it comes to tracing the roots of toleration. It would be ludicrous to suggest that no one before the modern age ever thought about religious freedom (or broader intel-lectual freedom, to widen the net) in the abstract. It is also perfectly clear that many premodern people became rather cross when the overseers of prevailing orthodoxies informed them that their in-terpretations of the Christian faith were wayward. No one enjoyed being called a heretic or being punished as a result. The crucial point is that earlier grumbles were not framed in the same terms as our own.

There were many daring Christian theologians during the an-cient, medieval, and early-modern eras — from Origen to Abelard to Calvin — and, as we have seen countless times already, there were many groups and individuals who caused sufficient uproar to be de-nounced as overly imaginative heretics. It would still be very sur-prising to discover that any of these people (even many of the most outlandish heresiarchs) held a modern belief in religious pluralism or an inalienable *right* to think and worship however they chose. Such concepts (modern rights theory most conspicuously) were inventions of the seventeenth and eighteenth centuries. This might seem like nitpicking: it is actually vital because it speaks to the chasm that separates the modern age from all those that came before.

This did not mean that there was no room for conjecture in the arenas of religious, philosophical, or intellectual endeavor: an-cient classical philosophy was full of such pursuits, after all. In the Christian experience, there were limits to such playfulness, and transgressing them had a habit of landing a thinker in trouble, but inside the parameters of acceptable debate there was a surprisingly generous space for speculation. Christianity often worked hard to differentiate between the essentials of faith and matters indifferent (*adiaphora* is the lofty theological term). In fact, it would be entirely possible to write a history of medieval theologizing anchored in an analysis of where the lines between inventive thought and errant, heretical posturing ought to be drawn.

It was even possible for pristinely orthodox scholars to riff on the idea of free inquiry in the safety of their studies. Thomas More, who turned out to be one of the most strident heretic haters of the sixteenth century, grappled rather adventurously with the concept in his most famous book, *Utopia*. In his faraway land King Utopos "decreed that every man might cultivate the religion of his choice, and might proselytise for it, too, provided he did so quietly, modestly, rationally, and without bitterness towards others."[1] The thing about Utopia, of course, is that it meant "nowhere." Back in the real world, More was delighted to pen denunciations of Lutheranism and to charge into the German immigrant communities of 1520s London, looking for books to burn. Heresy, as he wrote, demanded "clean cutting out" for "preservation not of the faith only but also of the peace among the people."[2]

He was not alone and, crucially, even those sixteenth-century thinkers who seemed to be articulating an expansive vision of religious freedom (one that, at face value, bears a striking resemblance to our own) can sometimes lead us down interpretative culs-de-sac. Read their words once, and they can look gloriously advanced and enlightened (in *our* terms). Read them twice, and one begins to realize that (in anyone's terms) other factors and considerations were still hard at work.

Often, such thinkers were dreaming up notions of toleration out of self-interest (to save themselves from imminent persecution, which was hardly blameworthy), or — and this is quite an interesting phenomenon — they were suggesting that there should be a temporary free-for-all so that the one single truth could be allowed to emerge. The devil, and the predictability, is in the detail of the second half of this proposition. There was no open-ended invitation to religious plurality.

The theory often went something like this: give it fifty years or so of frank debate, and everyone would realize what Christianity was truly all about. After that, presumably, the insistence upon this newfound orthodoxy would be just as fervent as before. Nothing much would have changed.

The same impossible goal — Christian unity — was still the target. Even for many of the fabled sixteenth- and seventeenth-century advocates of tolerationism. A season's chaos would lead to an eternity of certitude. It was a fleeting strategy that would allow a version of Christianity (almost always *their* idiosyncratic version) to emerge triumphant. After that, the foolish people who dissented from the new, obvious truth would once again be castigated as heretics: not slaughtered, perhaps, but still sneered at.

Make no mistake, there were rare birds who, during the Reformation era, pursued exceptionally radical thoughts about toleration and the role of coercion in matters of faith. We have already heard from Sebastian Castellio and his disgusted reaction to the execution of Servetus. The Dutch thinker Dirck Coornhert was equally troubled by the religious animosity of his times and in tracts replete with words like *love* and *forbearance* he went so far as arguing that "only God has the right to be master over man's soul and conscience; it is man's right to have freedom of conscience."[3] The fascinating thinker Sebastian Franck decided to draw the sharpest of distinctions between the crucial inner world of faith and the dismal, disputed workaday realm of rituals, competing dogmas, and confessional hatred. If a single error makes one a heretic, he once opined, then God help us all. For Franck, the path to authentic religious truth lay within the soul and conscience of the individual believer. This was the birth of a spiritualist tradition that would play an important role during subsequent Christian centuries.

Bold as such meditations were (and, even here, close examination sometimes reveals them to be less groundbreaking than we might imagine), they have to be seen as aberrant in their sixteenth-century context. Men like Coornhert and Franck sometimes seem to prefigure later nostrums in hard-to-resist ways, but (even we interpret them through a decidedly anachronistic filter) they were prophetic fish out of water and their impact on the general cultural mood was very limited. They have received vastly more attention from later historians than they did from contemporaries.

A widespread, genuinely indulgent, philosophically based approach to religious diversity still lay far in the future. This should warn us against constructing a simplistic narrative that charts the inexorable rise of religious toleration.

∽

Similarly, it is easy to mistake complaints about the *ways* in which heresy was pursued with the modern assumption that heresy shouldn't be pursued *at all*. Many of those who objected to the execution of Servetus, for example, were dismayed by the manner of his treatment: not by the fact that there had been an effort to silence him. It is tempting to suggest that this often came down to nothing more complicated than basic compassion — and it would be nice to suppose that this, at least, was something of a constant in human history.

In 1542 a Catholic student from Germany was present at religious executions in Paris, and he was horrified by what he saw.

> I saw two burnt there. Their death inspired in me differing sentiments. If you had been there, you would have hoped for a less severe punishment for these poor unfortunates . . . The first was a very young man, not yet with a beard . . . he was the son of a cobbler. He was brought in front of the judges and condemned to have his tongue cut out and burned straight afterward. Without changing the expression of his face, the young man presented his tongue to the executioner's knife, sticking it out as far as he could. The executioner pulled it out even further with pincers, cut it off, and hit the sufferer several times on

the tongue and threw it in the young man's face. Then he was put into a tipcart and was driven to the place of execution.[4]

There was little joy to be gained from witnessing such awful events, but a commitment to making the pursuit of heresy a little less gruesome was nothing new. Even Augustine, the architect of Christianity's coercive imperative, had been reluctant to see heretics killed. Even Calvin had tried to convince the Geneva authorities to behead Servetus rather than burn him alive. It was a stance shared by some of the most committed participants in the eighth-century iconoclastic controversy, and it would even be shared by the Catholic-hating John Foxe, who, for all his deep reserves of spleen and venom, was offended by the harsh treatment doled out to the Elizabethan missionary priest Edmund Campion. God dispensing horrendous divine punishments (and Foxe, as we've seen, delighted in such interventions) was one thing; human authorities behaving with undue cruelty was quite another.

This was kindly, but it was a long way from a plea for unfettered religious freedom. Heresy still had to be stamped out: just not so brutally. It should also be borne in mind that many of the calls for clemency were, at heart, self-serving: if you killed your religious enemy, then you gifted your opponents a martyr, out of whose gruesome death they would make endless bales of propagandist hay. Proving that the opposition was defined by cruelty was one of the long-standing objectives of sixteenth- and seventeenth-century Catholics and Protestants. A moment of restraint (the prison cell instead of the noose or the martyr's fire) was a point scored in this propagandist tussle.

We need to exercise similar caution whenever we come across early modern people who suggested that arguing over every last point of doctrine was a pointless, disruptive pursuit. Erasmus is the perfect example. In his writings he sometimes seems to be taking the very notion of heresy to task. In fact, he was simply objecting to the way the word was being abused. As he once wrote, in the "old days a heretic was listened to almost with respect and was absolved if he did penance . . . nowadays the accusation of heresy is a very different thing . . . on the slightest pretence all at once they are all crying 'heresy. heresy.'" The man who bad-mouthed Aquinas was instantly called a heretic; "indeed, if he disagrees with some new-fangled reasoning thought up yesterday by some sophister in the schools" he would find himself in trouble. "Anything we do not like, anything they do not understand is heresy."[5]

All that Erasmus was objecting to, however, was the misuse of the category of heresy. And he presumably found this so offensive because that category was so terribly important. Some things *were* beyond the theological pale, and this is why people using heresy as a rhetorical stick with which to beat their enemies was so regrettable: it clouded a vital issue. Erasmus dearly wanted the possible points of contention to be kept to a minimum. He disliked unnecessary squabbles, "like whether the second person of the divinity could have arrived as a donkey, a woman, a devil, or a gourd."[6] Like many other sixteenth-century luminaries, he was impressed by the notion of adiaphorism, which roughly meant not falling out over "indifferent" things of little importance. The so-called adiaphorists were rarely convinced, however, that the basics of Christian orthodoxy ought to be opened up to endless criticism and debate. They wanted there to be fewer lines in the theological sand, but the ones that remained lost none of their importance.

As Erasmus explained, "It is, I admit, a serious crime to violate the faith; but not everything should be forced into a question of faith." As he also wrote, "All error is not heresy . . . nor does something become heretical if this man or that disapproves of it. They do not always advance the cause of the faith who attach grand labels of this kind." Even Luther ought to be cut some slack: "I would rather he were set right than destroyed; for this agrees better with the example Christ has given us . . . as it is . . . [people] neither correct Luther nor instruct him; they merely traduce him with their crazy clamor before popular audiences and tear him to shreds with the most bitter and venomous denunciations, their mouths full of nothing but the words *heresy* and *heretic*."[7]

But all Erasmus was really saying was that theologians oughtn't be transfixed by trivialities. There was room, as he put it in one of his letters, for "courtesy and gentleness" when dealing with religious rivals. The people who attacked fundamental ideas, by contrast, deserved to be struck down.

శ

All of which leaves us in something of a quandary. The people of the Reformation — even the nicer ones — simply did not share our principled belief in toleration and religious pluralism and yet these very modern beliefs still had to originate somewhere.

They did not arrive overnight, but it cannot be denied that something very odd happened in seventeenth- and eighteenth-century Europe. A whole new historical narrative, populated by people like Locke, Voltaire, and Madison, began to unfold. A passionate philosophical commitment to religious freedom did, ultimately, emerge, and the oddities spouted by people like Sebastian Castellio began to garner general consent. Persecution was wrong, they said, simply wrong. The individual had a *right* (and there's that word again) to think about and worship God as he or she saw fit. Heresy became almost fashionable and the pursuit of heresy began to look like a stale, disreputable habit of the past.

This was a very curious turn in the tides of human history. We have already conjured up a hundred-year-old resident of Tudor England, so, in the same playful spirit, let's imagine a visitor from the other end of the galaxy surveying the course of Christianity since 1 B.C.E. For an awfully long time it was virtuous, even normative, to suggest that a single religious orthodoxy (however it was defined) ought to be pursued. It was hard to determine the precise lineaments of heresy, but few dissented from the idea that it was a blight and a menace that ought to be scrubbed out. This was as true of the Cathars as of their persecutors, as true of Reformation Protestants as Reformation-era Catholics. Some people were gentler than others, many of them were confused, and there were moments when pragmatic, level heads reined in the persecution. But hardly anyone went so far as to suggest that religious freedom and religious pluralism were *positive* goods.

And yet here we now are, in 2011, and such a suggestion would barely raise an eyebrow. More than that, to dissent from that notion would more than likely drop you into very hot water. You'd be called a bigot; you'd be termed medieval; you'd be told to flee the stage and dream noxious dreams of the bad old inquisitorial days.

Our alien would surely be perplexed and so should we. How on earth did it happen? The easy answer, and one to which (with some regret) I'll return, is that perhaps it never happened at all. Perhaps all we really have is a philosophical veneer: a very efficient one that almost everyone paints on their theological fences these days, but a veneer nonetheless. Deep down, do we really rejoice at the mavericks and feel glad to be alive because so many people are disagreeing with us? I hope so, but there is room for doubt.

Before thinking about conceding this point, we are obliged to interrogate the fairy tale, to decide if it is in fact a fairy tale at all. Perhaps things just did change and, against the currents of human history, they changed for the better. How did our modern notions of religious freedom, which seemed to sound the death knell for heresy, come into being? Whether you believe in this trajectory or not, whether you bask in its results or suspect that it is just too good to be true, it deserves our attention. For better or worse, and probably for a bit of both, it defines us.

As a first step we will have to return to the gruesome days of the Reformation and, as so often, we will discover that later grandstanding ideas started out very small indeed. Lofty philosophizing began life as workaday common sense. That indulgent mayor of Exeter and that constable in Cawthorne who refused to turn religious dissenters in to the authorities had no intention of inventing religious freedom — they were simply hoping for a quieter life — and yet, in a curious way, they set everything in motion. Such is the legerdemain of history.

PRAGMATISM

Long before the Reformation period, there had often been good reasons to stamp on the embers of religious controversy. As one of the most provocative theorists of the medieval period, Marsilius of Padua, explained in the fourteenth century, there were even times when heretics ought to be tolerated in the interests of social cohesion. Perhaps it was best to think of something like excommunication as a purely spiritual punishment: there was no need to combine it with temporal disenfranchisement. For a commonwealth to go down this route could often be counterproductive. On the most humdrum level, what if the religiously aberrant just happened to own all the best shops? Why lose the opportunity of "purchasing bread, wine, meat, fish, pots, or clothes from them, if they abound in such items and others of the faithful lack them?"[8]

Clearly, positing Marsilius of Padua as in any way typical of the medieval outlook would be preposterous. He was, for all his brilliance, an odd duck, and he was saying all these seemingly enlightened things as part of a career-long battle with the papacy. A battle, in fact, that earned him his own allegations of heresy. Behind the polemic, there was a sensible point, however. Political and social pragmatism sometimes trumped the obsession with hunting down heresy. Just occasionally, rulers of medieval polities and city-states were willing to put up with religious dissent because it made good economic sense (why banish people who made such welcome contributions to the public purse?), sound social sense (why cause riots and pesky neighborhood disputes when they could be avoided?), and excellent political sense.

The Reformation, with all its carnage and conflict, brought such concepts into the sharpest possible focus. We are still a long way from a principled belief in religious freedom here, but by the end of the sixteenth century, we are certainly entering the foothills.

Imagine being a magistrate in a town in middle Europe that was home to vibrant, opposing religious communities. Or, on a more expansive scale, imagine being the ruler of a country in which Calvinists and Catholics lived uneasily alongside each other. Early on, there had been a hope that the new religious groups would disappear or become so marginalized as to be little more than an irritant. This had almost always happened before, after all. This time around, however, the people defined as heretics — the Lutherans, the Calvinists, and all the rest — showed no sign of giving up the fight. By 1550, it was clear that they were here to stay. What was a ruler to do?

There were two options. You could escalate the persecution in the hope that you would eliminate the threat — and this logic certainly had more than its share of advocates; in some places it even seems to have worked. Alternatively, and much as this went against everything you had been taught, you could bow to the inevitable and try to conjure up some measure of religious coexistence.

You didn't do this because you enjoyed the religious turmoil, or because you believed in religious freedom as we'd now define it, but because it made political sense. Let's not forget: one of the main reasons for attacking heresy over the past fifteen hundred years, or at least since Constantine and his successors had made Christianity the privileged faith of the empire, had been the preservation of social and political order. This idea died hard. Here is the comment of one disgruntled Catholic in the sixteenth century who clearly believed that this logic was still operative. Allow heresy to flourish and "it will come to pass that the husband will be of one opinion and his wife of another, the children and servants will be of another, so that there will be nothing but disagreement and rebellion . . . heresy is such that as soon as it makes its way into a house, city, or kingdom, it brings . . . division and discord."[9]

But what if the opposite were true? What if the most dangerous source of social turmoil was the attempt to pursue heretics? Sometimes, in the wake of Reformation, the very best way to achieve stability and order was to hammer out a compromise.

It is surprising how often this thought occurred in Reformation Europe. We've already seen it happening in the "other Reformation," and the logic was replicated, time and again, in cities like Ulm, Regensburg, Erfurt, Cologne, and Augsburg, where savvy local politicians realized that they were charged with governing an irrevocably divided community. It made an awful lot of sense to force such fragmented communities to get along. The results were never perfect. In Augsburg, for instance, Catholics and Protestants continued to hate each other and, from time to time, their hatred spilled over into violence. However, there were also long stretches of time during which the two groups went relatively happily about their shared business. Such moves, backed up by municipal legislation, often drove the syndics of competing orthodoxies into paroxysms of anger. One gets the sense, however, that many of the citizens of a place like Augsburg were rather grateful. In the town of Biberbach, by the middle of the seventeenth century, it had all become surprisingly civilized. At St. Martin's Church a rota was in operation every Sunday: Catholics were to use the church between 5 and 6 A.M., between 8 and 11 A.M., and between 12 and 1 P.M., while Lutherans were to fit in their devotions, in the same building, between 6 and 8 A.M. or 11 A.M. and 12 P.M. Not that such coexistence was always without its problems. At one Biberbach church, in 1638, local Catholics were shocked to discover that someone (presumably a Lutheran) had irreverently blown their nose into the vessel in which holy water was stored.[10] Still, given the alternatives, it was possible to cope with such relatively minor gestures of confessional animosity.

Coexistence happened on the national stage too. The sixteenth-century Holy Roman Empire was a strange conglomeration of towns, city-states, and principalities. During the Reformation, some polities joined the Protestant camp; others remained loyal to Rome. It quickly became clear that imposing a uniform empirewide religious settlement was impossible. Instead, in 1555, it was decreed that each particular region, be it a small city, a prince-bishopric, or a vast territory, would simply have to abide by the theological decisions of its ruler. Some places would be Lutheran, others would be Catholic (Calvinism, for the time being, was excluded).

A similar process unfolded in France. Decades of internecine Christian strife led to the 1598 Edict of Nantes. Its decrees only remained operative for ninety years but, ahead of the edict's being revoked in 1685 (at which point tens of thousands of Huguenots fled the realm), those of Protestant sympathies were granted grudging acceptance. In certain places they would be permitted to worship as they saw fit. It happened in Poland too, with the 1569 Union of Lublin. A political merger with Lithuania was in the offing and, since such a merger was dependent upon Catholics, Protestants, and members of the Greek Orthodox Church putting up with one another, a healthy measure of religious toleration was extended to all the relevant parties.

And then there was the Dutch Republic. Until quite recently, it was fashionable to talk about the seventeenth-century Netherlands as a tolerationist paradise. It was no such thing: from the perspective of religious freedom the Dutch Golden Age was more an age of silver-gilt. Officially, the Dutch Reformed Church held absolute theological sway but, courtesy of the 1579 Union of Utrecht, those of different religious beliefs were granted freedom to *think* whatever they chose. Public worship was a different matter, and Lutherans and Jews had to wait for many decades before they were entitled to establish their churches and synagogues. For all this, Holland was one more example of the pragmatic approach to religious difference. Allowing those of competing theologies to coexist was astute. There would be fewer rows and everyone would be able to contribute to the community's economic well-being.

∽

If we are looking for the taproots of modern toleration, this official and unofficial exercise of restraint and curtailed toleration is the very best place to look. This coexistence — the "ecumenicism of everyday relations," as one historian has described it — had a tendency to crop up in even the most unlikely places.[11] What turned out to be a sacred philosophical shibboleth started out as day-to-day common-sense behavior in the parish and, from time to time, in the statute book. This is not the worst of pedigrees. One of the most wounding accusations that can be leveled against philosophizing is that it is based upon abstraction and otherworldly hopes. In this case it might just have derived from quotidian concerns. The avid pursuit of heresy became more trouble than it was worth.

THE GREAT LEAP

There had always been diversity and, in a way, Christianity had almost relished it. It made the "truth" stand out. Back in the fourth century, Epiphanius of Salamis had identified no fewer than eighty Christian heresies — some real, some long dead, and others the product of his fertile imagination — but he nimbly grouped them all together in his *Panarion*, his "medicine chest." They were all a little odd, all unlikely to captivate more than a small segment of the Christian fraternity, but they allowed him to become even more confident in his belief that a single Christian truth was a splendid idea. They brought clarity, through opposition, to his beliefs. Similarly, the Eastern Church, throughout the medieval era, routinely rolled out an official catalogue of orthodox positions and anathemas to be spat at those who dissented. Again, this made good sense. There were heresies, but they made the state-sponsored version of Christianity, in which everyone was expected to believe, instantly recognizable.

A similar logic prevailed in the West. Heresy, however irritating it might have seemed to the purveyors of orthodoxy, also had a certain utility. Just as important, the fonts of religious authority were few and far between, so imposing such an orthodoxy was a theoretical, if never quite achievable, goal.

The Reformation shattered any hope of sustaining such confidence. In the West, there was no longer a single dominant ecclesiastical authority, and so-called heresies had become the established faiths of entire countries: even in those places where they remained unpopular they had developed a rare talent for clinging to a perilous existence.

Not everyone accepted that limited coexistence was the solution to this problem. The eminent theorist Justus Lipsius was intimately acquainted with Reformation-era turmoil, and his own religious odyssey reflected the chaotic times in which he lived. Born a Catholic in 1547, Lipsius had a lofty academic career, which included professorial stints at the Lutheran university at Jena, the Calvinist university at Leiden, and, after reconciliation to the old faith, the Catholic university at Louvain. He was an advanced thinker in many ways, but he remained adamant that the very best way to preserve social cohesion and political order was to have a single established religion in any given country.

The pressures of pragmatism caused other theorists to disagree, and some of them were led down even more adventurous theological and philosophical avenues. The important thing to bear in mind is that the pragmatism I have described could ever achieve only so much. In very specific locations it had a certain appeal, but it was always, but always, vulnerable. Many times it sank without a trace. Frankly, if no one had taken a further step, turning pragmatism, compassion, and confusion into philosophical respectability, the goal of toleration might very well have vanished. This is where the much-bruited miracle comes into focus. A new philosophy emerged and it tried, and largely succeeded, to take over the world: at least in its dreams.

Some of the first stirrings of this transition are perceptible in the work of the influential French philosopher Jean Bodin. He had lived through the gruesome French wars of religion, so it is perhaps unsurprising that he advocated limited toleration as a wise political strategy. In some of his writings he reached much further. The *Colloquium of the Seven,* written in 1593 though not published until long after his death — a hint that it was controversial — imagined a debate between those of different faiths (Catholics, Jews, Muslims, Calvinists, and Lutherans included). They all put forward their ideas but, very unusually for a tract of this kind, no obvious winners and losers had emerged by the end of their discussion. The inference to be drawn was that a truth, most especially a religious truth, could not be achieved purely through the exercise of reason. As soon as any idea is disputed, it is immediately brought into question and this causes any sensible person to have doubts. This was a watershed moment in the history of Western theology and philosophy.

In a world where seemingly pious Christians (sometimes even good neighbors, friends, and kin) were coming up with all sorts of Christianities, there was much scope for puzzlement. The quarrels looked set to continue in perpetuity and there was no dominant source of theological authority to sort the wheat from the chaff. Beyond basic Christian essentials, was it ever possible to acquire doctrinal certainty? Skepticism and doubt gradually arrived on the philosophical stage.

Such thoughts clawed their way into many aspects of philosophical inquiry. Via thinkers such as Descartes and Spinoza they
laid the foundations for the modern suspicion of objectivism, but
they were especially potent in the realm of religious belief. After
all, Christians had long accepted that full access to the glories of
religious truth was far beyond the abilities of puny, intellectually
limited human beings.

Some seventeenth-century Christians wondered if it was best
to become what the history books call latitudinarian. Insist on a few
basics of Christian belief (a stance, let us stress, that still allowed
for the category — albeit much diminished — of heresy) but, for the
rest, bite your tongue. In many ways, this idea had already been
gaining ground during the sixteenth century — in the adiaphorism
and irenicism we have already encountered — but matters became
much more daring during the seventeenth.

Yet again, this shouldn't necessarily be confused with a passionate embrace of religious pluralism: it was sometimes the precise
opposite, in fact. It usually added up to a shrugging of the shoulders:
with so many options, who can possibly tell what the real Christian
truth is? It was very important, nevertheless. It was also a popular
resort of many seventeenth-century thinkers and one of them, the
endlessly fascinating William Chillingworth, will have to serve as
its representative.

෴

Chillingworth enjoyed a spectacularly chaotic intellectual odyssey, and if doubt was in the seventeenth-century air, Chillingworth
breathed deep. Born in 1602, he started out life as a Protestant but
after his years at university he became attracted to the Roman Catholic notion of doctrinal infallibility. He hoped that this would allow
him to silence the theological puzzles that insisted on cluttering up
his mind.

At university he had been much involved in disputes about whether it was possible to achieve certainty in matters of faith, and he had been very much on the side of skepticism. However, discussions with the Catholic priest John Fisher made him query the Church of England's orthodoxy and, much in need of some mechanism to calm his own constant questioning, he turned to Rome. He hoped, as he wrote, "that there was and must be always in the world some Church that could not err; and consequently, seeing all other Churches disclaimed this privilege of not being subject to error, the Church of Rome must be that Church which cannot err."

This commitment did not last for very long. After converting to Catholicism in 1629, Chillingworth decided that he was simply being made to "obey" rather than think for himself. He came home and, over the coming years, he set out to achieve a rational basis for his Christian belief — which was, in whatever variant, always very strong. He would reach this goal, he insisted, through the exercise of reason and his reading of scripture. His conclusions annoyed many people but, in his 1638 book, *The Religion of Protestants: A Safe Way to Salvation,* he set out his philosophical stall. "My desire is to go the right way to eternal happiness; but whether this way lie on the right hand, or on the left, or straight-forward; whether it be by following a living guide, or by seeking my direction in a book, or by hearkening to the secret whisper of some private spirit, to me is indifferent."

Indifferent was the key word. Ultimately, it was the quest for truth, not its acquisition, which truly mattered. And even when you imagined that you'd reached that elusive goal, there was precious little room for certainty or self-satisfaction. Any belief, even one derived from scripture, could only ever be probable. It was reasonable to treat such a belief as a pragmatic certainty — it would allow you to live your daily life as a Christian — but you should always see it for what it was: a hunch.

Unsurprisingly, such ideas offended their share of contemporaries and, when Chillingworth died in 1644, after rallying to the Royalist cause during the English Civil War, someone took the trouble to throw a copy of his infamous book into his open grave.[12]

In the longer perspective of history, however, Chillingworth had clearly opened a crack in the notion of orthodoxy. One more step was required, however: a move beyond skepticism to a positive belief in toleration. This required two maneuvers. First, there would have to be a reiteration of the notion that religious faith was always a matter of individual conscience. Coercion in any form was inevitably counterproductive: it would only produce a world of hypocrites who pretended to believe in the prevailing religion in order to avoid ostracism or punishment. As such, the state could never become directly involved in the policing of belief because, however kindly a political ruler might seem, there was always the latent threat of coercion behind his actions and pronouncements. Second, there would have to be a shift from grudging acceptance of religious diversity to a bold commitment to an unassailable right to freedom of conscience.

By the late seventeenth century some people were beginning to think in precisely these terms, including the philosopher John Locke, who entirely recast the standard approach to religious diversity. Locke talked about *rights* — the philosophical privileges that, for better or worse, we have been living with ever since. Even Locke had his limits, of course. He was resistant to the idea of extending total religious freedom to Catholics because, by his calculation, their overriding allegiance to the pope posed a risk to political stability. He was not enamored of atheists either, because they lacked a sense of eternal punishment, and this was an important concept: it tended to regulate your earthbound deeds. But still, for all the rest, he was ever so generous.

Civil interests, as he termed them, were easy to define: the ability to pursue life, liberty, and health (American readers will notice an echo of this triumvirate in their founding document). The magistrate was entitled, duty bound for that matter, to help people achieve such goals. People wanted to possess and hang on to "outward things, such as money, lands, houses, furniture, and the like," but the ruler's remit was strictly "bounded and confined to . . . the care of promoting these things." Never should his authority, and the threat of coercion that lay behind it, "be extended to the salvation of souls." "All the life and power of true religions consists in the inward and full persuasion" of the mind and, in consequence, "the care of souls cannot be given to the civil magistrate because his power consists only in outward force; but true and saving religion consists in the inward persuasion of the mind." As Locke wrote elsewhere, it was "part of my liberty as a Christian and as a man to choose of what church or religious society I will be of, as most conducing to the salvation of my soul, of which I alone am the judge."[13]

A less familiar, but perhaps even more striking example of this new philosophical attitude can be located in the writings of Pierre Bayle. He is especially important in a history of heresy because he took the foundational authority and the favorite text of Christian coercion directly to task. Augustine had turned to Luke's Gospel and its invitation to compel gainsayers to attend the feast. Bayle boldly and brilliantly argued that Augustine had got things very badly wrong.

As is so often the case, biography influenced philosophical preferences. Bayle was born the son of a Protestant minister in 1647: just in time to see the end of Europe's last and greatest confessional confrontation, the Thirty Years' War. By 1669, Bayle had converted to Catholicism — a choice for which his family never forgave him — but his affection for Rome was short-lived. He soon returned to the Protestant fold, although his unique speculations proved to be deeply unpopular among many of his co-religionists.

Bayle detested unnecessary religious bickering, and personal experience had taught him all about the potential cost of offending the ecclesiastical authorities. One of his books, a contribution to the history of Calvinism, was publicly burned by the official hang-man of Paris. Worse yet, Bayle's own brother was incarcerated in his stead and died in prison. The general culture of religious animosity was equally unpalatable to someone of Bayle's unusually inclusive sympathies. In the years leading up to the revocation of the Edict of Nantes — a development that robbed the Huguenots of the legal protections they had enjoyed for almost a century — France wit-nessed some especially vindictive anti-Protestant behavior. Catho-lics fumed against mixed-religion marriages, they campaigned to have Calvinist schools closed, and most egregiously of all they man-aged to have troops (the so-called *dragonnades* policy) billeted in Huguenot homes. The unfortunate householders not only had to support these troops out of their own pockets, but they also en-dured many instances of brutality at the soldiers' hands — tales of violence and sexual assault were not uncommon. When the Edict of Nantes was finally struck from the statute book in 1685, hundreds of thousands of French Protestants were forced to attend Catho-lic Masses against their will, and almost half a million Huguenots headed into exile.

For Bayle, this was the inevitable and deeply offensive con-sequence of religious coercion. It encouraged people to "kindle a deadly hatred to one another, force[d] them to traduce and slander each other and become mutually wickeder and worse Christians than they were before." To follow the Augustinian imperative was to risk producing "a continual scene of blood." "Thus we should see a continual War between People of the same country, either in the streets or in the open field, or between nations of different opin-ions; so that Christianity would be a mere hell upon earth to all who loved peace, or who happened to be the weaker side." This was Bayle as an old-fashioned pragmatist — he sought to contain vio-lence and social dislocation — but his attack on Augustine also rose to a different philosophical level.

Coercion in matters of faith was inappropriate because it trampled on the exercise of natural reason, the God-given natural light that showed the way to moral truths, which wait "on us at all seasons and in all places." This was far more than a call for pragmatic coexistence. It was an insistence that faith was always about the persuasion of the soul and "nothing can be more opposite to this spirit than dragoons, banishment, pillage, galleys, inflictions [and] tortures." To suggest, as Augustine had done all those centuries before, that faith could be given a nudge by means of force or coercion, was utterly "frivolous." Augustine and twelve centuries' worth of Christians had made a tragic miscalculation. "There is not, say they, a more dangerous pest in any government than multiplicity of religions; as it sets neighbour at variance with his neighbour, father against son, husbands against their wives, and the prince against his subjects. I answer that this, far from making against me, is truly the strongest argument for toleration; for if the multiplicity of religions prejudices the state, it proceeds purely from their not bearing with one another, but on the contrary endeavouring each to crush and destroy the other by methods of persecution." Genuine toleration, available to all (even atheists), was not the greatest threat to society: it was, in fact, its most vital guarantor.[14]

Hurrah! Religious freedom was on the royal road to victory. Nor was it simply a matter of philosophizing. Bayle's France might have suffered a setback with the 1685 revocation of the Edict of Nantes but, only four years later, Locke's England witnessed the arrival of its fabled Toleration Act. This did not represent good news for every kind of Christian. Catholics and those who questioned Trinitarian ideas were still stranded in the doldrums, but at least most Protestant nonconformists were now entitled to worship as they saw fit. All we now needed was an Enlightenment, during which ideas like Locke's and Bayle's would be toasted in Parisian salons and American studies and, for good measure, the obscurities and power-hungry antics of Christian priests and their secular overseers would be denounced. And so it came to pass. By 1699 Gottfried Arnold was suggesting that heresy had existed only because it served the vested interests of the ecclesiastical establishment. As the leading lights of the Enlightenment, the authors of the grand encyclopedia, saw it, grapefruits, voguish inventions, and the laws of physics deserved more column inches than the silly, distracting puzzlements provided by Christian theology.

The era did not see an end to confessional division and, sometimes, outright hatred, and it was certainly not without its heresies. France itself would witness the continuing theological tussle between Jansenists and their opponents, and new varieties of daring speculation would sustain their ability to offend the syndics of orthodoxy. Just as Bayle was writing his bold words, Miguel de Molinos and his ideas about the annihilation of all human desires and the virtues of a passive, quietist spirituality were causing uproar.

The traditional case against heresy and in favor of rigorous orthodoxy was still bruited loudly but, as the eighteenth century progressed, a more radical counterpoint became increasingly noticeable. By midcentury someone like Voltaire was pouring a huge amount of scorn on the fact that Europe was still home to moments of irrational persecution. He even offered room and board to some of the victims. The abbé Jean Martin de Prades had earned his doctorate in November 1751 but, only a few short months later, his thesis was labeled heretical by the Sorbonne. A warrant was issued for his arrest, but he took the sensible step of heading off to Potsdam, where Voltaire obligingly took him in.[15]

Voltaire did not like persecution, and one of his most splenetic outbursts was provoked by the Calas affair of 1762. Jean Calas had been accused of murdering his son to prevent him from becoming a Catholic. A Toulouse court sentenced the sixty-four-year-old to death: he was to be tied to a cross, the bones of his arms and legs crushed, the vertebrae in his neck dislocated by a winch and halter. Ahead of his horrendous execution Calas had been tortured; water was forced down his throat, in the hope that he would reveal his accomplices.

Voltaire turned these events into a cause célèbre, raising money for the family and pamphleteering with abandon. He refused to accept that religious hatred should still be allowed to produce such horrific episodes as the death and torture of Jean Calas. People, Voltaire insisted, had a right to liberty of conscience and "it is impossible to see how, following this principle one man could say to another, 'believe what I believe . . . or you will die.' That is how they talk in Portugal, Spain, and Goa."[16]

Many Europeans were starting to agree with such sentiments.

～

Unfortunately, and to play devil's advocate for a moment, we are obliged to ask whether this transformation was quite as momentous and complete as it seems. It is sometimes suggested that, behind the lofty sentiments and the dog-eared tracts of liberty, good old-fashioned pragmatism was still the root of most tolerationism. Perhaps we embraced religious freedom because, in the moment, it made good political and social sense. It served our purposes, just as it always had, and everything else was merely a gloss: a playground for brilliant thinkers like Locke and Voltaire but of precious little genuine interest or import for the bulk of Western humanity.

What, after all, is the alternative supposition? That we just matured, in ways that our forebears simply couldn't manage? We are entitled to be skeptical of the idea that this new, kindlier impulse (wonderfully transformed into high-level philosophizing) just lay hidden until one tiny corner of the globe discovered it in the seventeenth century. There is potential for colossal arrogance here, and the cynic would say "just wait and see if such ideas persevere" — and, frankly, you would not have to wait; you would just have a look around. Perhaps the default position is always there. My ideas trump yours, and I will impose them upon you if I can possibly get away with it.

This is a challenging thought, this notion that modern religious freedom is a sophisticated veneer, but perhaps it is only so troubling because we are in thrall to a philosophical invention of the seventeenth and eighteenth centuries. The new tolerance won all sorts of victories; it was enshrined in any number of constitutions and seductive philosophical tracts, but perhaps it was just a trick of the light. Perhaps we have been hoodwinked — and thank goodness we have — but we have been hoodwinked nonetheless.

I am a creature of my time and, as such, I would be delighted if the pipe dreams turned out to be true. As a matter of day-to-day existence, it does not matter hugely if modern tolerationist ideas and their seventeenth-century forebears are genuine or an elaborate smoke screen. The net result is that people are unlikely to be burned at the stake these days. We also have an obligation to dig a little deeper, however, if only to preserve the freedoms we now enjoy. If they are, in fact, precarious, if they are not much more than a philosophical patina, then we will have to work that much harder to shore them up. I started out by drawing a stark distinction between *our* ideas about religious belief and that of our forebears. It is worth considering whether the distinction is really so definitive. The safest conclusion is that, with us, in the here and now, these two ideas — a right to enjoy religious freedom and the deep-seated instinct to tear our theological or philosophical enemies to shreds, even if only via nasty rhetoric — sit together in an uneasy tension.

It is a notion well worth examining. A useful first port of call is America: a place that knew all about Locke and Bayle but also inherited the bitter rivalries of the Reformation. We seem to have been heading ever westward over the course of this book and, fortunately, the tension to which I just referred came into its own in colonies like Massachusetts and Pennsylvania, in the crucible of eighteenth-century religious debate, and in the creative turmoil that produced the American Republic. There were to be arguments about the future of heresy and orthodoxy, about how religious dissent ought to be treated, and about what role political authority should play in this age-old process. America had them all.

The history of heresy skipped across the Atlantic, and we are obliged to follow. Chronologically, this requires us to take one step back, for which I apologize, and then two forward, which will bring us into the modern age.

9

AMERICAN HERESY

The legitimate powers of government extend to such acts only as
are injurious to others. But it does me no injury for my neighbor
to say there are twenty Gods or no God. It neither picks my pocket
nor breaks my leg. —THOMAS JEFFERSON[1]

Heresy trials are foreign to our constitution. Men may believe
what they cannot prove. They may not be put to the proof of their
religious doctrines or beliefs. Religious experiences which are as
real as life to some may be incomprehensible to others. Yet the fact
that they may be beyond the ken of mortals does not mean that
they can be made suspect before the law.

—JUSTICE WILLIAM O. DOUGLAS, *United States v. Ballard*, 1944[2]

COLONIAL AMERICA WAS chock-full of religious diversity. This
delighted some and irked others. Traveling around in, let's say, 1650,
a curious observer would have encountered many signs that all the
old European religious battles were still raging, but he might also
have discerned some hefty hints that America was going to add
something very new to the history of Christianity and, by exten-
sion, the history of heresy.

He could visit the tobacco-rich Anglicans in Virginia, the Calvinistic Congregationalists in Massachusetts, or members of the
Dutch Reformed Church holding the reins of power in New Amsterdam (as New York was known in those days).

In all these places, the age-old quest for orthodoxy was still
alive and well, but our notional traveler could also spend time in
colonies where experiments in religious toleration were steadily un-

folding: the Rhode Island of Roger Williams, perhaps, or the colony of Maryland where, thanks to the founding vision of the Catholic George and Cecil Calvert, the first and second Lords Baltimore, even Catholicism had managed to secure a much-buffeted refuge in an otherwise Protestant heartland.

The colony's 1649 Toleration Act recommended tolerance for many species of Christian, at least on paper: "Whereas the enforcing of the conscience in matters of religion has frequently fallen out to be of dangerous consequence in those commonwealths where it hath been practised . . . [be it] enacted that no person . . . within this province . . . professing to believe in Jesus Christ, shall . . . be any ways troubled, molested, or discountenanced for or in respect of his or her religion, nor in the free exercise thereof." The person who decided "willfully to wrong, disturb, trouble, or molest" anyone who claimed to believe in Christ would meet with monetary fines and, if he persisted, such an offender "shall be severely punished by public whipping and imprisonment." Oddly, persecution itself was now the thing to be persecuted.[3] This shiny dispensation would not endure. By the end of the seventeenth century Maryland had become a royal colony, ruled directly from London and, a decade later, an Anglican religious establishment was introduced. Still, for its time, it was fairly remarkable.

A few decades after Maryland enacted its Toleration Act, the most noteworthy tolerationist adventure of them all, the Quaker fiefdom of Pennsylvania, would emerge. All sorts of so-called heretics (Mennonites, Moravians, Schwenkfelders, Pietists, and many others who had been stigmatized as wayward Christians back in Europe) were attracted by the words of the colony's Frame of Government, enacted in 1682: "All persons living in this province, who confess and acknowledge the one almighty and eternal god to be the creator, upholder and ruler of the world; and that hold themselves obliged in conscience to live peaceably and justly in civil society shall, in no ways, be molested or prejudiced for their religious persuasion, or practice, in matters of faith and worship, nor shall they be compelled, at any time, to frequent or maintain any religious worship, place, or ministry whatever."[4]

Colonial Pennsylvania was not nearly as indulgent as is often imagined. Challenges to authority and breaches of the prevailing moral code were routinely pounced upon but, in the context of its time, it was still an astonishing colony, and we might even be minded to conclude that, in such places, Christian diversity had never found a safer harbor.

Needless to say (since we'd surely be expecting it), many colonial Americans detested this mosaic of religious difference. For them, it was cause for infuriation, not celebration, and any number of residents and visitors grumbled, in the staunchest terms, about the plurality of sects. Still, for the purposes of a history of Christian heresy — which, when you come to think about it, only really adds up to the story of how different types of Christians have confronted each other — colonial America is an unusually exciting place to investigate. So far as the history of toleration is concerned, something new was quite obviously in the groundwater.

ᔥ

The gloomier news is that, while pre-Republican America can sometimes look like a veritable engine room of tolerationist initiative — Roger Williams offering up paeans to Soul Liberty, or William Penn insisting that coercion in matters of faith was a grotesque, misguided notion — the day-to-day lived reality in lots of places often represented the same intolerant old story.

It's best to think of these two trends operating in tandem. There were moments when the road toward tolerance was obviously being walked, and in more daring ways than ever before in Christian history. At the same time, nowhere was the tension between established ways of dealing with heresy and all the forward-looking talk more apparent. More often than not, the old ways triumphed. Colonial America never quite managed to escape the conflicts and cussedness of the Reformation: it simply moved the squabbles and rivalries several thousand miles to the west.

The familiar tale begins in New England, which, for all its bluster, ecclesiastical innovation, and talk of building cities on hills, wasn't really very new at all. Rather, it was essentially Geneva-by-the-Sea, with all the unhappy (or, by some accounts, necessary) consequences for those who stepped out of line: the very best example, in fact, of how Protestantism, once it achieved something approaching political plenitude, felt obliged to identify and eradicate its own heresies.

I hasten to add that I'm not blaming the New England Puritans for everything that followed: that's a tried, tested, but ultimately fatuous exercise. They simply lived when and where they did. But even Americans themselves couldn't help but notice the irony inherent in a colonial adventure that started off as a bid for religious freedom and ended up being decidedly persecutory. As the nineteenth-century jurist John Story remarked, it all added up to "a chapter as full of the darkest bigotry and intolerance as any which could be found to disgrace the pages of foreign annals." Or, as the eighteenth-century Baptist Isaac Backus (who knew a thing or two about the censorious nature of New England religion) explained, a hypocritical pretense lay behind the residents of somewhere like Massachusetts, suggesting that "there was this vast difference between these proceedings and the coercive measures which were taken against themselves in England."[5] We might allow ourselves to be a little more charitable and simply conclude that entrenched habits died hard.

New England

As all American schoolchildren are expected to know, their nation's religious enterprise began as an escape from persecution. They are invited to summon up images of the Pilgrim Fathers leaving behind an England that refused to countenance their particular interpretation of the Reformation and striking out on their own. And so they did, but regarding this as a breakthrough moment in the history of religious freedom is about as accurate as those painful Thanksgiving mini-plays (with colonists and "Indians" getting on awfully well) that parents make those same schoolchildren enact on a given Thursday in November. The first pilgrims were an inordinately intolerant bunch. Religious freedom, in the modern sense, was the furthest thing from their minds: they simply wanted, and found, an opportunity to divorce themselves from what they regarded as the corrupt church back in England. Having achieved this, they set about hating and sniping at every other religious alternative available.

A few years after the *Mayflower* bumped into Plymouth Rock, other English Protestants took to the seas. They were not quite as radical as their forerunners: instead of damning the entire Anglican enterprise, most of them held out hope that, from across the Atlantic, they could serve as an example to the church back at home — and it *was* still home, back then. These later pilgrims, the people who set up their theological stall in towns like Cambridge and Boston, were not lacking in bold visions, however.

When John Winthrop, who would serve as governor of the Massachusetts Bay Colony, traversed the ocean in 1630, he came up with some truly epic sentences. As ever, he pleaded for unity. *Mutatis mutandis,* it was Ignatius of Antioch all over again. "True Christians are of one body with Christ," he explained. "All the parts of this body being thus united are made so contiguous in a special relation as they must needs partake of each other's strength and infirmity, joy and sorrow, weal and woe." It was through these bonds of love that "they might be all knit more neatly together." The task was clear: "We must entertain each other in brotherly affection. We must be willing to abridge ourselves of our superfluities, for the supply of others' necessities. We must uphold a familiar commerce together in all meekness, gentleness, patience, and liberality. We must delight in each other, make others' conditions our own; rejoice together, mourn together, labor and suffer together, always having before our eyes our commission and community in the work, as members of the same body." Do all this and we shall "keep the unity of the spirit in the bond of peace. The Lord will be our God, and delight to dwell among us, as his own people, and will command a blessing upon us in all our ways."[6]

What a vision! And what a relief, after all the troubled times in England. Yes, there was a duty to teach the homeland lessons: to show what could be achieved. But there was also a firm sense of embarking upon a new chapter in Christian history. The task was to abandon Laodicea and go into the wilderness, to escape the dragon's rage and sacralize the newfound continent.[7]

There was a chance to leave the chaos of Europe behind, to produce a Christian pasture in which the theological soil could be easily tilled and old dissensions could be weeded out. Back home, Winthrop had lamented, the churches "are brought to desolation, and our sins, for which the Lord begins already to frown upon us . . . do threaten evil times to be coming." Perhaps America was a "refuge for many whom he means to save out of the general calamity." It was apparent that God had "some great work in hand which he hath revealed to his prophets among us whom he hath stirred up to encourage his servants to this plantation."

It was a mantra that encouraged many people to pack their bags in Stuart England. We shouldn't assume that all who traveled to New England during the 1630s and 1640s were searching for a promised land. As lots of recent historians have informed us, economic opportunity motivated many. But a solid majority were transfixed by this idea of jettisoning all the religious spats and disputes and erecting a quarrel-free commonwealth.

John Cotton, who would turn out to be the most influential

theologian of New England's first generation, serves as an excellent example. He was thoroughly disenchanted with life in his rural English parish. No one came close to calling him a heretic, but he always knew that he was on the losing side of a very important battle. He was certainly on the left-wing of English Protestantism and he had few doubts that the English church, for all its early potential, was still mired in the dregs of popery. Ministers still draped themselves in elaborate vestments, people were still kneeling for communion and making the sign of the cross, and the Book of Common Prayer that Cotton was obliged to use was not nearly radical enough for his tastes. He saw before him a church half-reformed.

For two decades, between 1612 and 1633, he worked hard to carve out an island of purity in the sea of Anglican compromise. In his church he refused to wear the proscribed surplice and made "selective" use of the prayer book. In his home he held informal seminars where people of more advanced Protestant sympathies could gather together. This all annoyed many of his parishioners, but it landed Cotton in a surprisingly limited amount of trouble: nothing more irksome than a couple of temporary suspensions.

Then, however, Cotton's concerns about "tarrying with the magistrate" — waiting for a king or queen to carry Reformation through to its pure and ultimate consequences — could no longer be ignored. During the first decade of the reign of Charles I, who ascended to the throne in 1625, something we now refer to as the Laudian ascendancy arrived in the English church. William Laud and his allies, despite what their enemies alleged, were not crypto-papists. They simply pursued a kind of Anglicanism that someone like Cotton couldn't stomach. The Laudians had serious doubts about the extremes of Calvinist predestinarianism, they liked a little bit of glamour in their worship, and while they respected the pulpit, they also cherished the altar — so much so that they rescued it from the fringes of English worship and brought it back to the heart of devotional life.

This was unacceptable to Cotton. His worst fears had been realized. The half-reformed church was now heading backwards, returning blindly to the empty rituals and offensive opulence of Rome.

In 1633 Laud became archbishop of Canterbury. At around the same time Cotton, whose theological ideas were becoming increasingly unfashionable, found himself in jeopardy. He was called before the Court of High Commission, where he was sure to receive a more stinging slap on the wrist than he had so far suffered. For Cotton, the game was up. He resigned his Lincolnshire living and, in 1633, he hopped aboard a ship headed for the New World.

He must have been excited. He had shown interest in the Bay Colony for several years and the prospect of living in a place where his theological vision was shared by the entire populace must have entranced him. Sadly, the Winthropian notion of all these righteous strangers in a foreign land, effortlessly getting along, didn't have the slightest hope of coming to fruition. When Cotton disembarked in Boston he was met with open arms and was immediately provided with a lofty position in the New England ecclesiastical firmament. The initial signs were excellent. Unfortunately, the 1630s turned out to be a bitter disappointment — for both Cotton and Winthrop. Everything quickly fell apart and the dream became a nightmare.

Dissenters and heretics (as defined by New England orthodoxy) were more than capable of boarding the ships that crossed the Atlantic. The rhapsodic words of someone like Winthrop quickly morphed into bitter denunciations (and worse) of theological enemies. The persecuted became the persecutors. Cotton fetched up in Massachusetts, but so did Roger Williams and Anne Hutchinson.

HUTCHINSON

> Therefore take heed what you go about to do unto me, for you have no power over my body, neither can you do me any harm, for

> I am in the hands of the eternal Jehovah, my Saviour. I am at his
> appointment. The bounds of my habitation are cast in heaven. No
> more do I esteem of any mortal man than creatures in his hand. I
> fear none but the great Jehovah, which hath foretold me of these
> things, and I do verily believe that he will deliver me out of your
> hands. Therefore, take heed how you proceed against me, for I
> know that for this you go about to do to me, God will ruin you and
> your posterity, and this whole state.
>
> — ANNE HUTCHINSON, at her trial[8]

There was colossal (even enviable) hope and expectation at the
heart of the New England experiment: an almost palpable sense
that the new land was a place of promise, a wilderness to be turned
to advantage, the place of righteous exiles. When he crossed the
ocean in 1630 Winthrop wasn't idly churning out bloated rhetoric:
he meant, and felt, every word. But in his very confidence, behind
all those hypnotic sentences, we can also sense some trepidation.
The dream was there, but so was the potential nightmare. What if
it all went wrong? There was a constant fear in seventeenth-century
New England that Satan would try to wreak havoc. The devil would
find it easy to cross an ocean and, if news reached him of some
godly commonwealth springing up, he would be sure to seek it out
and spread his mischief. Heresy and dissent would doubtless be his
weapons of choice.

Fear and dread of this awful possibility turned out to be one
of the defining characteristics of New England Protestantism, and
rhetoric got you only so far. There was also a need for rules, regula-
tions, and vigilance. This was not good news for heresy.

Massachusetts was built on the idea of congregationalism. No
bishops here, just an assemblage of individual congregations who
were often fiercely proud of their independence. There still had
to be order, however. Massachusetts took an extreme approach.
Church membership was everything in the colony by the bay. At
least in the early years, residents had to provide definitive proof that

they had undergone an authentic conversion experience. There had to be firm, or at least convincing, evidence that you were a member of the Calvinistic elect. This was the Visible Church writ large: the people in the pews had to be God's chosen ones. If they were not (if the tares and the wheat were still sitting next to each other), then there would have been no point in leaving all the perdition-bound hypocrites behind in England.

Sometimes the stakes (both figurative and literal) were raised. This nagging fear of impostors warming themselves by the godly hearth was the main reason why New England endured a frantic witch-craze just as western Europe was recovering from such excesses. For the most part, however, the penalty for failing to prove that you were not clubbable, in New England's theological terms, was exclusion. You were not a full member of civil society.

This was an unremittingly exclusivist outlook. It also heightened the sense that you were living on a battleground, fought over between God and Satan. As the minister Nathaniel Ward put it, there was liberty in New England: the liberty either to conform or keep away from us. Understandably, whenever there was a whisper of religious dissent — heresy, for all intents and purposes — it was pounced upon. As bad luck would have it, this happened almost immediately.

ॐ

Anne Hutchinson started badly. During her sea crossing, aboard the *Griffin* in 1634, she found time to criticize the seaboard preaching of Zachariah Symmes. Come landfall she seems to have apologized and, for a little while, her midwifery skills proved very useful in a medically impoverished colony. The thing about Hutchinson, however, was that she had a very specific theological vision, and it didn't sit at all well with some of the leaders of Massachusetts.

Mention has already been made of the puzzling Calvinistic

understanding of the arrival of grace and the promise of salvation that accompanies it. For all the arbitrariness of Calvin's vision, however, there were resolute attempts within the Calvinist fraternity to attenuate the overwhelming sense of being a plaything within the salvific economy. Such attempts were very popular in some corners of 1630s Massachusetts. It would have been very useful, for instance, if a person's good works could be taken as an indication that they might be destined for salvation. This, in strictly orthodox Calvinist terms, wasn't necessarily theologically disreputable. You were not arguing that your actions in any way influenced your eternal prospects (grace was a random gift from God, which had nothing to do with human agency), but simply that piety and devotion might offer vague hints that this or that individual was among the elect.

For Hutchinson, however, this exercise in soteriological forensics was being taken to extremes in the Bay Colony. People were patting themselves on the back for behaving piously, and this led them into the trap of believing that their righteous behavior and good works granted them some sense of *assurance* that they were saved. Again, for Hutchinson this was intolerable. The risks of inappropriate certainty (which could easily morph into perilous smugness) were obvious and it was also wise to remember that the dissembling, irreligious hypocrite was perfectly capable of acting like a saint if it suited his or her purposes.

Good behavior and piety were, at best, unreliable indicators of a person's eternal prospects. To Hutchinson's eye, people were crossing a very important line by turning them into a *proof* or anything approaching a dependable yardstick. Instead of this suspicious "covenant of works," Hutchinson urged her fellow-colonists to adopt a more spiritist approach to grace: to feel for its presence within, rather than seek clumsy, workaday evidence of its arrival.

These were old arguments, but Hutchinson had significant counts against her, and that represented a lot of ammunition in the unstable, censorious climate of seventeenth-century Massachusetts.

First, she hadn't kept her thoughts to herself: she had established theological discussion groups in her home, where these puzzling issues could be debated, and the last thing Massachusetts wanted was unregulated debate. Second, she had managed to win over some rather influential Massachusetts politicians to her point of view: something of a body blow to Winthrop's dream of concord. Third, she hadn't been shy about voicing her dissent. She had publicly declared that almost every political or religious dignitary in the colony was doused in theological error. Finally, and perhaps most important, she was a woman. As the appeal of Hutchinson's ideas amply demonstrates, many people were thinking along lines similar to hers, but her gender was the clinching argument against her amateur theologizing. Mainstream Protestantism advanced many ideas, but it usually clung to the certainty that it was not a woman's place to preach or pontificate about theological matters.

In truth, the situation might have been contained. Hutchinson's position actually won a great deal of support and represented, albeit in quite radical form, a reasonably widespread theological position: dislike of the covenant of works was shared by many local luminaries. Unfortunately, some of those who challenged Hutchinson, most notably the minister Thomas Shepard, seemed determined to stir up controversy. A curious series of events unfolded, and this theological dispute began to disrupt the smooth running of the colony: it infected political debates and elections, it led to new measures by which fresh arrivals in the colony were quizzed about their beliefs, and, for all the attempts to calm the waters in meetings and synods, some kind of solution had to be found.

So it was that Anne Hutchinson came to trial in 1637, accused of acting in ways unbecoming to her sex and of being "one of those that have troubled the peace of the commonwealth and the churches here." The legal process actually went quite well for her at first but, fatally, she suggested that she and her followers received direct revelations from God. This last move was idiotic: hardly anyone in the seventeenth century queried the notion that direct revelations from God had ended in the days of the apostles. A heretic in all but name, Hutchinson was "banished from out of our jurisdiction as being a woman not fit for our society." Hutchinson had asked the simplest question of her judges: Why have you done this to me? John Winthrop's reply was blunt: "Say no more, the court knows why and is satisfied."[9]

∽

For a long time Hutchinson continued to be regarded as the American Jezebel: the patriarchal notion that women oughtn't to have much to do with intricate matters of faith died hard — it hasn't breathed its last in some circles. In the past few decades many books and articles have been written about Hutchinson, but the vast majority have focused on her status as a pilloried woman. And this is all to the good: that is what she was, after all. The trouble is, the actual theologizing — which had nothing much to do with gender — can get lost in the mix. Hutchinson's religious ideas are deeply fascinating. They were never worked out in intricate detail: she wasn't a professional theologian, after all. But, in their way, they managed to expose many of the more obvious fault lines within Calvinism. Massachusetts was supposed to be the place where pure Calvinism would finally find a home. As it turned out, when one version of Calvinism became a little too undiluted, this caused uproar.

For all its bold prognostications, New England's theological stance was a long way from being settled or neatly defined. There was trouble in the earthly paradise. Winthrop's dream was in jeopardy before it even had a chance to weave its magic. One could only imagine what would happen if someone had suggested that the whole New England enterprise, only a few years after it had embarked upon its journey, was rotten to the core or advised people to seek out new and better pastures. And just imagine if he were a *man,* who couldn't be dismissed as a hysterical, overreaching woman. Enter Roger Williams, the man whom John Cotton (more courageous, this time around) didn't hesitate to damn to the depths as a boisterous and arrogant spirit. Here was a genuine American heretic — the first in a long line.

WILLIAMS

When Cotton and Winthrop crossed the Atlantic, their fervor only blossomed. When Hutchinson sailed, she only grew grumpier. And so it was with Roger Williams. When he arrived at Nantasket on February 5, 1631, on board the *Lyon,* he was full of hell, and one half-wonders why he had bothered to make the trip.

Almost as soon as he set foot on land he launched into extravagant denunciations. He was greeted by none other than John Winthrop, who lauded Williams as a "godly minister" — a stock formulation that meant Williams was considered as someone possessed of a good education and reputation — and he was offered a position at Boston's First Church. This was quite the billet, but Williams declined it. He wanted nothing to do with parishioners who still held the corrupt English church in any affection. These were the people who remained "unseparated," who were engaged in "middle walking." Here was an indication both of Williams's high standards and of the many troubles that lay ahead.

Williams did take up positions in Plymouth (as assistant to the pastor Ralph Smith) and subsequently at Salem (helping out the minister Samuel Skelton). These were both towns of more separatist tastes, which Williams could just about tolerate. Safe (or so he thought) in such harbors, Williams launched into withering critiques of many of the Bay Colony's policies. He lambasted the way in which indigenous peoples were being stripped of their lands; he objected to patently ungodly people being allowed to take oaths (what blasphemy was this!); and, most provocative of all, he fumed against local secular powers directly interfering in the affairs of God. He wondered what could possibly entitle magistrates to punish breaches of the first four commandments. Coercion had no place in the realm of faith. As Williams memorably put it, forced worship stank in the nostrils of God.

The colony's General Council (the embodiment of everything Williams detested) endeavored to silence Williams on several occasions, but to no avail and, in July 1635 his "erroneous and very dangerous" ideas were denounced. By October he had been banished from the colony for spreading sedition and heresy.

After spending time on the eastern bank of the Seekonk River, Williams and a small band of supporters entered Narragansett territory. On land bought, not seized (Williams was insistent on this point), from the local leaders Miantonomo and Canonicus, the exiles began to establish a new home that would later be known as Providence — given the circumstances, a very good name for a town.

⮶

The debate was far from over, however. By 1638 what would turn out to be the colony of Rhode Island was signing up to a social compact that required residents to obey public orders in the interests of sustaining harmony — but only in secular, beyond-the-temple matters. Their religious beliefs were their own and there was to be no forced uniformity. In a series of tracts — none more memorable than the mid-1640s *Bloudy Tenent of Persecution* — Williams set about defending his notion of "soul liberty." All the "weapons which are used by persecutors," all the stocks, whips, prisons, swords, gibbets, and stakes were blunted tools in the work of religious instruction or correction. One had to rely, instead, on "spiritual artillery and weapons."

History offered full and appalling evidence of what happened when force intruded on the religious world: just look, Williams advised, at "the blood of so many hundred thousand souls of Protestants and Papists spilled in the wars of present and former ages." Christ had never asked that "a uniformity of religion be enacted and enforced in any civil state." Such "enforced uniformity (sooner or later) is the greatest occasion of civil war, ravishing of conscience, persecution of Christ Jesus in his servants, and of the hypocrisy and destruction of millions of souls." As for secular magistrates, like those back in Massachusetts, they had a single, simple rubric to follow: they were to enjoy "no power of setting up the form of church government, electing church officers, [or] punishing with church censures."[10]

Bold words, indeed.

⸎

Hutchinson and Williams posed a massive threat to Winthrop's dream of a snug and unified Massachusetts Bay Colony. They certainly provoked a dynamic response. Many of Williams's books and tracts were replied to by John Cotton, who stuck loyally to an older party line. There were times, he insisted, when the religious dissenter publicly and repeatedly undermined the theological consensus and threatened to provoke disorder. He or she had to be punished. Williams's conceptualization of "liberty" was misguided. True liberty was not license: it was the freedom to serve God. "It is no impeachment of church liberty, but an enlargement of its beauty and honour, to be bound by strict laws and holy commandments, to observe the pure worship of God, and to be subject unto due punishment for gross violation of the same."[11]

As for the Hutchinson affair, Winthrop was adamant that he had God on his side: "After we had escaped the cruel hands of persecuting prelates and the dangers of the sea ... [the] commonwealth began to be founded and our churches sweetly settled in peace."

Then, however, there had been a new storm of "unsound and loose opinions." Because of them, ministers had argued against each other, husbands had squabbled with wives. Mercifully, God had heard "our groans to heaven and freed us from this great and sore affliction." Even the unfortunate end of Hutchinson and her family — the "last act of her tragedy" — seemed, to Winthrop, strangely appropriate. Not too long after being banished from Massachusetts "the Indians set upon them and slew her and all her family . . . her daughter and her daughter's husband and all their children save one that escaped." The Indians had behaved badly before, Winthrop concluded, but this time around "God's hand is the more apparently seen herein, to pick out this woeful woman, to make her and those belonging to her" an "example of their cruelty."[12]

This was a harsh adjudication, but one grounded in an age-old logic. It was reminiscent of Ambrose delighting in the fetid demise of Arius, or John Foxe relishing the divine retribution doled out to persecutory Catholics. Religious dissenters and heretics had to be cast out of the godly commonwealth and, if their lives ended tragically, they only had themselves to blame. It was certainly the logic that Massachusetts (and it wasn't alone in this) clung to over the coming decades. In 1651, three Baptists, John Clarke, Obadiah Holmes, and John Crandall, arrived in the town of Lynn after a three-day walk from Rhode Island. After engaging in a spot of preaching and baptizing, they were arrested and offered the option of paying fines or facing more gruesome punishment. Two of the men raised the necessary cash, but Holmes refused to pay. He was tied to a post and whipped in Boston's marketplace. Not much later, the Quaker Mary Dyer (an old associate of Anne Hutchinson) was arrested and banished from the colony. She returned and, in October 1659, she was sentenced to death by the General Court, along with her fellow Quakers William Robinson and Marmaduke Stevenson. The two men went to the gallows but Dyer was granted a last-minute reprieve and was merely cast out of the colony. Undeterred, Dyer was back in Boston by 1660 but, on this occasion, there was no escape. In May 1660 she was hanged on Boston Common.

QUAKERS

> And thou, Philadelphia, the virgin settlement of this province, named before you were born, what love, what care, what service, and what travail has there been to bring you forth, and preserve you from such as would abuse and defile you. Oh that you may be kept from the evil that would overwhelm you . . . My soul prays to God for you, that you may stand in the day of trial, that your children may be blessed of the Lord, and your people saved by his power.
>
> — WILLIAM PENN, Farewell Address to Philadelphia, 1684[13]

Nothing much had changed, at least not in Massachusetts. Elsewhere, though, things were most certainly in flux. The theorizing of Roger Williams oughtn't to be misread, though it almost always is. In many ways he was an unlikely champion of religious freedom. As he demonstrated as soon as he set foot in the New World, he was a religious snob, with precious little patience for those whose religious beliefs he disliked. He did not believe that the state had the power to crush them, but he was no advocate of chaotic religious pluralism. More to the point, his notion of soul liberty had nothing whatsoever to do with modern ideas about a "right" to religious freedom. Still, the colony he founded became a refuge for all manner of alienated and persecuted Christians and, as the rest of seventeenth-century colonial history would demonstrate, there were many other movements in this tolerationist direction.

One of the more spectacular strides was taken in New Netherland. Given that this was a Dutch colonial enterprise, it might be imagined that pragmatic toleration was the order of the day: what was good enough for the homeland was surely good enough for the overseas dependency. It rather depended on who was in charge.

Peter Stuyvesant became director general of New Netherland in 1647. Two things can be said with certainty about him. First, he adored wielding power, and his regular pompous parades through the streets of New Amsterdam quickly earned him a fitting nickname: the peacock. Second, he was as religiously intolerant a man as the seventeenth century produced. He was a strict Calvinist and he hated anyone who wasn't. He despised Baptists, which is why William Wickenden was banished for performing adult baptisms on Long Island. He despised Lutherans and took every possible step to prevent their theological poison from infecting his colony — even to the extent of stopping them from holding private ceremonies in their homes. Most of all, however, he hated the Quakers — as we've seen, a far from unusual quality in the mid-seventeenth century.

Individual acts of Quaker baiting were pleasing to someone of Stuyvesant's sensibilities, which is why Robert Hodgson would be hauled to Manhattan in a cart and sentenced to jail and hard labor. Overarching legal policies were even more satisfying. Stuyvesant declared that there would be steep fines for those who sheltered a Quaker in their home; any ships that brought Quakers into the colony would be confiscated. Then, though, another of those extraordinary moments of seventeenth-century tolerationism took flight. It was another of those examples of older certainties and newer speculations clashing head-on.

The people of Flushing did not applaud Stuyvesant's anti-Quaker ordinances, and by means of a remonstrance they informed the director general of their disgust. "You have been pleased to send up unto us a certain prohibition or command that we should not receive or entertain any of those people called Quakers because they are supposed to be by some seducers of the people." Flushing was determined to mount a protest. "For our part, we cannot condemn them in this case, neither can we stretch out our hands against them, to punish, banish, or persecute them." What goes around, comes around, they suggested, so it was best "not to judge lest we be judged, neither to condemn lest we be condemned, but rather let every man stand and fall to his own master." A much safer policy was to be "good unto all men especially those of the household of faith."

Stuyvesant would doubtless perceive all this as an act of disobedience: in fact, the people of Flushing insisted, it was a "case of conscience betwixt God and our own souls." All who claimed to follow Christ were welcome in their town: "our desire is not to offend one of his little ones, in whatsoever form, name, or title he appears in, whether Presbyterian, Independent, Baptist, or Quaker." Ultimately, "if any of these said persons come in love unto us, we cannot in conscience lay violent hands upon them, but give them free egress and regress unto our towns and houses, as God shall persuade our consciences."[14]

Stuyvesant was furious and he had various Flushing officials arrested. Still, the whole episode had been something of a propaganda coup for the Quakers and, in a few years, they would enjoy an even more significant one: the establishment of their very own colony on and around the banks of the Schuylkill and Delaware rivers. This is our last example of what might be termed the bright side of seventeenth-century American religious history. After visiting it, all that remains is to reach some speculative conclusion about what we should make of the gnawing tension between old-fashioned persecution (which certainly wasn't limited to Massachusetts or Stuyvesant's New Amsterdam) and forward-looking tolerationism (which, as becomes ever clearer, was turning into something of a colonial stock-in-trade).

❦

Whenever heresy was mentioned in seventeenth-century America, there was always an excellent chance that the Society of Friends was the intended target. The "abominable heresy called Quakers," as Stuyvesant referred to them, put many theological noses out of joint, on both sides of the Atlantic.

The Quakers were the brainchild of George Fox. From the mid-1640s he began traveling around the north of England, talking about direct encounters with Christ and suggesting that the traditional churches were pursuing a foolish theological and ecclesiological trajectory. On Pendle Hill, Lancashire, in 1652, Fox enjoyed a vision in which Christ complained about the profusion of bickering sects that had been established in his name. He told Fox about the inner light and the possibility of encountering God's immediate presence without any need for parish churches, salaried ministers, or the dispensing of sacraments. The quietist Quaker vision was born and, from that day to the present, members of the Society of Friends would gather at silent meetings and wait for Christ's voice to speak from within. Only then was there any point in shattering the calm with the sound of human utterance. Better yet, this was a religious route available to anyone who chose to embark upon it: no one was predestined to burn in the sulfurous pit of hell.

There is something mildly irritating about modern perceptions of the Quakers. They are often thought of as rather bland, pacifistic folk and it is not unknown for uncommitted people to attend their meetings in an almost recreational way, to escape from the hurly-burly of contemporary life. It is a shame that Quakerism is treated this way — much as it's a pity that people go and gawk at the Amish without any tangible sense of how, long ago, they (just like the Quakers) were at the cutting edge of theological speculation. Yesterday's heresy — the sort of thing that made orthodox theologians spit feathers — becomes today's tourist attraction.

Back in the seventeenth century, the Quakers were unfeasibly radical and roundly condemned by all and sundry. They dared to talk about direct divine revelation, they abandoned centuries' worth of ritualistic rigmarole, and, into the bargain, they were deemed to be extremely socially disruptive. They refused to take oaths or pay

tithes, their pacifism prevented them from offering military service, and their agenda of social equality was breathtaking. There
was to be no doffing of hats to social superiors, and everyone was
to be addressed with a simple *thee* or *thou,* rather than the titles of
rank deployed by everyone else. Worse yet — as Mary Dyer's habit
of returning time and time again to an unwelcoming Massachusetts
clearly demonstrated — they had tremendous missionary zeal.

Unsurprisingly, such attributes brought a great deal of suffering down on the Quakers' heads. By 1680 ten thousand Quakers
had endured spells in English jails — 243 had died there. Perhaps
the greatest of the early Quakers, William Penn, also knew the inside of a prison cell. When he questioned the doctrine of the Trinity
in his 1668 tract, *The Sandy Foundation Shaken,* he received eight
months in the Tower for his trouble. In 1671 he was incarcerated in
Newgate but, during his enforced leisure, he found time to compose
his most treasured work: *The Great Case of Liberty of Conscience.* In
this and a host of other writings he mounted a formidable defense
of the Quakers' ideas.

He based his pleas for toleration on the "possession of these
freedoms to which we are entitled by English birthright." This was
not just about belief: "By liberty of conscience we understand not
only a mere liberty of the mind, in believing . . . this or that principle
or doctrines, but the exercise of ourselves in a visible way of worship." In a direct echo of Roger Williams he argued that coercion in
matters of faith was a pointless exercise. Only God could influence
the human conscience and, therefore, "we say that the restraint and
persecution for matters relating to conscience directly invades the
divine right, and robs the Almighty of that which belongs to none
but himself."[15]

Penn worked hard to further the Quaker cause, helping those
who had been arrested for attending illegal Quaker meetings and
making missionary tours on the continent, but even greater opportunities began to appear across the Atlantic. Penn had been show-

ing interest in the colonies since the mid-1670s, helping to compose some of the foundational documents of New Jersey, for instance. As the colony's charter explained:

> No men, nor number of men on earth, has power or authority to rule over men's consciences in religious matters; therefore it is consented, agreed and ordained, that no person or persons whatsoever within the said province, at any time or times here-after, shall be any ways upon any pretence whatsoever, called in question, or in the least punished or hurt, either in person, estate or privilege, for the sake of his opinion, judgment, faith or worship towards God in matters of religion. But that all and every such person, and persons may from time to time, and at all times, freely and fully have and enjoy his and their judg-ments, and the exercises of their consciences in matters of reli-gious worship throughout all the said province.[16]

Penn had still more extravagant plans in mind, however: a veritable "Holy Experiment" and a colony of his very own.

What came to be known as Pennsylvania was the result of two seemingly ill-matched ambitions. Penn wanted to build a society in which his vision of religious tolerance could be fully realized, and he also wanted to make some money. Bailing out so many Quaker friends had created some hefty debts. As Penn put it, "Though I desire to extend religious freedom, yet I want some recompense for my trouble."[17] Such dreams might never have come to fruition if the English king, Charles II, had been able to settle a £16,000 debt owed to Penn's late father, but he was either unable or willing to do this and, instead, in March 1681, he granted Penn a charter for lands north of Maryland. Over the next few years these would be extended by land purchases from the local Delaware Indians and, as early as the autumn of 1682, Penn arrived in his new colony.

By 1685 eight thousand people had settled in Pennsylvania. Re-grettably, Penn became increasingly disillusioned with the whole

enterprise over the coming decades. He had to contend with border disputes, and the financial strain of establishing a colony clearly
took its toll. As Penn lamented, "I cannot but think it hard measure,
that while it has proved a land of freedom . . . it should become to
me, by whose means it was principally made a country, the cause of
grief, trouble, and poverty."[18] Those who didn't have to cope with
Penn's pocketbook would prove to be more sanguine. So far as Voltaire was concerned, Penn deserved to be remembered as the man
who, in his tireless quest for religious freedom, had brought down
upon the earth a golden age.

It wasn't quite as pure as Voltaire imagined. Penn himself had
his moments of old-fashioned intolerance. He was never keen
on Catholics and, when Lodowick Muggleton and his attendant
Muggletonians strolled into the colony, Penn complained about the
ragbag of "whimsies, blasphemies, and heresies" that they carried
with them. Nor was Pennsylvania a place that always tolerated dissent, something that George Keith and his printer learned when
they were accused of spreading sedition after criticizing Penn.[19]

For all this, Pennsylvania was still an astonishing experiment
in religious freedom. At first, anyone who traveled there would
have noticed that Quakerdom was culturally dominant and the in-
tense religiosity of the colony was clear for all to see. Residents were
strongly encouraged to observe the Sabbath in suitable ways and
if, on any day of the week, they fell short of accepted standards of
morality — by indulging in card or dice playing, theatergoing, or
cockfighting, for instance — they would face hefty punishments.
None of this, however, prevented Pennsylvania from becoming a
world-renowned haven for religious exiles, and it was no coincidence that, during the eighteenth and nineteenth centuries, a host
of denominations, both old and new, made the city of Philadelphia
their home. It was where the Protestant Episcopal Church was later
constituted and where the African Methodist Episcopal church
would have its origins.

REVOLUTIONS GREAT AND SMALL

By the dawn of the eighteenth century colonial America was in the midst of a discombobulating process. It was being pulled in two antithetical directions. In many locales there were established, state-sponsored churches: some were relatively indulgent of religious difference, others much less so. There was still much room for complaint, which is why, for the remainder of the century, a group such as the Baptists grumbled endlessly about the legal disadvantages and unfair fiscal impositions they had to endure. On the other hand, colonies such as Pennsylvania and Rhode Island went from strength to strength.

Seismic events came and went, but they often served only to exacerbate the tension between these two impulses. The Great Awakening of the mid-eighteenth century, for example, opened up devotional possibilities for all sorts of new groups, but it also, by revitalizing Calvinist thinking, closed down many theological possibilities. The one thing that could be said with certainty was that, by the eve of revolution, America was home to a dizzying plurality of sects. Thomas Barton, a missionary for the Society for the Propagation of the Gospel in Foreign Parts, visited Pennsylvania in the 1750s, and he was flabbergasted and appalled by what he saw. In Lancaster County alone, he reported, he had come across "German Lutherans, Calvinists, Mennonites, Moravians, New Born, Dunkers, Presbyterians, Seceders, New Lights, Covenanters, Mountain Men, Brownists, Independents, papists, Quakers, [and] Jews."[20]

In spite of Barton's outrage, and for all the battles still to be fought, there is still a sense that colonial America was moving forward to more expansive religious freedom. Nowhere was someone like John Locke more adored and nowhere was the pragmatic need to cope with the swarm of sects, as Barton described it, more urgent. Perhaps all that was really needed was a revolution. Shake off the yoke of British rule and all would be set fair. Religious freedom would finally find a home.

~

This, of course, is where one of the great American myths arrives on the scene. America loves its legends and, being a young nation, it still has the absolute right to believe in them, even if they fly in the face of the evidence. The revolution itself has long been mythologized to an absurd extent. As soon as the guns of the Revolutionary War fell silent, America set about dreaming up a specious historical narrative in which words like *liberty* and *providence* played a starring role. The freedom-loving colonists had all rallied together to defeat the redcoats; the great American experiment had begun. In fact, Americans had not been united in their quest for independence: at first, most of them wanted the relationship between Britain and its American colonies to be readjusted, not destroyed. As late as 1775 almost everyone concerned thought of themselves as British, and one of the chief catalysts of revolution was an obsession with having one's rights as a British subject respected, not some imperative to make things new. It was distaste for the lunatic decisions of specific parliaments and ministers, not a rejection of the entire constitutional apple cart, that created the United States.

When it comes to religious freedom, a similarly slanted analysis has often come to the fore: as part of their great quest for freedom, the founding fathers naturally had liberty of religious conscience in their sights and, at the first opportunity, they enshrined this lofty goal in the religion clauses of the First Amendment. It is crucial to realize, however, that (1) there was no consensus among those founding fathers on the issue of religious freedom, that (2) enshrining the variety of religious freedom that some of them sought was a complicated process, and that (3) even when it had been so enshrined it was not a magic wand that instantly banished the bad old days of religious persecution.

These are three very important points, and we'll return to them very soon, but there is still an opportunity to let people like James Madison and Thomas Jefferson enjoy their day in the sun. They scored some notable victories and they represented significant milestones in the history of both heresy and religious freedom. Many objected to the fact, but Locke and the European Enlightenment set down roots in American soil. Troubled waters lay ahead, but the trip out of the harbor was rather wonderful.

JEFFERSON AND MADISON

Jefferson's true religious identity is opaque: a surprise, given how much he wrote on the subject.[21] Claiming him as an atheist is almost certainly wrong-headed, so some have chosen to think of him as a classic eighteenth-century deist. According to that position, any God who existed was not of the interventionist variety: he had set the universe in motion, long ago, but he neither desired nor warranted the superstitious worship of organized religion that was lavished upon him. Jefferson was also deeply skeptical about the role of the established Christian churches. As he explained in a letter of 1814, "In every country and in every age, the priest has been hostile to liberty. He is always in alliance with the despot, abetting his abuses in return for protection to his own." But while Jefferson had little patience for ritual, dogma, or a priestly caste, he was a long way from being hostile to Christianity per se. In fact he regarded it as a reliable ethical anchor. "Of all the systems of morality, none appear to me so pure as that of Jesus." He merely objected to the "artificial vestments . . . [and] speculations of crazy theologians which have made a Babel of a religion the most moral and sublime ever preached to man."[22]

Jefferson enjoyed poring over the New Testament, searching

for its edifying moral core. "I have made a wee little book," he wrote in 1813, "which I call the Philosophy of Jesus. It is a *paradigma* of his doctrines, made by cutting the text out of the book, and arranging them on the pages of a blank book, in a certain order of time or subject. A more beautiful morsel of ethics I have never seen." As Jefferson once wrote to a friend, his genuine beliefs constituted something very different "from that antichristian system imputed to me by those who know nothing of my opinions." He was against the "corruptions of Christianity . . . but not the genuine precepts of Jesus himself."[23]

The key point was that while Jefferson saw nothing wrong with Christianity providing the bedrock for moral law, he was wary of it intersecting directly with human *positive* law — the actual rules and statutes that governed society. On this issue Jefferson was clear: the direct entanglement of religion and politics, of what later Americans would call church and state, was among the worst ideas in the world. He summed this notion up in a famous 1802 letter to the Baptists of Danbury, Connecticut: "Believing with you that religion is a matter which lies solely between man and his God, that he owes account to none other for his faith or his worship, that the legitimate powers of government reach actions only, I contemplate with sovereign reverence that act of the whole American people which declared that their legislature should 'make no law respecting an establishment of religion or prohibiting the free exercise thereof,' thus building a wall of separation between church and state."[24]

Reaching this point, by which time Jefferson's ideals had been encapsulated in nothing less than an amendment to the U.S. Constitution, had been a struggle. It had begun in the mid-1770s with Jefferson's attempt to promote a statute of religious freedom in Virginia. This measure wouldn't be enacted until 1786, but even in its 1777 draft version it neatly sums up Jefferson's aspirations and ideals.

Proving himself a devoted follower of the philosophy of John

Locke, Jefferson opined that God created people with free and open minds. Evidence pours in, and opinions and beliefs are subsequently developed. This was Locke's tabula rasa in all its glory. For a government or any human authority to try to coerce such minds — by threats or punishments — was simply wrong-headed. The best you would achieve was hypocrisy: people pretending to believe in things in order to avoid censure or persecution. It was crucial to remember that God, being an omnipotent divinity, could easily have forced humanity to hold to a specific set of opinions. He didn't and, Jefferson opined, we ought to have the good sense to follow suit. To dictate faith was absurd: just look at all the conflicts and false religions such efforts had produced over the course of human history.

Similarly, forcing people to pay for ministers they didn't believe in (the existing taxation system in Virginia) was grotesque. Nor should religious affiliation have any impact on your access to civil rights, or your ability to hold political office. You might as well say that only believers in a certain kind of geometry or physics were eligible. All such policies should be abandoned, and it ought to be realized that "the opinions of men are not the object of civil government, nor under its jurisdiction." The magistrate should never "intrude his powers into the field of opinion."

Of course, if a specific religious viewpoint looked likely to provoke "overt acts against peace and good order," then government was obliged to step in. This was just common sense and, in fact, it would represent the balancing act between protecting religious freedom and preserving order and the common good that American jurisprudence would have to confront over the subsequent two centuries. In the absence of glaring threats, however, there wasn't the slightest reason to police people's beliefs or impose orthodoxy and conformity upon them. Virginia should become a place where "no man shall be compelled to frequent or support any religious worship place or ministry whatsoever, nor shall be enforced, re-

strained, molested or burdened in his body or goods, nor shall otherwise suffer on account of his religious opinions or belief, but that
all men shall be free to profess, and by argument to maintain their
opinions in matters of religion, and that the same shall in no wise
diminish, enlarge, or affect their civil capacities."[25]

⌇

The man who helped to follow through this vision was another Virginian, James Madison.[26] From early in life, Madison had exhibited
a strong dislike for any kind of religious persecution. In 1771 he denounced the flogging of Baptists in Orange County and, in 1774,
he became very annoyed when the Anglicans of Culpepper parish
secured the arrest of Baptist preachers. In the same year he wrote to
his friend William Bradford in Philadelphia, contrasting the state
of affairs in their two colonial locales. In Virginia, he complained,
the "diabolical hell-conceived principle of persecution rages among
some, and to their eternal infamy the clergy can furnish their quota
of imps for such business. This vexes me the most of anything whatever. There are at this time in the adjacent county not less than five
or six well meaning men in close gaol for publishing their religious
sentiments which in the main are very orthodox."

A few months later he admitted to being very envious of
Bradford:

> You are happy in dwelling in a land where those estimable priv-
> ileges [of religious freedom] are fully enjoyed and [the] public
> has long felt the good effects of this religious as well as civil
> liberty. Foreigners have been encouraged to settle among you.
> Industry and virtue have been promoted by mutual emulation
> and inspection, commerce and the arts have flourished and I
> cannot but help attributing those continual exertions of genius
> which appear among you to the inspiration of liberty and that
> love of fame and knowledge which always accompany it. Reli-

gious bondage shackles and debilitates the mind and unfits it for every noble enterprise.[27]

Madison would have many opportunities to pursue this vision. In 1776, in the heat of rebellion, he was elected to Virginia's revolutionary convention. The delegates discussed the question of whether religious toleration should be enshrined in the proposed constitution. George Mason came up with a draft phrase that insisted that "all men should enjoy the fullest toleration in the exercise of religion." Naturally, Madison liked this clause a great deal, but he called for a seemingly minor (but in fact quite major) amendment, which would replace the word *toleration* with *free exercise*. This was a hugely important moment.

To speak of tolerance, from Madison's perspective, suggested that the state was *allowing* individuals to think and behave in certain ways and this, in turn, implied that the state, at some time in the future, might remove this permission and make some varieties of religious expression illegal. If you referred to free exercise, however, you recognized that people enjoyed a natural right (in perpetuity) to believe and worship whatever they chose. Just as important, you turned a negative into a positive. The word *toleration* always carried a judgmental charge: we don't like you, but we'll *put up with you,* for now. As Goethe later said, to tolerate is always to insult. The notion of genuine religious freedom, by contrast, has the potential to embrace religious difference. I've talked a lot about the profound difference between modern and premodern ways of confronting religious variety. The paradigm shift is encapsulated by this linguistic shift from tolerance (which was always about pragmatism) to religious freedom (which was grounded in philosophical principle).

Madison got his way in 1776, and there were many victories ahead. A decade later he was the driving force behind bringing his friend Jefferson's statute for religious freedom to the Virginian statute book. The debates were hard fought in 1786. There was a broad consensus that the old model — whereby a single religious establishment (Anglicanism) was paid for through everyone's taxes, regardless of their personal beliefs — should be abandoned. Some politicians (with Patrick Henry leading the charge) only wanted to tinker, however. They floated the idea of multiple establishments: every person would be allowed to direct his tax dollars to a denomination of his choice. For Madison, this did not go nearly far enough. It still involved the entanglement of church and state.

In his *Memorial and Remonstrance,* Madison pleaded with his contemporaries to embrace the idea that religious belief should be "wholly exempt" from the cognizance of civil society. A state demanding taxes to support churches, even in a more equitable way, was still a state demanding taxes. This, as Jefferson and Williams had insisted already, brought the threat of force into the business of religious belief. States, since they were built on the idea of potential coercion, couldn't help but do this and this posed a potential challenge to a person's "inalienable right" to let conscience guide religious beliefs. Into the bargain, taking the state completely out of the question might just turn out to be excellent news for Christianity. We should remember, Madison suggested, that before the days of Constantine "this religion both existed and flourished, not only without the support of human laws, but in spite of every opposition from them." The church did not require the crutch of state support and, as history showed, when such support had arrived the results had been parlous: centuries' worth of persecution overseen by a proud and indolent clergy.

It was time for America to remember the best parts of its colonial history, when it had provided "an asylum to the persecuted and oppressed of every nation and religion." This, Madison sang, was a "lustre to our country." The rival legal model Madison was trying to defeat — multiple establishment — was a step backward: "from the Inquisition it differs . . . only in degree." If it was enacted, it would deter the seeker after religious freedom from settling in Virginia. It would be "a beacon on our coast, warning him to seek some other haven."[28]

Madison (with lots of help, notably from Baptists like John Leland) won the day. He would achieve even greater triumphs, most memorably his role, in September 1789, in defining the federal government's attitude toward religious freedom and state-church relations: as the First Amendment confidently put it, "Congress shall make no law respecting an establishment of religion, or prohibiting the free exercise thereof." Still, for Madison, looking back in later life, his greatest success, his proudest achievement in the work of creating religious freedom, still lay in Virginia. "Some of the states," he lamented, "have not embraced this just and this truly Christian principle in its proper latitude," but "there is one state at least, Virginia, where religious liberty is placed on its true foundation."[29]

∽

There were still battles for men like Jefferson and Madison to fight. When Jefferson ran for president in 1800, it became clear that their dream — that people would not worry about a candidate's religious ideas — was still a distant prospect. Jefferson endured all sorts of accusations of atheism and infidelity — a "reckless extravagance of calumny," as someone wrote. He was denounced by one New York preacher as the "profane philosopher and an infidel," and if he made it to the presidency, the preacher warned his flock, this would be a gross "insult to yourselves and your Bibles."[30]

And yet, of course, Jefferson triumphed, and perhaps this was cause for optimism. If so, it was to be short-lived. Fourteen words of a constitutional amendment could not overturn the habits of centuries quite so easily.

THE REPUBLIC

The First Amendment seemed to inaugurate a new way of dealing with religious difference. Unfortunately, that amendment has always been hard to interpret. First, we have to ponder why it was enacted in the first place: for some people — Madison, certainly — it represented the articulation of a heartfelt philosophical stance. For others, it was still very much about pragmatism (and, though this is sometimes forgotten, the need to contain the social perils of religious diversity was also part of Madison's thinking). By the end of the eighteenth century, as we've seen, America was home to countless Christian denominations. Many were very influential, with robust congregations, and there was considerable risk of chaos among the sects. This — just as in the sixteenth-century Holy Roman Empire, or just as in one of those tolerant Reformation-era German cities — had to be alleviated. This was one of the reasons, and a very sensible one, for the arrival of the First Amendment. There was more to it than that, of course, but an older logic still played its part.

There was also the question of what the First Amendment actually meant. Based on one reading, it applied to only the federal government: it was aimed at preventing a *national* establishment of religion. It said nothing specifically about the states. This seems to be borne out by the first few decades of the nineteenth century. During these years exclusionary measures remained enshrined in many state constitutions, requiring oaths and preventing those of various faiths from holding public office. Long-established, state-sponsored churches clung to their primacy. It was not until 1833 that the last of them, the Congregationalism of Massachusetts, was disestablished. Church-state entanglement died hard and this made someone like James Madison very cross: late in life he lambasted those "states of America, which retain in your constitutions or codes any aberration from the sacred principle of religious liberty, by giving to Caesar what belongs to God." It was time for them to "hasten to revise and purify your systems."[31]

Perhaps even more surprising, it was not until the arrival of the Fourteenth Amendment that an individual's right to religious freedom became fully operative at the state level. And, in legal terms, it was another century before the Supreme Court actually applied the consequences of the Fourteenth Amendment to specific cases involving religious freedom and the separation of church and state.

Far more important, a statutory protection of religious freedom was very different from the practice of such freedom in day-to-day life. Nineteenth-century America could still be a wildly intolerant place. At the very best it remained a de facto Protestant republic. There was a pervasive belief that Christianity — and this usually meant Protestant Christianity — should guide the American ship of state. It was to be the privileged moral compass: in many ways, it still is. For John Adams, religion established "the principles upon which freedom can securely stand." A "decent respect for Christianity," and he meant Protestant Christianity, was "among the best recommendations for the public service."[32]

Some late-eighteenth- and early-nineteenth-century luminaries went even further. In 1811, James Kent, chief justice of New York's highest court, confidently declared that "we are a Christian people and the morality of the country is deeply ingrafted upon Christianity and not upon the doctrines or worship of . . . impostors." Kent put his gavel where his mouth was. In the case of *People v. Ruggles* the accused was indicted for profaning Christ and the Virgin Mary. There was no specific New York law against blasphemy but, from Kent's perspective, this was of little consequence. The crime had long been denounced in the English common law tradition, and this was good enough for Kent. Ruggles had uttered "wicked and malicious" words "in the presence and hearing of diverse good and Christian people . . . to wit: 'Jesus Christ was a bastard and his mother must be a whore.'"

Such statements were always going to cause offense, Kent suggested, because "the people of this state, in common with the people of this country, profess the general doctrines of Christianity, as the rule of their faith and practice; and to scandalize the author of these doctrines is not only, in a religious point of view, extremely impious, but even in respect to the obligations due to society, is a gross violation of decency and good order."[33]

∽

As for which types of Christianity deserved such lavish protections, there was room for debate: not, perhaps, at the legal level but, in the broader culture, there were those with very definite opinions. Roman Catholicism didn't do too badly out of the American Revolution: Catholics had fought boldly for the cause and even France (that most Catholic of countries) had come to the rescue. Old animosities had been forgotten, but not for very long. The treatment of Catholics in nineteenth-century America was sometimes horrendous. At Charlestown, Massachusetts, in 1834 an Ursuline convent was burned down. With little indication of brotherly love, anti-Catholic riots engulfed Philadelphia in 1844 and, in 1854, the residents of Ellsworth, Maine, stoned the house of the Jesuit John Bapst, then undressed, tarred, and feathered him.

The rhetoric could be every bit as pernicious. At midcentury, there was heated talk of a vast Catholic conspiracy to take over the new territories of the West. As Lyman Beecher explained, the old Church was "in full organization, silent, systematized." Beecher was quick to assure his readership that he stood by the protections of the First Amendment, but some of his utterances reveal a deep hatred of what he would have called Romanism: "Clouds like the locusts of Egypt are rising from the hills and plains of Europe and on the wings of every wind are coming over to settle down upon our fair fields."[34] Others blamed the Catholics for the Civil War and, subsequently, for Lincoln's assassination. They fulminated against the tides of Catholic immigration and, most crucial of all, they insisted that Catholicism, with its overriding allegiance to the pope, was at odds with the whole project of American democracy.

The famous Samuel Morse was really the infamous Samuel Morse. He launched ugly tirades against Catholic immigration, talking of the arrival of mindless automatons, "senseless machines" who "obey orders mechanically" and follow "their priests as demigods." "Popery is opposed in its very nature to Democratic Republicanism; and it is therefore as a political system as well as religious, opposed to civil and religious liberty, and consequently our form of government." Morse was horrified by the spectacle of Catholicism "spreading itself into every nook and corner of the land." "Churches, chapels, colleges, nunneries and convents are springing up as if by magic everywhere."[35]

The telling point is that such sentiments had a wide appeal. In 1849 Charles Allen organized the Order of the Star-Spangled Banner, out of which the Know-Nothing political party emerged. In the mid-1850s, most notably in the congressional elections of 1854, it scored some sensational victories on the back of its xenophobic, anti-Catholic platform. Nor would popular suspicion of politically active Catholics quickly disappear. It was the single most important factor behind Al Smith's failure to secure the presidency in the early twentieth century and it still counted for something when John Kennedy ran for the White House five decades later.

A constitutional amendment did not a tolerant land make. And even those of Protestant ideas sometimes suffered from the consequences. All manner of new denominations sprang up in the early Republic: many of them, the Shakers, the Millerites, the Adventists, the Campbellites, had to endure no end of criticism and condemnation. And when America came up with a genuinely original idea of its own — Mormonism — a passion for religious freedom was not much in evidence.[36]

However you judge Mormonism's theology—and I'd happily conclude that it is decidedly quirky—it demonstrated that persecution and the category of heresy were still alive and well in nineteenth-century America. As they moved ever westwards, the Mormons endured some horrible times. There were violent clashes in Jackson County, Missouri, in the fall of 1833. The Mormons crossed the river but, over in Caldwell County, worse days lay ahead. In October 1838, a 250-strong mob shot 20 Mormons dead, just days after Governor Lilburn Boggs had ordered them out of his territories: "Mormons must be treated as enemies and must be exterminated or driven from the state, if necessary, for the public good."[37]

If this was religious freedom, it wasn't worth a light, and the Mormons said as much. As John Green told a crowd in Cincinnati in 1839:

> Fellow Citizens . . . Turn not a deaf ear to this cry of the oppressed! The Mormons are outlawed, exiled, robbed . . . they ask of your justice and charity that you befriend them. They have suffered these outrages from mob violence; they bid you beware, lest licentiousness unreproved bring ruin to your own privileges. Law has been trampled down and liberty of conscience violated, and all the rights of citizenship and brotherhood outraged by the house-burnings, the field-wastings, insults, whippings, murders, which they have suffered; and in the name of humanity and heaven, they pray you to utter the indignant condemnation merited by such crimes.[38]

The call was not heeded and, more tragic still, the Mormons themselves proved more than capable of inflicting violent outrages on their opponents. The "lustre to our country" sometimes seemed to lack sheen during America's nineteenth century.

10

THE POLITE CENTURIES

IT WOULD BE EASY to invoke these nineteenth-century outrages and suggest that nothing had really changed in tolerating a spectrum of religious belief. This clearly is not the case. Outrages are precisely what they were: exceptional events. For every Mormon hater or anti-Catholic nativist there was an American who believed in the rubrics of the First Amendment and found the idea of religious pluralism highly satisfactory. We should be cautious about describing the nineteenth-century Republic as a tolerationist paradise, but we should be equally wary of becoming overly cynical. Religious hatred had not vanished, and mutual cross-confessional respect was often more about style than substance, but there *were* now legal protections in place, and these assuredly prevented any number of bloody confrontations. Heresy's greatest foe had always been the partnership of religious and secular power. In the United States, this was at least theoretically abandoned and the ancient dream of Constantine and Augustine was coming under ever greater scrutiny. For most of the time, rival Christians grew accustomed to getting along, and even when they fell to squabbling, the old solutions — stakes and such — were no longer available.

What was true of America sometimes held good in Europe too. By the end of the nineteenth century, the martyr's pyre and the auto-da-fé were becoming distant memories: no one had been burned at the stake for heresy in England since Edward Wightman went to his reward in 1612, and the Spanish Inquisition's last capital victim had been garroted in Valencia as long ago as 1826. The intermingling of secular and sacred power was rather more resilient in Europe though, especially in Catholic nations. The disconcerting events of the French Revolution put the Roman hierarchy on to the back foot, and it spent most of the nineteenth century fighting a rearguard action against the currents of modernism: church-state separation, rationalism, liberalism, and a host of modish philosophies were bitterly attacked on the banks of the Tiber. When Roman Catholics evinced signs of sympathy for such trends (and many did, not least in the United States), the Vatican was in the habit of scolding them very severely. This agenda relied heavily on old ideas of orthodoxy and a firm commitment to the continuing love affair between secular and religious power — or throne and altar, as it was put in those days.

None of this could quite hold back the tides of history. The long-standing clerical monopoly in education came under siege in many places, church attendances began to dwindle, and, by some accounts (often overstated), Europe entered the age of secularism. Nineteenth-century Europe also carried forward the ideas of earlier philosophers and, in the religious arena, any number of bold new initiatives were launched. Scripture began to be dissected like any other historical document, theologies that chimed in with fashionable rationalist philosophies began to dominate many university faculties, and dialogue between different denominations (even between Christian and non-Christian faiths) moved on apace.

By 1893 a world's parliament of religions was being staged in Chicago. It was, to be fair, something of a disappointment but, suddenly, the spectacle of rival faiths sitting down together and engaging in respectful conversations (the dream long ago summoned up by Pierre Bayle) had become a reality. Not everyone was pleased with the events that unfolded on the banks of Lake Michigan: the

pope, the archbishop of Canterbury, the leaders of American Pres-
byterianism, and the sultan of Turkey all refused to send representatives. Still, there were Jews, Lutherans, American Catholics, Unitarians, Hindus, Jains, Confucians, and many others in attendance
and, along with rousing speeches and illuminating discussions,
they even found time to put aside their doctrinal differences and
idiosyncratic prayers and join together in what they called an act of
common worship to almighty God. It was easy to sense which way
the religious wind was blowing.

Whether religious pluralism was being embraced out of genuine commitment, savvy strategy, or a vague obligation to move
with the times remains an open and very important question, but
one thing is abundantly clear. In this new landscape, orthodoxy and
heresy did not count for nearly as much as they once did. The heresy
trial (and even America had lots of these during the nineteenth and
twentieth centuries) was now usually a matter of internal church
discipline and of ever diminishing interest to the wider culture. Internecine Baptist and Presbyterian squabbles and Vatican-inspired
slaps on the theological wrist were commonplace, but those who
were not directly involved began to shrug their shoulders. Moreover, while heresy still existed in the minds of many, it now had to
be punished by the sideways glance, the snub in the street, or sanctions that paled in comparison with the punishments of past ages.

EMERSON AND PARKER

We started our tour of American heresy in Massachusetts, so we
might as well end there — a fillip to those who still think that
Boston was once the hub of the universe and, given the contours
of American religious history, they might just have a point. The
colony-turned-state saw its share of religious controversy during
the nineteenth century. First there was Unitarianism. The Unitarians were committed to pursuing a universalist agenda. At least

in theory (though one often betrayed by some of their theological snootiness), they were happier to dwell on the things that all Christians had in common rather than becoming fixated with all the petty doctrinal details. Their aim was to limit the potential points of discord. This was something of a Trojan horse, given that their central tenets — a denial of the Trinity and a rejection of traditional Calvinistic concepts of predestination — were always likely to raise eyebrows, but there is no harm in giving them the benefit of the doubt.

Unfortunately, the arrival of Unitarianism caused theological havoc in New England. In 1805 two rival candidates were up for the Hollis Chair of Divinity at Harvard. Henry Ware, a liberal figure, was elected, and the anti-Unitarian camp launched a fierce propaganda campaign that endured for decades. Understandably, the Unitarians fought back. The crucial point, though, is that a mean-spirited rhetorical battle was all it ever really became. In 1815 William Ellery Channing, dismayed by all the cruel things people were saying about Unitarianism, put it like this: "Are we not authorized . . . to repel these charges with some degree of warmth? Are we not called to speak in the language of indignant and insulted virtue?"[1] The critical phrase was this: "some degree of warmth."

Religious rivalry was now usually limited to shouting the odds. Crucially, it was an internal matter for religious denominations. There was no longer a power-wielding Constantine to adjudicate the disputes. The U.S. federal government had washed its hands of such chores and, over the next century and a half, most governments around the world (at least those of similar liberal democratic sympathies) would follow suit.

Heretics used to be the people sent to the galleys and those whose houses were torn down. Now they were simply the people lambasted from the pulpit or in the pages of newspapers.

Massachusetts learned this lesson well. Out of Unitarianism came Transcendentalism, an even more provocative school of thought most often associated with Ralph Waldo Emerson. For those of more orthodox tastes there was something rotten in the Transcendentalist vision: the spiritual communion with nature, the cultivation of the subjective conscience, the insistence that the true habitation of religious belief was not the established churches or hoary old traditions, but the individual soul. On July 15, 1838, Emerson pulled many of these strings together in his address to the senior class of Harvard Divinity School. His speech (a thing of wonder) was perceived, quite rightly, as an assault on tradition and the activities of the established churches, but in the new America there was precious little that Emerson's enemies could do about it.

Emerson talked, in soaring prose, about the "universal decay and now almost death of faith in society," of a "sleep of indolence" that had descended on the United States. This, he suggested, was the responsibility of the organized churches. For them, it was all about rules, idle formalism, and preachers who "make [Christ's] Gospel not glad, and shear him of the locks of beauty and the attributes of heaven." What was lacking was any sense of the intuitive truths about religion that Transcendentalism was so eager to promote. "Historical Christianity," Emerson barked, had "fallen into error that corrupts all attempts to communicate religion . . . it is not the doctrine of the soul, but an exaggeration of the personal, the positive, the ritual."

True religious inspiration was to be found all around, in nature: "The faith should blend with the light of rising and of setting suns, with the flying clouds, the singing bird, and the breath of flowers." Any remnants of "dry creaking formality" had to be abandoned and Emerson implored his audience — the cream of the next generation of America's clergymen, no less — to become "newborn bard[s] of the Holy Ghost," to reject conformity. "Let the breath of new life be breathed by you," he advised, and this required only one inner guide: "first, Soul, and second Soul, and evermore Soul."[2]

Emerson's beautiful and deliberately provocative speech caused uproar. In a single address he had managed to attack the idea of biblical miracles, he had poured scorn on the caliber of the entire religious establishment, and he had launched into rhapsodies of Transcendentalist theology. Andrews Norton, an orthodox Unitarian (if that isn't a contradiction in terms), did not regard this as legitimate theology at all. It was merely the "latest form of infidelity." In the *Boston Daily Advertiser,* Norton launched a withering attack on Emerson. "Such false preachers could have a disastrous effect upon the religious and moral state of the community," he warned. Out of a "restless craving for notoriety and excitement," Emerson had mounted a "general attack upon the clergy" and an "insult to religion." Such outrage was echoed in newspaper columns around the country. A year later Norton chastised Emerson for striking "directly at the root of faith in Christianity and, indirectly, of all religion, by denying miracles attesting to the divine mission of Christ."[3]

But that was as bad as things got in civilized nineteenth-century Boston. The place that had whipped Obadiah Holmes in its marketplace now had to make do with splenetic journalism.

⟆

Needless to say, some people adored Emerson's speech. Theodore Parker shared many of Emerson's beliefs — not least his suspicion of biblical miracles — and he praised Emerson's "Divinity School Address" as the "noblest, the most inspiring" thing he had ever heard. Emerson had long since abandoned a career within the Unitarian Church, but Parker managed to sustain one, aiming at achieving reform from within. In 1841 he delivered a sermon of his own that was every bit as punchy as Emerson's.

"Jesus of Nazareth believed the religion he taught would be eternal, that the substance of it would last forever," Parker reminded his congregants. Unfortunately, Christianity had forgotten the difference between its eternal, central truths and its always-shifting outward forms. The church was obsessed with monitoring these petty details and ensuring that everyone conformed to them. The slightest deviation from orthodoxy was met with outrage: "There are some who are affrighted by the faintest rustle which a heretic makes among the dry leaves of theology; they tremble lest Christianity itself should perish without hope."

Make no mistake, the decline of Christianity would have appalled Parker. Like the vast majority of nineteenth-century Americans, he wanted it to play a dominant role in every aspect of American life: "Silence the voice of Christianity, and the world is well nigh dumb, for gone is that sweet music which kept in awe the rulers and the people, which cheers the poor widow in her lonely toil, and comes like light through the windows of morning, to men who sit stooping and feeble with failing eyes and a hungering heart." But, Parker continued, it was ludicrous to focus all attention on upholding a particular version of Christianity that just happened to flourish in a given time and place. Christianity had always been mutable, and it was absurd for Unitarians to imagine that their new version of Christianity had any more chance of achieving stability than its predecessors. Was there really such a "difference between the nineteenth century and some seventeen that had gone before it"?

There were two Christianities: one defined by mankind's folly, and a second that was utterly dependent upon the eternal truth of God. All too often, he said, the New England churches were purveyors of the former. In these parts, "transient things form a great part of what is commonly taught as religion. An undue place has often been assigned to forms and doctrines, while too little stress has been laid on the divine life of the soul, love to God, and love to man." "We never are Christians, as he was the Christ, until we worship, as Jesus did, with no mediator, with nothing between us and the Father of all. He felt that God's word was in him; that he was one with God . . . The Christianity of sects, of the pulpit, of society, is ephemeral — a transitory fly. It will pass off and be forgot."[4]

Such comments, delivered from one of Unitarianism's own pulpits, were much resented. But, once again, the sanctions available to Parker's foes were severely limited. In the coming years many within the Unitarian fraternity refused even to speak with Parker in the street. Behind his back they called him an atheist, an infidel, and, yes, a heretic, and when Parker tried to arrange the traditional pulpit exchanges with his fellow ministers (swapping congregations on a given Sunday in order to spread a different articulation of the Word), they snubbed him. This was doubtless irksome, but Parker remained a leading light in New England intellectual life: loved by some, detested by others. Heretics were simply not what they used to be.

જી

Nineteenth-century America would witness many other moments when words like *heresy* were flung about with abandon, just as they always had been. Such episodes were often only of real interest to the members of a specific denomination: the notion that such tussles had the potential to tear the political commonwealth apart was fast disappearing. In this new world, there was even scope to abandon acrimony entirely.

The events at Andover Theological Seminary — a bona fide modern heresy trial — in the last decades of the nineteenth century make this point especially well. In 1886, five Andover professors, including Egbert Coffin Smyth, the editor of the *Andover Review,* were brought to trial before the seminary's Board of Visitors for holding opinions that seemed to contradict the Andover Creed, to which all professors were expected to conform. Though it dealt with some decidedly obscure points of Protestant theology, the trial became something of a cause célèbre at the time (occasionally these internal squabbles could still gobble up column inches). The legal process rumbled on, via the appeals process of the Massachusetts Supreme Court, until 1892. On New Year's Eve, 1886, a reporter from the *New York Times* was in attendance. There was much excitement: "The same eager and expectant audience braved the blistering snow storm today to attend the trial of the Andover professors," he revealed. Once the trial got underway there was a great deal of earnest theological cut and thrust, but also a staggering lack of animosity. As the *New York Times* explained it, "Socially, the trial of the Andover professors has been, and is, of the friendliest character. This was exemplified today after adjournment, when Professor Smyth and Dr. Dexter, who might be called the heretic and the chief inquisitor, were engaged a long time in friendly conversation and discussion. Among all the participants at this famous trial it seemed as if an era of good feeling had suddenly burst forth and that no enmity was left."

"The solemn attributes of the tribunal at once disappeared," the *Times* continued, and everyone "forgot the antagonism of the hearing, and the differences between the Andover creed and the new theology, and fraternised with keen enjoyment." Whatever else might happen, the reporter from the *Times* was "certain that it will not in any event impair the personal relations of the parties to the controversy."[5]

How times had changed.

THE SUM OF ALL HERESIES

Having a collegial drink with your opponents after a heresy trial can sensibly be categorized as an improvement on sulfurous flames atop the head. Things were not always so cordial (there was still much bickering ahead) but a new attitude toward heresy was clearly emerging.

It was a development that quickly sought to conquer the Western world. Even the Roman Catholic Church (one among many institutions that still claimed a monopoly on religious truth and that scowled at many of the philosophical developments of the modern era) was obliged to negotiate the shifting situation.

The nineteenth-century church often expressed hatred of the nineteenth century. This, for obvious reasons, was decidedly awkward. Ideas like democracy, liberalism, and the separation of church and state routinely offended Rome. It responded with gusto. It finally committed itself, on paper, to the notion of papal infallibility; it poured scorn on modern theologizing by trying to reinvigorate the legacy of Thomas Aquinas; and, in its famous Syllabus of Errors, it attacked more or less every notion that was winning intellectual assent in the minds of contemporary Europe.

A lot of nonsense is written about nineteenth-century Catholicism, and denouncing it as nothing more than an addict of deluded revanchism is well wide of the mark. As it goes, Catholics (even if their musings invited censure) often took the lead in pushing the boundaries of theological and biblical study, and the church's response to the dark side of the capitalist incursion was (regardless of the motivation) quite impressive. It is also a little unfair to single out Catholicism. In the bonkers post-Enlightenment era, every Christian denomination had to take stock, many presumed that their back was against the wall, and not only Roman Catholicism fulminated accordingly or clung to exclusivist ideals.

That said, Catholicism felt itself to be in an especially precarious position, and the hierarchy was often determined to silence what it regarded as internal dissent. Within the Catholic fraternity there were people who rather enjoyed the cut and thrust of contemporary philosophical debate. Rome was not best pleased. At the beginning of the twentieth century, the Vatican shouted "Heretic!" with alarming frequency. But shout was really all it could do: that, and the imposition of forced redundancies, the withdrawal of the papal imprimatur, and other measures that were far less drastic than the tools previously available.

～

The Americans came into the crosshairs first. For all the moments of anti-Catholic violence, many American Catholics were rather pleased by the protections provided by the First Amendment. They were never going to re-create the glory days of Europe, when the spiritual lives of entire countries were dominated by the established Catholic Church, but, at least in theory, federal law allowed Catholics to go about their devotional business unmolested.

Church leaders such as John Ireland, archbishop of St. Paul, and Cardinal James Gibbons of Baltimore thought it best to reconcile the ambitions of Catholicism with the political reality of the United States. Even the concept of church-state separation was sometimes embraced.

It was a very American affair, at least for a while: Rome fumed and insisted that various individuals should be silenced or stripped of their jobs but, at first, the rest of Europe showed little interest. Then, however, a fairly harmless book by Isaac Hecker, founder of the Paulists and very much in sympathy with the attempt to carve out a uniquely American Catholicism, was translated into French. Uproar ensued. Rome accused some of the loftiest American ecclesiastical dignitaries of caving in to the pretensions of the modern world, of watering down orthodoxy in order to fit in with the errant obsessions of liberal democracy. This so-called Americanism was declared to be a heresy.

More was to follow. Historians talk about Catholic modernism, the school of thought (of which Americanism was certainly a constituent part) that aggravated Rome during the first decades of the twentieth century. It was not nearly as easily defined as Rome insisted (nor was Americanism, for that matter) but its basic propositions can usefully be delineated.

First, it tried to reconcile Catholic theologizing with modern philosophical notions of rationality. Old metaphysical certainties were to be thrown out, the sainted Aquinas was resolutely pushed to the sidelines, and some brave souls even dared to put thinkers like Kant into the mix. Second, and in direct consequence, it pursued the goal of reading the Bible in new ways. Forensic examinations of the scriptures were embarked upon, and some suggested that regarding them as historically accurate was often misguided: allegorical interpretations sometimes made more sense. Third, and perhaps most fatally, it encouraged lay activism within the church.

Rome was not happy. In the decree *Lamentabili* and the 1907 encyclical *Pascendi Dominici Gregis* it struck back. Modernism was nothing less than "the synthesis of all heresies." These are among the most astonishing of papal documents. They turned modernism, which at best (or worst) was only ever a loose coalition of like-minded theologians, into a full-fledged heretical movement. They also did an excellent job of exaggerating and misrepresenting the modernist case. For all that, they were still impressive exercises in propaganda. They were very, very truculent.

The 1907 encyclical started with a bold claim. The papacy's duty, it said, was to guard "with the greatest vigilance the deposit of the faith delivered to the saints, rejecting the profane novelties of words and the gainsaying of knowledge, falsely so called." Such a task was now urgent. The devil was always causing mischief, but "it must, however, be confessed that these latter days have witnessed a notable increase in the number of the enemies of the Cross of Christ, who, by arts entirely new and full of deceit, are striving to destroy the vital energy of the Church."

The tragedy was that these enemies were installed in the

church's very bosom: among the laity and "what is much more sad [in] the ranks of the priesthood itself." The danger was "present almost in the very veins and heart of the Church." Rome had tried to be charitable: "Once, indeed, we had hopes of recalling them to a better mind, and to this end we first of all treated them with kindness as our children," but it had then proven necessary to treat "them with severity; and at last we have had recourse, though with great reluctance, to public reproof."

The reproof was severe: "There are Catholics, yea, and priests too, who say these things openly; and they boast that they are going to reform the Church by these ravings . . . Blind, they are, and leaders of the blind, puffed up with the proud name of science, they have reached that pitch of folly at which they pervert the eternal concept of truth and the true meaning of religion; in introducing a new system." This "system means the destruction not of the Catholic religion alone, but of all religion."

They had called into question the very notion of immutable truth, Christianity's obsession for nineteen hundred years; they had trampled on old notions of tradition, authority, and revelation, and they had done so out of self-love and a thirst for novelty. "It is pride which fills Modernists with that self-assurance by which they consider themselves and pose as the rule for all. It is pride which puffs them up with that vainglory which allows them to regard themselves as the sole possessors of knowledge."

Harsh words indeed, and, by mentioning pride as the lodestone of heresy, very familiar ones, but what was to be done? First, it was important to return to the theological staples: "We will and strictly ordain that scholastic philosophy be made the basis of the sacred sciences." Next, "anyone who in any way is found to be tainted with Modernism is to be excluded without compunction from these offices, whether of government or of teaching, and those who already occupy them are to be removed." Censorship was also key: "It is also the duty of the bishops to prevent writings of Modernists, or whatever savors of Modernism or promotes it, from being read when they have been published, and to hinder their publication when they have not. No books or papers or periodicals whatever of this kind are to be permitted to seminarists or university students." An iron hand was required.[6]

᠅

Tough talk, but what did it mean in practice? The consequences were awful for some of those involved. Many lost their jobs and many were obliged to take anti-modernist oaths of which they disapproved. Heresy was still there to be condemned. The Catholic Church, and it was certainly not alone in this (just think of twentieth-century Baptists or Presbyterians in America), continued to criticize those of supposedly heretical tastes. The importance of such actions should not be underestimated, but something had obviously altered. Heresy now warranted harsh words, the arched eyebrow aimed at a theological adversary, perhaps the loss of academic tenure. In this sense, heresy (while still taken very seriously and still capable of provoking sentences as harsh as excommunication) now seemed a shadow of its former self.

Perhaps the most extraordinary development of all occurred within the Catholic Church itself. It continued to insist (as it was perfectly entitled to do) that it offered the surest route to eternal bliss and, as many Catholic theologians learned over the course of the twentieth century, Rome had not abandoned the habit of censoring or silencing troublesome thinkers. By the early 1960s, however, the extraordinary events of the Second Vatican Council were beginning to unfold. A lot was accomplished between 1962 and 1965, but one of the more striking transformations involved Catholicism's approach to other faiths and to divergent opinions within its own ranks. Many of the leading lights at the council were men who, only a few years earlier, had been denounced as troublemakers. More staggering still, Protestants were invited to observe the council's proceedings. There were some radical declarations too. The council committed itself to the cause of religious freedom and, in the documents concerning interaction with other religions, it got positively ecumenical. Catholicism, it averred, was still the best horse to back, but there was sense in seeking dialogue with good men and women of other faiths (or no faith at all) in the pursuit of bettering the world. Other faiths could even be respected: "The Catholic Church rejects nothing of what is true and holy in these religions. It has a high regard for the manner of life and conduct, the precepts and doctrines which, although differing in many ways from its own teaching, nevertheless reflect a ray of that truth which enlightens all men and women." Such soaring, pope-supported words did not please everyone within the Catholic fraternity (and the arguments continue) but one thing is certain: those words would have been unthinkable a century earlier. We all seemed to have moved on.

11

CONCLUSION

> Two conditions must obtain before one is considered a heretic in the proper and complete sense. The first is if one holds in the intellect or the mind erroneous views concerning the faith, and this is the beginning of a disposition toward heresy. The second is if one stubbornly clings to these errors in the will or the affect, and this act fulfills or completes the heresy. These two conditions, that is, render one a heretic in the full sense of the term.
>
> — *DIRECTORIUM INQUISITORUM*, 1575[1]

> *Heresy:* A Greek word, signifying belief or elected opinion. It is not greatly to the honour of human reason that men should be hated, persecuted, massacred, or burnt at the stake, on account of their chosen opinions.   —VOLTAIRE[2]

THE TERM *HERESY* derives from a Greek phrase meaning "to choose." Long ago, it was a word that usually lacked negative connotations: it was applied to the members of rival philosophical schools and even, in a boffin-filled metropolis like ancient Alexandria, to supporters of different approaches to medical science. The word lost its innocence within Christianity. It found new meaning, valence, and vitality, but also became much darker.

Needless to say, Christianity does not hold a monopoly on provoking theological and devotional alternatives, and it is certainly not alone when it comes to dealing with the consequences. Other contenders in the monotheistic sweepstakes have also witnessed their share of conflict and division. The quarrels that arose in Islam after the Prophet's death are with us today. Sunni and Shiite Muslims still compete and, throughout Islamic history, there has been no shortage of animosity.

There have also been poignant moments that rank alongside anything the Christian tradition has to offer. Sufism (one of the world's more intriguing religious experiments) traced its theological pedigree back to the days of the Prophet. By the tenth century its spirituality was adjudged, by some, to be a thorn in the side of Islamic orthodoxy. The Sufi thinker al-Hallaj was seen as an especially disruptive presence. His emphasis on interior devotions was deemed irresponsible and heretical by many of his fellow Muslims. For his pains al-Hallaj would endure eleven years in a Baghdad prison, brought to an end by his death as a heretic and as a threat to political stability in 922 — a punishment to which al-Hallaj is said to have responded by dancing his way to the place of execution.

The Judaic heretical canvas is also broad but markedly different. At many moments assumptions were challenged: the long and conflicted history of Jewish false messiahs testifies to this. What Judaism often lacked was the political wherewithal and theological inclination to impose a single vision too strenuously. There has never been a Jewish state overseen by some equivalent of Constantine. There has never been an exact Jewish analogue to Christianity's church councils, and no rabbinic courts have acquired the power and pretensions of Christianity's inquisitions. A recurring theme in Jewish history (though it has been queried from within the faith) is that the apostate and heretic will find their punishment in the hereafter, and even when an earthbound assault has been launched against heresy, it has usually been a local affair. It has largely been a story of isolated denunciations of *minim* and the impositions of *herem* (Judaism's feared censure, which bans all social intercourse with the accused party, removes the possibility of marrying the guilty party, and obliterates all hope of receiving traditional burial rites).

For all this, Judaism has, *mutatis mutandis*, had its anti-heretical incidents, and the sentences could sometimes be ferocious. When Baruch Spinoza offended the Jewish mainstream during the seventeenth century, a synagogue on Amsterdam's Houtgracht handed down a swingeing punishment. As reward for his "monstrous deeds . . . evil opinions and abominable heresies" Spinoza was utterly cast out from the Jewish faith: "Cursed be he by day and cursed be he by night; cursed be he when he lies down and cursed be he when he rises up. Cursed be he when he goes out and cursed be he when he comes in . . . the Lord shall blot out his name from under heaven."[3]

Heresy has played a starring role in the history of other religions, and more comparative studies are sorely needed. There was no room to pursue this important goal here. Christianity has been our focus, but this little book has still left a lot unsaid. It has, for the most part, homed in on Western Christianity, which leaves us a world of Asiatic, African, and South American heterodoxies still to explore, and it has not found time to delve into any number of head-spinning technical heresies that would take us deep into the territory of abstruse theologizing. One conclusion is robust, though. The former bishop of Bristol who, back in 1556, compared heretics to millers' blind horses turning the millstone, thinking they were moving forward when they were really just plodding "round and round, feeding on the coarse bran of their pride and damnable opinions," was only, at best, half right.[4] There were heretical lunatics and dullards, but there were also heretics who helped to define, enliven, and complicate Christianity.

This book has been about these odysseys and, after spending a little time with the Donatists, Iconoclasts, Cathars, and Anabaptists (not to mention those who opposed them with such passion), we'd hope to be a little closer to answering some of the questions and solving some of the conundrums with which we began. That is a lot to ask, but I think we can sensibly conclude that the extraordinary perseverance of Christian heresy must, in large part, be put down to the mutability of the Christian message. This is not intended as an insult. It might, when one comes to think of it, inspire us to compliment all those decent Christians who have worked inordinately hard to sustain a coherent version of their faith and who have erected impressive devotional and theological architecture on shaky foundations. There have been cruelties and crusades, but there have been cathedrals and cantatas too. It has, God knows, been a strange journey, but diversity, whatever Celsus might have said back in the second century, does not necessarily signal a lack of authenticity. We should not mistake a muddle for a mess, still less for a misadventure. There have been dozens (more like hundreds) of different Christianities, but that is precisely why the history of Christianity is so fascinating.

This still leaves us with the bothersome issue of how Christianity has confronted its fractures and fragmentations. Here, as I mentioned at the outset, we enter treacherous terrain, and I would not suggest for a moment that we are out of the thicket. Throughout this book I have worked hard to sustain a sense of historical objectivity, which, as grandiloquent as that might sound, only means allowing bygone eras to speak for themselves and avoiding the temptation to impose present-day nostrums on the past. I fully accept that this is easier said than done, especially when it comes to a provocative subject like heresy.

I have nonetheless set out my stall. The keystone of my analysis has been the supposition that a specific culture's moral and philosophical postures are fleeting, contingent, and historically determined, and that this has profound consequences for how we interpret the history of Christian heresy, or any other history, for that matter. This will provoke dissent in some quarters (and that's one very good reason to refer to it as a supposition: I'm open to rival arguments) but, for present purposes, it has served as a workable interpretative lodestone.

I've no desire, however, to play the hermeneutic tyrant (another sign of the times, no doubt), so I must point out that alternatives are available and that it is entirely possible to construct a narrative of heresy in which everything looks very different. Some of these narratives strike me as ludicrous, though. Any teleological trawl through the history of heresy that treats current philosophical proclivities as glorious inevitabilities should be shown the door. Such a pursuit requires unhealthy doses of anachronism and arrogance. Other, more subtle theses are well worth a look, however. I've erred on the side of cautious relativism because I can't quite see who or what is able or entitled to define eternal moral verities. That said, this approach risks ignoring shared ground between the past and the present, and it makes tracing long-term historical processes a good deal more difficult.

I have stressed differences; others look for commonalities, and they deserve their day in court. There might, as many worthwhile scholars remind us, be opportunities to dig deep for the roots of modern tolerationism in some sectors of Greek and Roman classical culture and the more adventurous corners of medieval and early-modern Western thought, or to identify a variety of natural rights theory that took shape in the European Middle Ages. My response (as you'd expect) would be that classical conceptions of, let's say, free inquiry were very different from our own and that medieval rights theory didn't have a great deal in common with its modern cousin. But the last thing I want to do is close down debate. The history of Christian heresy *should* make us think long and hard about how human beings construct their belief systems and how they react to those with whom they disagree. It *should* make us interrogate our ways of analyzing that process. It *should* be a battlefield and no one should emerge unscathed, and that includes me.

Here I am, criticizing others for imposing modish, overarching theories on the past, while I myself commit a comparable sin. My approach to the study of history looks eminently levelheaded, but it too is one more product of those aforementioned fleeting, contingent, and historically determined circumstances. I can bleat about objectivity but, with no small amount of paradox and irony, the very bleating is subjective, and in a hundred years it might look preposterous. Worse yet, this particular understanding of objectivity wouldn't have made much sense to the people about whom I've been writing. This is a trap from which there is no obvious escape unless we shrug our shoulders and decide that writing history is more trouble than it is worth.

This, clearly, is not an acceptable option, so we have to accept that, as historians, we can't help but be creatures of our time and that we have to start somewhere. The best we can do is to identify (self-defined) blind alleys or promising avenues and try to prove our points. My rule of thumb (as frangible as all the rest) is that it might be best to dispense with Olympian judgments when it comes to considering the history of the Christian heretics. This doesn't remove the possibility of looking askance at the self-serving medieval ruler (the very worst proponent of orthodoxy) who exploited the fear of heresy; it doesn't prevent us from raising an eyebrow when some deluded demagogue (the very worst kind of heretic) turned Christianity's fault lines to personal advantage; and it certainly doesn't mean that we can't feel sorry for people who were tortured, mangled, or burned at the stake. Such responses are legitimate and, crucially, they were sometimes shared by our forebears. The excesses did not represent the whole story, however, and we should be wary of an adamantine black-and-white adjudication of the entire history of Christian heresy and orthodoxy. Choosing sides is very easy. Confronting the past on its own terms is much more difficult, but a little humility goes a very long way. I'll always concede that if the story of heresy doesn't render you befuddled, then you have missed the point. My fondest hope is that someone will disagree violently with my musings and let me know.

Mention of humility, befuddlement, and violent disagreement leads us to one final issue. We still have to cope with the concept of heresy in the here and now: not as historians, but as puzzled residents of the twenty-first century. We have to wonder if the battle between heresy and orthodoxy is dead or dying (as many claim and hope) and, rather more daringly, if we'd really want to be invited to the funeral. At this point, and with your indulgence, I'll let my hair down and allow myself a partial and idiosyncratic opinion from 2011.

In 1540s Scotland the specter of heresy permeated the whole of society, and it was the job of the Edinburgh Parliament to destroy it and impose orthodoxy. As the loyal subjects of James V declared, it was absolutely necessary, "to the confusion of all heresy," "that all the sacraments be held and honoured as they have been in all times bygone within this realm" and that they "conform to the laws and doctrine of Holy Kirk." This was a political imperative, as was the commandment that "the glorious Virgin Mary, mother of our blessed saviour Jesus Christ, be over all this realm reverently worshipped and honoured and that prayers be made to her to make intercession to God almighty, Father, Son and Holy Ghost for the succession, health, welfare and prosperity of the king's grace, his queen our sovereign lady and their prosperous successes, peace, unity and concord betwixt our said sovereign lord and all Christian princes."

No species of religious dissent was to be tolerated. It was crucial that "no manner of person argue nor impugn the pope's authority under the pain of death and confiscation of all their goods, movable and unmovable." Even discussing theology was a perilous hobby: no one was to "hold nor let be held in their houses nor other ways congregations or conventicles to commune or dispute of the Holy Scripture" unless "they be theologians approved by famous universities or admitted thereto." And if a heretic surfaced, "no man, of whatsoever state or condition" should "cherish or favour" him. In fact, the good citizen was expected to "denounce and accuse them to the next officer of justice they see." Into the bargain, if you managed to expose a heretical sect you could anticipate rich rewards: a share of the loot or, as the 1540s legislation put it, "any part of the confiscated goods."[5]

We like to think that we are a long way from 1540s Scotland or 1630s New England or 1530s Cologne, where the city council could speak about arsonists, prostitutes, and heretics as comparable menaces to public safety.[6] Not too long ago, heresy was the boil that emperors and kings were obliged to lance. Now, at least in the West, it can sometimes seem like cultural flotsam. Heresy used to be condemned in the most excoriating terms, by Pope Gregory IX in his *Libra Extra,* for example: "There is no doubt that all heretics and schismatics will burn in eternal fire with the devil and his angels."[7] These days popes and many other religious leaders still talk in terms of orthodoxy and heresy, they even mention Cyprian's musings on the unity of the church from time to time, but they also devote considerable energy to apologizing for earlier anti-heretical mistakes: popes admitting, 350 years after the event, that Galileo was probably right, and conceding that, 700 years ago, their predecessors were a tad too tough on the Templars.

Jolly good, but for the rest of us, the present-day manifestations of religious heresy (and the trials and strictures they still provoke) can sometimes seem like a bad joke. Whenever it claws its way into the news cycle, talk of heresy is more likely to invite guffaws than panic. Throughout the twentieth century (and into the twenty-first) suspicions and accusations of heresy continued to crop up in many Christian denominations. Issues like biblical interpretation, homosexual clerics, the availability of salvation outside a specific faith, the limits and benefits of religious pluralism, and even the ancient tussle over Christ's divinity (or lack thereof) stirred up animosity and division.

It would be grotesquely insensitive to belittle the impact such internecine battles can have on the participants. As always, there have been excesses, but in many cases the word *heresy* is used in a technical sense as part of an attempt to codify the beliefs of a specific branch of Christianity. This, when handled with subtlety, is not inherently blameworthy, but those watching from the sidelines might conclude that the battles are decidedly parochial and culturally discordant. Disputes about the resurrection, the virgin birth, or the salvific potential of non-Christian faiths can seem arcane. When, in 2004, the American presidential candidate John Kerry found himself under a ludicrous heretical cloud for his views on abortion, the gulf between old mechanisms and new cultural nostrums could not have been wider. When confronted with such curious incidents, it becomes much easier to adopt a cozy rallying call: we are all heretics now. There is, we're told, a duty to carve out our own vision of what the world and the moral universe should look like. Not to do so is regarded as lazy. The old rules, the veneration of tradition are candles guttering out. Make it new, make it yours, be a maverick: these are the dominant cultural mantras. To believe in heresy is now the heresy.

Make no mistake — I exploit this new way of looking at things every day, but it is worth wondering if we are really so very far from 1540s Scotland after all. It is vital that we don't bask, a little too smugly, in our allegedly improved way of looking at the world. Those of faith have to consider how secure the burgeoning commitment to religious pluralism really is. I have no doubt that impassioned advocates of cross-confessional and interreligious dialogue often mean every word that they say, and we should all thank them for their efforts, but I also wonder if their ranks are quite as well populated and enduring as they (or we) would like to think. Sectarian hatred (let alone well-mannered antagonism) is still with us.

As for those who speak so loudly about the decline of religion and announce that we now live in rosier, secularized times — well, they too should tread carefully. Heresy is not moribund: it has simply shifted shape. This should come as no surprise. The battle between orthodoxy and heterodoxy represents a dynamic that has defined every worthwhile philosophical project under the sun: the quest for unattainable truth and the habit of criticizing those with whom you disagree. Though the Christian tradition brought this conflict to full fruition, it does not possess a monopoly. The methods change, and (as Christianity knows only too well) the stakes are always higher when an idea secures political support, but to suppose that the process is defunct would be silly.

Furthermore, to single out Christianity for behaving in predictable ways would be a little unfair. Even without Christianity, people would have found things to fight about, and even without Christianity, the convenient (perhaps even necessary) concepts of heresy and orthodoxy would have carved out an existence. The squabbles and the terminology would have differed, but the logic (regardless of whether you applaud or denounce it) would have prospered.

That logic is alive and well and, for all my dismissals of historical constants, it seems a safe bet that people are always going to quarrel. We should therefore continue to take the notion of heresy (and its history) very seriously. We tend not to. I Googled "heretic" recently and I saw it being applied to an unlikely cast of characters: a chef who argued (against prevailing orthodoxy) that beef should be served well done; a gardener who never pruned his roses; a fashion designer who broke some obscure rule of haute couture. This is flippant but harmless, provided that we don't forget the inordinate power, menace, and promise a word like *heresy* enshrines.

What, then, of the future of heresy? We can heartily agree, between ourselves and for a little while, that persecuting and killing our adversaries has no place in the modern world (though neither pursuit has gone entirely out of fashion: let's not forget that the supposedly godless twentieth century was the bloodiest on record). Whether we should entirely dispense with the notions of heresy and orthodoxy is a different matter, though we could perhaps conjure up less loaded, less battered words to describe the phenomena.

Here's the thing. It would be a shame if we forgot how to snarl (that far, and no farther) at those with whom we disagree. The alternative — some cozy planet on which everyone pretends to get along, with a population of polite cowards who are terrified of causing offense — sounds very dull, and more than a little delusional, to me.

To suppose that this would make for a better world is bonkers, and so, with excruciating punishments consigned to the past, I wish both heresy and orthodoxy (or the struggle they encapsulate) an interesting future. Not that they require my blessing. They are, for better or worse, a fundament of who we are. Both are flawed concepts, because they orbit around the notion of stable truth in a moral universe so often defined by flux. They are, however, also very useful ideas because we are always likely to grope toward such a truth. In order to live our lives usefully and authentically, we have to pretend that the conclusions we have reached are, at the very least, the best ones we can muster: blowing in the historical wind, perhaps, but also worth defending.

Even if we sense that, in the grander scheme of things (not that one exists), it is all a crapshoot, and even if we swallow the gospel of moral relativism undiluted, we still have urgent moral, political, and intellectual decisions to make. We might accept that most of our choices and assumptions are dictated by accidents of time and place, and we might feel a little hard done by because of all the determinism in our lives, but we still have to live them as if they were the best possible reflection of our chosen beliefs. There's far less choice than we'd like, and accepting this state of affairs should most definitely engender respect for alternative points of view, but even if there's a little intellectual dishonesty and sleight of hand involved, we have to be able to say "I'm right" and "you're wrong," even if neither of us is really sure. Else what's the point? Though we want no more burnings at the stake, absolutely and obviously, we really should feel free to bicker, call each other names, and hate our enemies. We should have a few heretics and purveyors of orthodoxy in our lives, and we should relish the possibility of being a heretical or orthodox thorn in someone else's side: not in the realms of cookery, horticulture, or high fashion, but in the places that really matter.

This isn't how our forebears understood heresy or orthodoxy, but the words have always changed with the times, and there's no good reason why we shouldn't benefit from them in our turn. This very modern perspective would offend almost all of the characters in this book, but I don't see this as unduly problematic. I've urged you to examine earlier attitudes toward heresy on their own terms and to have the good grace to accept that the past saw things differently; it's bizarre to cheer for heretical or orthodox ideas as they were understood in the fourth, eleventh, or sixteenth century. As historians, we have to allow the past to be the past. The present is different. In the pub, at the dinner party, on the train, when sitting next to some fool, we can be as bullish and provocative as we'd like. These are our times to define, and I know for certain that during my decades in the vale of tears, heresy and orthodoxy will arise in a thousand different guises. Outside the study I relish them both equally because I recognize them as the price we pay for being flawed, inquisitive, puzzled human beings looking for certainties where none exist. It is quite the quagmire, but would we really want it any other way? Whenever we examine the *history* of heresy and orthodoxy, we should aim for nuance and respect and try, however feebly, to cultivate objectivity. When we wake up tomorrow, different rules apply. So, yes, please send in the heretics. Don't bother, they're here.

ACKNOWLEDGMENTS

Thanks to my agents George Lucas and Peter Robinson; to Andrea Schulz, Christina Morgan, and Rebecca Springer at Houghton Mifflin Harcourt; and to my copyeditor, Susanna Brougham.

Over the past couple of years there have been extended periods during which I was unable to travel to my usual library haunts in Oxford, Edinburgh, and London. I'm very grateful to friends and colleagues who spent fortunes on photocopying and postage (all reimbursed, I hope) and performed various other tasks without which the writing of this book would have been impossible.

Notes

I have taken an economical approach to references. For the most part, the following notes are limited to identifying direct quotations from primary and secondary sources.

Quotations from the writings of the early Christian era are usually taken from the familiar nineteenth-century translations of the Ante-Nicene and Nicene and Post-Nicene Fathers series (indicated by ANF and NPNF in the notes). These editions are the most easily accessible and they are more than serviceable, but I have sometimes slightly altered the translations in the interests of making things more palatable for the modern reader. For the sake of convenience, references to these texts are limited to the author, title, book, designation of section or paragraph, and a volume number in the ANF or NPNF series.

In later sections, chiefly the chapters dealing with the medieval and Reformation eras, I have opted to modernize spelling and grammar in the main text, but I have retained original orthography when it comes to book titles.

1. The Heretics

1   Charles H. Parker, *Faith on the Margins: Catholics and Catholicism in the Dutch Golden Age* (Cambridge, Mass.: Harvard University Press, 2008), 7.

2   James Simpson, *Burning to Read: English Fundamentalism and Its Reformation Opponents* (Cambridge, Mass.: Belknap Press, 2007), 20.

3   "Exposition of the Christian Faith," book 1, chapter 19 (NPNF, second series, 10).

4   Raymond Mentzer, *Heresy Proceedings in Languedoc, 1500–1560* (Philadelphia: American Philosophical Society, 1984), 113–123.

5   Edward Peters, *Heresy and Authority in Medieval Europe: Documents in Translation* (Philadelphia: University of Pennsylvania Press, 1980), 4.

6   Beverly M. Kienzle, "Holiness and Obedience: Denouncement of Twelfth-Century Waldensian Lay Preaching," in *The Devil, Heresy, and Witchcraft in the Middle Ages: Essays in Honor of Jeffrey B. Russell,* ed. Alberto Ferreiro (Leiden: Brill, 1998), 272.

7   Tertullian, "The Prescription Against Heretics," chapter 3 (ANF 3).

8   David Loewenstein and John Marshall, introduction to *Heresy, Literature, and Politics in Early Modern English Culture,* eds. Loewenstein and Marshall (Cambridge, UK: Cambridge University Press, 2006), 1.

2. THE INVENTION OF HERESY

1   "The Martyrdom of Ignatius," chapter 2 (ANF 1).

2   "Epistle to the Ephesians," chapters 2, 3, 6; "Epistle to the Trallians," chapter 6 (ANF 1).

3   "Epistle to the Romans," chapter 4; "Martyrdom," chapters 6, 7 (ANF 1).

4   Cited in James M. Robinson, *The Nag Hammadi Library in English* (San Francisco: Harper and Row, 1988), 5.

5   "Anti-Marcion," book 1, chapter 1 (ANF 3).

6   "Epistle to the Magnesians," chapter 10; "Epistle to the Philadelphians," chapter 9 (ANF 1).

7   Cary J. Nederman, *Worlds of Difference: European Discourses of Toleration, c. 1100–c. 1550* (University Park: Pennsylvania State University Press, 2000), 14.

8   "Ad Nationes," book 2, chapter 47 (ANF 3).

9   "The Prescription Against Heretics," chapter 29 (ANF 3).

10 Karen L. King, *What Is Gnosticism?* (Cambridge, Mass.: Belknap Press, 2003), 8.

11 David G. Hunter, *Marriage, Celibacy, and Heresy in Ancient Christianity: The Jovinianist Controversy* (Oxford: Oxford University Press, 2007), 147.

12 James Clark, *Montanus Redivivus; or, Montanism Revised* (Dublin, 1760), 10.

13 David Aune, *Prophecy in Early Christianity and the Ancient Mediterranean World* (Grand Rapids, Mich.: Eerdmans, 1983), 313.

14 Ronald Heine, ed., *The Montanist Oracles and Testimonia* (Macon, Ga.: Mercer University Press, 1989), 7.

15 Vincent of Lérins, "Commonitorium," chapter 18 (NPNF, series 2, 11).

16   William Tabbernee, *Fake Prophecy and Polluted Sacraments: Ecclesiastical and Imperial Reactions to Montanism* (Leiden: Brill, 2007), 339.

17   William Tabbernee, *Montanist Inscriptions and Testimonia: Epigraphic Sources Illustrating the History of Montanism* (Macon, Ga.: Mercer University Press, 1997), 1.

18   "On the Unity of the Church," paragraphs 5, 6, 9 (ANF 5).

19   Erasmus, Letter 1301, to the theologians of Louvain, in *Collected Works*, eds. Richard J. Schoeck and Guy Bedouelle (Toronto: University of Toronto Press, 1989), volume 9, 134.

20   "Contra Celsus," book 4, chapter 23; book 1, chapter 63, 7 (ANF 4).

21   "Letter to Donatus," epistle 1 (ANF 5).

22   "To the Martyrs," chapter 2 (ANF 3).

23   Robert McQueen Grant, *Second-Century Christianity: A Collection of Fragments* (Louisville, Ky.: Westminster John Knox Press, 2003), 8.

24   Eusebius, "Church History," book 5, chapter 1 (NPNF, second series, 1).

3. CONSTANTINE, AUGUSTINE, AND THE CRIMINALIZATION OF HERESY

1   Often referred to as Malchus in some versions of the story.

2   B. S. Merrilees, ed., *La Vie des Set Dormanz* (Oxford: Anglo-Norman Text Society, 35, 1977), passim.

3   A. F. Norman, *Libanius: Selected Works* (Loeb Classical Library, 1977), oration xxx, 8–10.

4   Rowan Williams, *Arius: Heresy and Tradition* (London: Darton, Longman and Todd, 1987), 32.

5   Maurice F. Wiles, *Archetypal Heresy: Arianism Through the Centuries* (Oxford: Clarendon Press, 1996), 10.

6   Socrates Scholasticus, "Church History," book 1, chapter 7 (NPNF, second series, 2).

7   "Life of Constantine," book 3, chapter 6 (NPNF, second series, 1).

8   Ibid., chapter 17.

9   Socrates Scholasticus, "Church History," book 1, chapter 9 (NPNF, second series, 2).

10   John B. Henderson, *The Construction of Orthodoxy and Heresy: Neo-Confucian, Islamic, Jewish, and Early Christian Patterns* (Albany: State University of New York Press, 1998), 8.

11   See Ramsay MacMullen, *Voting About God in Early Church Councils* (New Haven: Yale University Press, 2006).

12   "Letter to Victorianus," [letter 111] (NPNF, first series, 1).

13   "Letter to Boniface," [letter 185] (NPNF, first series, 1).

14   John Coffey, "The Martyrdom of Sir Henry Vane the Younger: From Apoc-

alyptic Witness to Heroic Whig," in *Martyrs and Martyrdom in England, c. 1400–1700,* ed. Thomas Freeman and Thomas Mayer (Woodbridge, UK: Ashgate, 2007), 228.

15 Edmund S. Morgan, *Roger Williams: The Church and the State* (New York: Norton, 2006), 96.

16 "Commonitorium," chapters 11, 18 (NPNF, series 2, 11).

17 "The Prescription Against Heretics," chapter 1 (ANF 3).

18 Gerard H. McCarren, "Development of Doctrine," in *The Cambridge Companion to John Henry Newman,* ed. Ian Ker and Terrence Merrigan (Cambridge, UK: Cambridge University Press, 2009), 119.

4. The Heresy Gap

1 Dmitri Obolensky, *The Bogomils: A Study in Balkan Neo-Manichaeism* (Cambridge, UK: Cambridge University Press, 1948), 35.

2 Janet Hamilton et al., eds., *Christian Dualist Heresies in the Byzantine World* (Manchester, UK: Manchester University Press, 1998), 66–77.

3 Alain Besançon, *The Forbidden Image: An Intellectual History of Iconoclasm* (Chicago: University of Chicago Press, 2000), 152; Cyril Mango, *The Art of the Byzantine Empire, 312–1453: Sources and Documents* (Toronto: University of Toronto Press, 1986), 152.

4 Francis E. Peters, *Judaism, Christianity, and Islam: The Classical Texts and Their Interpretation* (Princeton, N.J.: Princeton University Press, 1990), 59.

5 Mango, *Art of the Byzantine Empire,* 153.

6 Besançon, *Forbidden Image,* 166–168.

7 Oliver J. Thatcher and Edgar Holmes McNeal, eds., *Source Book for Mediæval History* (New York: Scribners, 1905).

8 Mango, *Art of the Byzantine Empire,* 159.

9 Besançon, *Forbidden Image,* 131.

5. Medieval Heresy I

1 Michael Frassetto, *Heretic Lives: Medieval Heresy from Bogomil and the Cathars to Wyclif and Hus* (London: Profile, 2007), 30–33; Walter Wakefield and Austin Evans, *Heresies of the High Middle Ages* (New York: Columbia University Press, 1991), 77–79.

2 Mark Gregory Pegg, *A Most Holy War: The Albigensian Crusade and the Battle for Christendom* (Oxford: Oxford University Press, 2008), 24.

3 Merrall Llewelyn Price, *Consuming Passions: The Uses of Cannibalism in Late Medieval and Early Modern Europe* (London: Routledge, 2003), 49.

4   Jeffrey Burton Russell, *Witchcraft in the Middle Ages* (Ithaca, N.Y.: Cornell University Press, 1972), 91.

5   Socrates Scholasticus, "Church History," book 1, chapter 8 (NPNF, second series, 2).

6   M. T. Clanchy, *Abelard: A Medieval Life* (Oxford: Blackwell, 1999), 290.

7   Heinrich Fichtenau, *Heretics and Scholars in the High Middle Ages, 1000–1200* (University Park: Pennsylvania State University Press, 1998), 1.

8   Clanchy, *Abelard,* 302.

9   See J. M. M. H. Thijssen, *Censure and Heresy at the University of Paris, 1200–1400* (Philadelphia: University of Pennsylvania Press, 1998).

10   James B. Given, *Inquisition and Medieval Society: Power, Discipline, and Resistance in Languedoc* (Ithaca, N.Y.: Cornell University Press, 1997), 23.

11   Carol Lansing, *Power and Purity: Cathar Heresy in Medieval Italy* (New York: Oxford University Press, 1998), 4.

12   Jeffrey Richards, *Sex, Dissidence, and Damnation: Minority Groups in the Middle Ages* (London: Routledge, 1994), 59.

13   Robert Moore, *The Origins of European Dissent* (London: Allen Lane, 1977), 115–138.

14   Charles T. Wood, ed., *Philip the Fair and Boniface VIII* (Huntington, N.Y.: Robert E. Krieger, 1976), 64.

15   Fourth Lateran Council (1215), canon 3.

16   Frassetto, *Heretic Lives,* 85. I am much indebted to Frassetto's account of the Albigensian Crusade.

6. MEDIEVAL HERESY II

1   Fourth Lateran Council (1215), canon 3.

2   Christopher Daniell, *Death and Burial in Medieval England, 1066–1550* (New York: Routledge, 1997), 103–104; Alfonso de Salvio, *Dante and Heresy* (Boston: Dumas, 1936); *Inferno,* volume 1, canto ix, 127–129.

3   Debra Strickland, *Saracens, Demons, and Jews: Making Monsters in Medieval Art* (Princeton, N.J.: Princeton University Press, 2003), 9.

4   Aquinas, ST.SS.Q11.

5   See David Burr, *The Spiritual Franciscans: From Protest to Persecution in the Century After Saint Francis* (University Park: Pennsylvania State University Press, 2003).

6   David G. Hunter, *Marriage, Celibacy, and Heresy in Ancient Christianity: The Jovinianist Controversy* (Oxford: Oxford University Press, 2007), 1.

7   Walter Simons, *Cities of Ladies: Beguine Communities in the Medieval Low Countries, 1200–1565* (Philadelphia: University of Pennsylvania Press, 2001), 35.

8   Katherine A. Lynch, *Individuals, Families, and Communities in Europe, 1200–1800* (Cambridge, UK: Cambridge University Press, 2003), 84.

9   Council of Vienne, 1311–1312, decree 16.

10 Emilie Amt, *Women's Lives in Medieval Europe: A Sourcebook* (New York: Routledge, 1993), 264.

11 Marshall, *Locke*, 198.

12 James Hannam, *God's Philosophers: How the Medieval World Laid the Foundations of Modern Science* (London: Icon Books, 2009), 127–130.

13 L. S. Davidson and J. O. Ward, eds., *The Sorcery Trial of Alice Kyteler* (Binghamton, N.Y.: Medieval and Renaissance Texts and Studies, 1993); Brian Levack, *The Witchcraft Sourcebook* (London: Routledge, 2004), 39.

14 Alain Boureau, *Satan the Heretic: The Birth of Demonology in the Medieval West* (Chicago: Chicago University Press, 2006).

15 *Summis desiderantes.* December 5, 1484.

16 Larissa Taylor, *The Virgin Warrior: The Life and Death of Joan of Arc* (New Haven, Ct.: Yale University Press, 2009), 108.

17 Larissa Taylor, *Soldiers of Christ: Preaching in Late Medieval and Reformation France* (Oxford: Oxford University Press, 1992), 182.

18 John C. Olin, *Catholic Reformation, Savonarola to Ignatius Loyola: Reform in the Church, 1495–1540* (New York: Fordham University Press, 1992), 31ff.

7. REFORMATIONS

1   J. H. Pollen, ed., "The Conclusions of the Autobiography of Father William Weston, SJ, 1589–1603," CRS Miscellanea (Catholic Record Society, volume 1, 1905), 79.

2   Miles Hogarde, *The displaying of the Protestantes* (1556), fols 15–15v.

3   John Foxe, *Acts and Monuments*, ed. George Townsend (8 volumes, London: Seeley and Burnside, 1837–1841), 8:635.

4   E. H. Burton and J. H. Pollen, eds., *Lives of the English Martyrs* (London: Longmans, Green and Co., 1914), 128–129.

5   John Bayley, *The History and Antiquities of the Tower of London* (1830), 390.

6   Diarmaid MacCulloch, *Tudor Church Militant: Edward VI and the Protestant Reformation* (London: Penguin, 1999), 102.

7   *Calendar of State Papers Venetian*, ed. H. F. Brown and A. B. Hinds (11 volumes, 1894–1912): *1534–1554*, 555.

8   J. A. Muller, ed., *The Letters of Stephen Gardiner* (New Haven, Ct.: Yale University Press, 1970), 311.

9   N. Breton, "A Mad World my Masters," in A. B. Grosart, ed., *The Works in Verse and Prose of Nicholas Breton* (2 volumes, 1879), volume 2, section I.8.

10 George Gifford, *A dialogue betweene a papist and a protestant* (1582), folio 2.

11   W. T. MacCaffrey, *Exeter, 1540–1640: The Growth of an English County Town* (Cambridge, Mass.: Harvard University Press, 1958), 189.

12   A. Peel, ed., *The Seconde Parte of a Register being a calendar of manuscripts under that title intended for publication by the Puritans about 1593* (2 volumes, Cambridge, 1915), volume 2, 31.

13   A. Kenny, ed., *The Responsa Scholarum of the English College, Rome* (2 volumes, Catholic Record Society, 54–55, 1962–1963), volume 1, 57–58; H. Foley, *Records of the English Province of the Society of Jesus* (7 volumes, 1875–1883), volume 3, 555–556.

14   D. Quinton, "Life Imprisonment and Torture of Catholics Under Elizabethan Law," *Ushaw Magazine,* volume 42 (1932), 124.

15   Knaresborough Collection (Ushaw College, Durham), volume 1, 246.

16   T. Nashe, "Christ's Teares Over Jeruslame," in R. B. McKerrow, ed., *The Works of Thomas Nashe* (5 volumes, Oxford, 1958), volume 2, 133.

17   *Temporis filia veritas: A mery devise called the troublesome travel of tyme* (1589), sigs A3, A4, A4v, B1v.

18   J. Bale, *Select Works,* ed. H. Christmas (Cambridge, UK: Parker Society, 1849), 242.

19   Foxe, 5:466; Foley, 3:112; F. A. Gasquet, *Hampshire Recusants* (London: J. Hodges, 1895), 51–52.

20   Foxe, 8:376.

21   Exsurge Domine, issued June 1520.

22   P. Janelle, *L'Angleterre catholique à la veille du schime* (Paris: Beauchesne, 1935), 539–540.

23   J. Lamb, *A Collection of Letters, Statutes, and Other Documents* (London: J. W. Parker, 1838), 185.

24   Benjamin Kaplan, "Dutch Religious Tolerance: Celebration and Revision," in *Calvinism and Religious Toleration in the Dutch Golden Age,* ed. R. Hsia and H. Van Nierop (Cambridge, UK: Cambridge University Press, 2002), 486.

25   Raymond Mentzer, "Communities of Worship and the Reformed Churches of France," in *Defining Community in Early Modern Europe,* ed. Michael J. Halvorson and Karen E. Spierling (Aldershot: Ashgate, 2008), 26.

26   Abraham Friesen, "Medieval Heretics or Forerunners of the Reformation: The Protestant Rewriting of the History of Medieval Heresy," in *The Devil, Heresy, and Witchcraft in the Middle Ages,* ed. Albert Ferreiro (Leiden: Brill, 1998), 166.

27   Foxe, volume 4, passim.

28   Susannah Brietz Monta, *Martyrdom and Literature in Early Modern England* (Cambridge, UK: Cambridge University Press, 2005), 41.

29   Grell, *Tolerance,* 4.

30   Robert Scribner and Tom Scott, eds., *The German Peasants' War: A History in Documents* (London: Humanities Press, 1991), 254–255.

31   Martin Luther, "Against the Robbing and Murderous Hordes," in *Luther's Works,* volume 46, ed. Robert Schultz (Philadelphia: Fortress Press, 1967), 49–50.

32   Carter Lindberg, *The European Reformation* (Oxford: Blackwell, 2000), 131.

33   G. H. Williams, *The Radical Reformation* (Philadelphia: Westminster Press, 1962), 362–375.

34   On Servetus, see Ronald Bainton, *Hunted Heretic: The Life and Death of Michael Servetus, 1511–1553* (Boston: Beacon Press, 1953); Andrew Pettegree, "Michael Servetus and the Limits of Tolerance," *History Today* 40 (1990), 40–45.

35   Marian Hillar, "Sebastian Castellio and the Struggle for Freedom of Conscience," in *Essays in the Philosophy of Humanism,* ed. D. R. Finch and M. Hillar, volume 10 (2002), 31–56.

36   John Dryden, *The Hind and the Panther,* volume 2, 150–155, cited in *Christianity's Dangerous Idea: The Protestant Revolution, a History from the Sixteenth Century to the Twenty-first,* by Alister McGrath (London: SPCK, 2007), 209.

37   Marshall, *Locke,* 198.

38   Lori Anne Ferrell, *The Bible and the People* (New Haven: Yale University Press, 2008), 127–157.

39   Robert Kolb, *Martin Luther, Confessor of the Faith* (Oxford: Oxford University Press, 2009), 18.

8. THE DEATH OF HERESY?

1   Andreas Höfele and Stephan Laqué, introduction to *Representing Religious Pluralization in Early Modern Europe,* ed. Höfele et al. (Berlin: Lit Verlag, 2007), ix.

2   Glenn Burgess, *British Political Thought, 1500–1660* (Basingstoke, UK: Palgrave Macmillan, 2009), 18–19.

3   Gerrit Voogt, *Constraint on Trial: Dirck Volckertsz Coornhert and Religious Freedom,* Sixteenth Century Essays & Studies 52 (Kirksville, Mo.: Truman State University Press, 2000), 4.

4   Bruce Gordon, *John Calvin* (New Haven, Ct: Yale University Press, 2009), 182.

5   Erika Rummel, *The Erasmus Reader* (Toronto: University of Toronto Press, 1990), 204.

6   Alan Jacobs, *Original Sin: A Cultural History* (New York: HarperOne, 2008), 107.

7   *Erasmus Reader,* 199; H. C. Porter, "Fisher and Erasmus," in *Humanism, Re-*

form, and the Reformation: The Career of John Fisher, eds. B. Bradshaw and E. Duffy (Cambridge, UK: Cambridge University Press, 1989), 92.

8   Cary Nederman and John Christian Laursen, *Difference and Dissent: Theories of Toleration in Medieval and Early Modern Europe* (Lanham, Md.: Rowman and Littlefield, 1996), 31.

9   Andrew Pettegree, *The Book in the Renaissance* (New Haven, Ct: Yale University Press, 2010), 212.

10 Benjamin Kaplan, *Divided by Faith: Religious Conflict and the Practice of Toleration in Early Modern Europe* (Cambridge, Mass.: Belknap, 2007), 214.

11 See Guido Marnef, "Belgian and Dutch Post-War Historiography on the Protestant and Catholic Reformation in the Netherlands," in *Reformationsforschung in Europa und Nordamerika: Eine historiographische Bilanz*, ed. Anne Jacobson Schutte, Susan C. Karant-Nunn, and Heinz Schilling (Gütersloh: Gütersloher Verlagshaus, 2009), 289.

12 *The Continuum Encyclopedia of British Philosophy*, ed. Anthony Grayling and Andrew Pyle, volume 1 (London: Continuum, 2006).

13 John W. Yolton, ed., *The Locke Reader* (Cambridge, UK: Cambridge University Press, 1977), 246; Richard Ashcroft, "Locke and the Problem of Toleration," in *Discourses of Tolerance and Intolerance in the European Enlightenment*, ed. Hans Erich Bödeker, Clorinda Donato, and Peter Hanns Reill (Toronto: University of Toronto Press, 2009), 58.

14 Pierre Bayle, *A Philosophical Commentary* (1686), 102, 144, 440, 71, 242.

15 Ian Davidson, *Voltaire: A Life* (London: Profile, 2010), 258.

16 Lynn Hunt, *Inventing Human Rights: A History* (London: Norton, 1960), 70–75; David Bien, *The Calas Affair: Persecution, Toleration, and Heresy in Eighteenth-Century Toulouse* (Princeton, N.J.: Princeton University Press, 1980).

9. AMERICAN HERESY

1   Gary Scott Smith, *Faith and the Presidency: From George Washington to George W. Bush* (Oxford: Oxford University Press, 2006), 70.

2   Marvin E. Frankel, *Faith and Freedom: Religious Liberty in America* (New York: Hill and Wang, 1994), 87.

3   William H. Browne, ed., *Archives of Maryland*, volume 1 (Baltimore, 1883), 244–247.

4   J. F. Maclear, *Church and State in the Modern Age: A Documentary History* (Oxford: Oxford University Press, 1995), 52.

5   Joseph Early Jr., *Readings in Baptist History: Four Centuries of Selected Documents* (Nashville, Tenn.: B&H Publishing Group, 2008), 51.

6   Andrew Delbanco, *Writing New England: An Anthology from the Puritans to the Present* (Cambridge, Mass.: Harvard University Press, 2001), 7.

7   A. Zakai, *Exile and Kingdom: History and Apocalypse in the Puritan Migration to America* (Cambridge, UK: Cambridge University Press, 1992), 122.

8   Francis J. Bremer, *Puritanism: A Very Short Introduction* (Oxford: Oxford University Press, 2009), 88.

9   Amy Lang, *Prophetic Woman: Anne Hutchinson and the Problem of Dissent in the Literature of New England* (Berkeley: University of California Press, 1987).

10   Os Guinness, *The Great Experiment: Faith and Freedom in America* (Colorado Springs, Colo.: NavPress, 2001), 64–65; Edmund S. Morgan, *Roger Williams: The Church and the State* (New York: Harcourt, Brace and World, 1967); Edwin Gaustad, *Liberty of Conscience: Roger Williams in America* (Grand Rapids, Mich.: Eerdmans, 1991).

11   J. Rosenmeier, "The Teacher and the Witness: John Cotton and Roger Williams," *William and Mary Quarterly* 25.3 (1968), 408–431.

12   Alden T. Vaughan, *The Puritan Tradition in America, 1620–1730* (New York: Harper and Row, 1972), 212.

13   Robert Proud, *The History of Pennsylvania* (Philadelphia, 1797), 289.

14   Milton Martin Klein, *The Politics of Diversity: Essays in the History of Colonial New York* (Port Washington, N.Y.: Kennikat Press, 1974), 191.

15   John J. Patrick and Gerald P. Long, eds., *Constitutional Debates on Freedom of Religion: A Documentary History* (Westport, Conn.: Greenwood, 1999), 17.

16   Howard L. Green, *Words That Make New Jersey History: A Primary Source Reader* (Piscataway, N.J.: Rutgers University Press, 1995), 12.

17   Frank Lambert, *The Founding Fathers and the Place of Religion in America* (Princeton, N.J.: Princeton University Press, 2003), 103.

18   James Bowden, *The History of the Society of Friends in America* (Carlisle, Mass.: Applewood Books, 2009), 144.

19   Edwin Bronner, *William Penn's Holy Experiment* (New York: Columbia University Press, 1962); J. William Frost, *A Perfect Freedom: Religious Liberty in Pennsylvania* (Cambridge, UK: Cambridge University Press, 1990).

20   John J. Patrick and Gerald P. Long, eds., *Constitutional Debates on Freedom of Religion: A Documentary History* (Westport, Conn.: Greenwood, 1999), 24.

21   Edwin Gaustad, *Sworn on the Altar of God: A Religious Biography of Thomas Jefferson* (Grand Rapids, Mich.: Eerdmans, 1996).

22   Charles B. Sanford, *The Religious Life of Thomas Jefferson* (Charlottesville, Va.: University of Virginia Press, 1984), 124.

23   Bernard Mayo, *Jefferson Himself: The Personal Narrative of a Many-Sided American* (Charlottesville, Va.: University of Virginia Press, 1970), 231.

24   James H. Hutson, ed., *Religion and the New Republic: Faith in the Founding of America* (Lanham, Md.: Rowman and Littlefield, 2000), 74.

25 John J. Patrick and Gerald P. Long, eds., *Constitutional Debates on Freedom of Religion: A Documentary History* (Westport, Conn.: Greenwood, 1999), 53–55.

26 Robert Alley, ed., *James Madison on Religious Liberty* (Buffalo, N.Y.: Prometheus, 1985); Lance Banning, "James Madison, the Statute for Religious Freedom, and the Crisis of Republican Convictions," in *The Virginia Statute for Religious Freedom: Its Evolution and Consequences in American History,* ed. Merril D. Peterson and Robert C. Vaughan (Cambridge, UK: Cambridge University Press, 1988).

27 Edwin Gaustad and Leigh Schmidt, *The Religious History of America* (New York: Harper San Francisco, 2002), 46; Robert S. Alley, ed., *The Constitution and Religion: Leading Supreme Court Cases on Church and State* (Amherst, N.Y.: Prometheus, 1999), 17.

28 John J. Patrick and Gerald P. Long, eds., *Constitutional Debates on Freedom of Religion: A Documentary History* (Westport, Conn.: Greenwood, 1999), 48–53.

29 John T. Noonan Jr., *The Lustre of Our Country: The American Experience of Religious Freedom* (Berkeley: University of California Press, 1998), 83–84.

30 Corwin Smidt et al., *The Disappearing God Gap* (Oxford: Oxford University Press, 2010), 21.

31 Lambert, *Founding Fathers,* 269.

32 James H. Hutson, *The Founders on Religion: A Book of Quotations* (Princeton, N.J.: Princeton University Press, 2005), 59.

33 *People v. Ruggles.* http://press-pubs.uchicago.edu/founders/documents/amendI_religions62.html.

34 Lyman Beecher, *A Plea for the West* (Carlisle, Mass.: Applewood Books, 2009), 79.

35 Edwin Gaustad and Mark Noll, *A Documentary History of Religion in America* (Grand Rapids, Mich.: Eerdmans, 2003), 460.

36 Richard L. Bushman, *Joseph Smith and the Beginnings of American Mormonism* (Urbana: University of Illinois Press, 1984); Jan Shipps, *Mormonism: The Story of a New Religious Tradition* (Urbana: University of Illinois Press, 1985).

37 Michael Van Wagenen, *The Texas Republic and the Mormon Kingdom of God* (College Station: Texas A&M University Press, 2002), 18.

38 Clark V. Johnson, *Mormon Redress Petitions* (Salt Lake City, Utah: Brigham Young University Religious Study Center, 1992), 8.

10. THE POLITE CENTURIES

1 Thomas Belsham, *American Unitarianism* (Boston, 1816), 17.

2 Peter Norberg, *Essays and Poems by Ralph Waldo Emerson* (Spark Educational Publishing, 2005), 70–72.

3 Perry Miller, *The Transcendentalists: An Anthology* (Cambridge, Mass.: Harvard University Press, 1950), 210.

4 Ibid., 279.

5 *New York Times,* January 1, 1887, page 5.

6 *Pascendi Dominici Gregis,* September 8, 1907.

11. CONCLUSION

1 Christopher Black, *The Italian Inquisition* (New Haven, Ct.: Yale University Press, 2009), 69.

2 Voltaire, *A Philosophical Dictionary, from the French* (London, 1843), volume 3, 1.

3 Steven Nadler, *Spinoza's Heresy: Immortality and the Jewish Mind* (Oxford: Clarendon Press, 2001), 1–2.

4 William Wizeman, "Martyrs and Anti-Martyrs in Mary Tudor's Church," in *Martyrs and Martyrdom,* edited by Freeman and Mayer, 172.

5 K. M. Brown, et al., eds. *The Records of the Parliaments of Scotland to 1707* (St. Andrews, 2007–2010), 1540/12/55-62, available at www.rps.ac.uk. Last accessed 7 March 2010.

6 Janis M. Gibbs, "Immigration and Civic Identity in Sixteenth-Century Cologne," in *Ideas and Cultural Margins in Early Modern Germany: Essays in Honour of H. C. Erik Midelfort,* ed. Marjorie Elizabeth Plummer and Robin Barnes (Farnham: Ashgate, 2009), 52.

7 Given, *Inquisition and Medieval Society,* 17.

SUGGESTED READING

The scholarly literature on Christian heresy is vast. In what follows I have simply provided a few pointers for those who might want to study certain aspects of the story in more detail. The majority of these books are still in print, all are anglophone, and many contain extensive notes and bibliographies for those who are eager to dig even deeper.

Alley, R., ed. *James Madison on Religious Liberty* (Buffalo, N.Y.: Prometheus Books, 1985).

Audisio, G. *The Waldensian Dissent: Persecution and Survival, c. 1180–c. 1570* (Cambridge, UK: Cambridge University Press, 1999).

Ayres, L. *Nicaea and Its Legacy* (Oxford: Oxford University Press, 2004).

Bagchi, D., and D. Steinmetz, eds. *Cambridge Companion to Reformation Theology* (Cambridge, UK: Cambridge University Press, 2004).

Bailey, M. D. *Battling Demons: Witchcraft, Heresy, and Reform in the Late Middle Ages* (University Park: Pennsylvania State University Press, 2003).

Bainton, R. *Hunted Heretic: The Life and Death of Michael Servetus, 1511–1553* (Boston: Beacon Press, 1953).

Baker, D., ed. *Schism, Heresy, and Religious Protest.* Studies in Church History, volume 9 (Cambridge, UK: Cambridge University Press, 1972).

Barber, M. *The Cathars: Dualist Heretics in Languedoc in the High Middle Ages* (London: Longman, 2000).

———. *The Trial of the Templars* (Cambridge, UK: Cambridge University Press, 1995).

Bauer, W. *Orthodoxy and Heresy in Earliest Christianity* (Philadelphia: Fortress Press, 1971).

Benedict, P. *Christ's Churches Purely Reformed: A Social History of Calvinism* (New Haven, Ct.: Yale University Press, 2002).

Besançon, A. *The Forbidden Image: An Intellectual History of Iconoclasm* (Chicago: University of Chicago Press, 2000).

Bien, D. *The Calas Affair: Persecution, Toleration, and Heresy in Eighteenth-Century Toulouse* (Princeton, N.J.: Princeton University Press, 1960).

Bireley, R. *The Refashioning of Catholicism, 1450–1700* (Washington, D.C.: Catholic University of America Press, 1999).

Bödeker, H. E., C. Donato, and P. H. Reill, eds. *Discourses of Tolerance and Intolerance in the European Enlightenment* (Toronto: University of Toronto Press, 2009).

Boureau, A. *Satan the Heretic: The Birth of Demonology in the Medieval West* (Chicago: University of Chicago Press, 2006).

Brown, P. *Augustine of Hippo: A Biography* (Berkeley: University of California Press, 2000).

Burr, D. *The Spiritual Franciscans: From Protest to Persecution in the Century After St. Francis* (University Park: Pennsylvania State University Press, 2003).

Bushman, R. L. *Joseph Smith and the Beginnings of Mormonism* (Urbana, Ill.: University of Illinois Press, 1984).

Cameron, E. *Waldenses: Rejections of Holy Church in Medieval Europe* (Oxford: Blackwell, 2000).

Clanchy, M. T. *Abelard: A Medieval Life* (Oxford: Blackwell, 1999).

Clasen, C.-P. *Anabaptism: Social History, 1525–1618* (Ithaca, N.Y.: Cornell University Press, 1972).

Cohn, N. *Europe's Inner Demons: The Demonization of Christians in Medieval Christendom* (Chicago: University of Chicago Press, 1993).

———. *The Pursuit of the Millennium: Revolutionary Millenarians and Mystical Anarchists of the Middle Ages,* 3rd ed. (New York: Oxford University Press, 1970).

Curry, T. J. *The First Freedoms: Church and State in America to the Passage of the First Amendment* (New York: Oxford University Press, 1986).

Davidson, I. *Voltaire: A Life* (London: Profile, 2010).

Davis, L. D. *The First Seven Ecumenical Councils (325–787): Their History and Theology* (Collegeville, Minn.: Liturgical Press, 1990).

Drake, H. *Constantine and the Bishops: The Politics of Intolerance* (Baltimore: Johns Hopkins University Press, 2000).

Ehrman, B. D. *Lost Christianities: The Battles for Scripture and the Faiths We Never Knew* (Oxford: Oxford University Press, 2003).

Evans, G. R. *A Brief History of Heresy* (Oxford: Blackwell, 2002).

Ferreiro, A., ed. *The Devil, Heresy, and Witchcraft in the Middle Ages: Essays in Honor of Jeffrey B. Russell* (Leiden: Brill, 1998).

Fichtenau, H. *Heretics and Scholars in the High Middle Ages, 1000–1200* (University Park: Pennsylvania State University Press, 1998).

Forrest, I. *The Detection of Heresy in Late Medieval England* (Oxford: Clarendon Press, 2005).

Frassetto, M. *Heretic Lives: Medieval Heresy from Bogomil and the Cathars to Wyclif and Hus* (London: Profile, 2007).

Frend, W. H. C. *The Donatist Church: A Movement of Protest in Roman North Africa* (Oxford: Clarendon Press, 1952).

Frost, W. *A Perfect Freedom: Religious Liberty in Pennsylvania* (New York: Cambridge University Press, 1990).

Fudge, T. *The Magnificent Ride: The First Reformation in Hussite Bohemia* (Aldershot: Ashgate, 1998).

Gaddis, M. *There Is No Crime for Those Who Have Christ: Religious Violence in the Christian Roman Empire* (Berkeley: University of California Press, 2005).

Garsoian, N. *The Paulician Heresy* (The Hague and Paris: Mouton, 1967).

Gaustad, E. *Liberty of Conscience: Roger Williams in America* (Grand Rapids, Mich.: Eerdmans, 1991).

———. *Sworn on the Altar of God: A Religious Biography of Thomas Jefferson* (Grand Rapids, Mich.: Eerdmans, 1996).

Given, J. B. *Inquisition and Medieval Society: Power, Discipline, and Resistance in Languedoc* (Ithaca, N.Y.: Cornell University Press, 1997).

Gordon, B. *John Calvin* (New Haven, Ct.: Yale University Press, 2009).

Grell, O. P., and R. Scribner. *Tolerance and Intolerance in the European Reformation* (Cambridge, UK: Cambridge University Press, 1996).

Grodzins, D. *American Heretic: Theodore Parker and Transcendentalism* (Chapel Hill: University of North Carolina Press, 2002).

Hall, D. *The Antinomian Controversy 1636–1638: A Documentary History* (Durham, N.C.: Duke University Press, 1990).

Hamilton, B. *The Medieval Inquisition* (New York: Holmes and Meier, 1981).

Hamilton, J., et al., eds. *Christian Dualist Heresies in the Byzantine World* (Manchester: Manchester University Press, 1998).

Hanson, R. P. C. *The Search for the Christian Doctrine of God: The Arian Controversy, 318–381* (Edinburgh: T&T Clark, 1988).

Harvey, S. A., and D. G. Hunter, eds. *The Oxford Handbook of Early Christian Studies* (Oxford: Oxford University Press, 2008).

Heal, F. *Reformation in Britain and Ireland* (Oxford: Oxford University Press, 2003).

Henderson, J. B. *The Construction of Orthodoxy and Heresy: Neo-Confucian, Islamic, Jewish, and Early Christian Patterns* (Albany, N.Y.: State University of New York Press, 1998).

Hoepfl, H., ed. and trans. *Luther and Calvin on Secular Authority* (Cambridge, UK: Cambridge University Press, 1992).

Hsia, R. Po-chia. *The World of Catholic Renewal, 1540–1700* (Cambridge, UK: Cambridge University Press, 1998).

———, ed. *The German People and the Reformation* (Ithaca, N.Y.: Cornell University Press, 1988).

Hsia, R. Po-chia, and H. Van Nierop, eds. *Calvinism and Religious Toleration in the Dutch Golden Age* (Cambridge, UK: Cambridge University Press, 2002).

Hudson, A. *The Premature Reformation: Wycliffite Texts and Lollard History* (Oxford: Oxford University Press, 1988).

Hurtado, L. W. *Lord Jesus Christ: Devotion to Jesus in Earliest Christianity* (Grand Rapids, Mich.: Eerdmans, 2003).

Israel, J. I. *Radical Enlightenment: Philosophy and the Making of Modernity, 1650–1750* (Oxford: Oxford University Press, 2001).

Jodock, D., ed. *Catholicism Contending with Modernity: Roman Catholic Modernism and Anti-Modernism in Historical Context* (Cambridge, UK: Cambridge University Press, 2000).

Kamen, H. *The Spanish Inquisition: A Historical Revision* (New Haven, Ct.: Yale University Press, 1998).

Kaminsky, H. *A History of the Hussite Revolution* (Berkeley: University of California Press, 1967).

Kaplan, B. *Divided by Faith: Religious Conflict and the Practice of Toleration in Early Modern Europe* (Cambridge, Mass.: Belknap Press, 2007).

King, K. L. *What Is Gnosticism?* (Cambridge, Mass.: Belknap Press, 2003).

Knight, J. *Orthodoxies in Massachusetts: Rereading American Puritanism* (Cambridge, Mass.: Harvard University Press, 1994).

Kolb, R. *Martin Luther, Confessor of the Faith* (Oxford: Oxford University Press, 2009).

Lambert, M. *The Cathars* (Oxford: Blackwell, 1998).

———. *Medieval Heresy: Popular Movements from the Gregorian Reform to the Reformation*, 3rd ed. (Oxford: Blackwell, 2002).

Lansing, C. *Power and Purity: Cathar Heresy in Medieval Italy* (New York: Oxford University Press, 1998).

Lerner, R. *The Heresy of the Free Spirit in the Later Middle Ages* (Berkeley: University of California Press, 1972).

Loewenstein, D., and J. Marshall, eds. *Heresy, Literature, and Politics in Early Modern English Culture* (Cambridge, UK: Cambridge University Press, 2006).

MacCulloch, D. *Reformation: Europe's House Divided* (London: Allen Lane, 2003).

Marshall, J. *John Locke, Toleration, and Early Enlightenment Culture* (Cambridge, UK: Cambridge University Press, 2006).

McGrath, A. *Heresy: A History of Defending the Truth* (New York: HarperOne, 2009).

McKim, D. K., ed. *The Cambridge Companion to John Calvin* (Cambridge, UK: Cambridge University Press, 2004).

Moore, R. I. *The Formation of a Persecuting Society: Power and Deviance in Western Europe, 950–1250* (Oxford: Blackwell, 1987).

———. *The Origins of European Dissent* (London: Allen Lane, 1977).

Morgan, E. S. *Roger Williams: The Church and the State* (New York: Harcourt, Brace and World, 1967).

Nederman, C. J. *Worlds of Difference: European Discourses of Toleration, c.1100–c.1550* (University Park: Pennsylvania State University Press, 2000).

Nederman, C., and J. C. Laursen. *Difference and Dissent: Theories of Toleration in Medieval and Early Modern Europe* (Lanham, Md.: Rowman and Littlefield, 1996).

O'Collins, G. *Christology: A Biblical, Historical, and Systematic Study of Jesus* (Oxford: Oxford University Press, 1995).

O'Donnell, J. *Augustine: A New Biography* (New York: Ecco, 2005).

Ozment, S. *Mysticism and Dissent: Religious Ideology and Social Protest in the Sixteenth Century* (New Haven, Ct.: Yale University Press, 1973).

Pegg, M. G. *A Most Holy War: The Albigensian Crusade and the Battle for Christendom* (Oxford: Oxford University Press, 2008).

Peters, E. *Heresy and Authority in Medieval Europe: Documents in Translation* (Philadelphia: University of Pennsylvania Press, 1980).

Raven, S. *Rome in Africa* (London: Routledge, 1993).

Rees, B. R. *Pelagius: A Reluctant Heretic* (Woodbridge: Boydell and Brewer, 1988).

Richardson, R. D. *Emerson: The Mind on Fire* (Berkeley: University of California Press, 1995).

Roach, A. *The Devil's World: Heresy and Society, 1100–1300* (London: Longman, 2005).

Robinson, J. M. *The Nag Hammadi Library in English* (San Francisco: Harper and Row, 1988).

Russell, J. B. *Witchcraft in the Middle Ages* (Ithaca, N.Y.: Cornell University Press, 1972).

Rutland, R. A. *James Madison: The Founding Father* (Columbia: University of Missouri Press, 1987).

Schwartz, S. *"A Mixed Multitude": The Struggle for Toleration in Colonial Pennsylvania* (New York: New York University Press, 1987).

Scribner, R., and T. Scott, eds. *The German Peasants' War: A History in Documents* (London: Humanities Press, 1991).

Simons, W. *Cities of Ladies: Beguine Communities in the Medieval Low Countries, 1200–1565* (Philadelphia: University of Pennsylvania Press, 2001).

Strayer, J. *The Albigensian Crusades* (Ann Arbor: University of Michigan Press, 1992).

Thijssen, J. M. M. H. *Censure and Heresy at the University of Paris, 1200–1400* (Philadelphia: University of Pennsylvania Press, 1998).

Tierney, B. *The Idea of Natural Rights: Studies on Natural Rights, Natural Law, and Church Law, 1150–1625* (Atlanta: Scholars Press, 1997).

Tilley, M. A. *Donatist Martyr Stories: The Church in Conflict in Roman North Africa* (Liverpool: Liverpool University Press, 1996).

Trevett, C. *Montanism: Gender, Authority, and the New Prophecy* (New York: Cambridge University Press, 1996).

Voogt, G. *Constraint on Trial: Dirck Volckertsz Coornhert and Religious Freedom*. Sixteenth Century Essays and Studies, volume 52 (Kirksville, Mo.: Truman State University Press, 2000).

Wakefield, W., and A. Evans. *Heresies of the High Middle Ages* (New York: Columbia University Press, 1991).

Wiles, M. F. *Archetypal Heresy: Arianism Through the Centuries* (Oxford: Clarendon Press, 1996).

Williams, G. H. *The Radical Reformation* (Philadelphia: Westminster Press, 1962).

Williams, M. A. *Rethinking "Gnosticism": An Argument for Dismantling a Dubious Category* (Princeton, N.J.: Princeton University Press, 1996).

Williams, R. *Arius: Heresy and Tradition* (London: Darton, Longman and Todd, 1987).

Winship, M. *The Times and Trials of Anne Hutchinson: Puritans Divided* (Lawrence: University Press of Kansas, 2005).

Zagorin, P. *How the Idea of Religious Tolerance Came to the West* (Princeton, N.J.: Princeton University Press, 2003).

Index

Aachen, Council of (799), 85
Abel (victim of English religious quarrel), 173
Abelard, Peter, 103, 104–5, 141, 213
Adams, John, 272
Ad extirpanda (papal decree), 128
Adiaphora, 10, 213, 218, 228
adoption heresy, 84–85
Adventists, 274
Affair of the Placards, 187
African Methodist Episcopal church, and Philadelphia, 261
Ailly, Pierre d', 154
Aldebert of Soissons, 6
Alexius, Saint, 107
Allen, Charles, 274
Ambrose, Saint, 1, 254
Ameaux, Pierrre, 202
America, 236–37, 238–41
   Catholicism in, 273, 286–87
   18th-century movement in, 262
   and First Amendment, 263–64
     difficulties in interpretation and application of, 271–73
     and Jefferson, 264–67, 270
     and Madison, 267–70, 271–72
   New England, 241–45
     Baptists and Quakers in, 254–55
     Dyer in, 254–55

Anne Hutchinson in, 245–50, 253–54
   Parker in, 283
   Roger Williams in, 251–53
New Netherland under Stuyvesant, 255–57
19th-century bigotry and persecution in
   against Catholics, 273–74
   against Mormons, 274–75
   against Protestant denominations, 274
19th-century pluralism in, 276
Pennsylvania, 259–61, 262
   Madison's praise for, 267
Revolutionary War, 263
Amish, 258
Anabaptists, 182, 196–99, 205
Andover Theological Seminary, trial in, 283–84
Antichrist, 112–13, 168
   Bale on, 181
   in Foxe's account, 190, 191
   in Olivi's account, 140
   pope(s) as, 122, 153, 190
Antipopes, 118
Apollinarius of Laodicea, 65
Apostolici (apostolic brethren), 112, 137
Apostolic succession, 188
   Montanism threatens, 32

Aréfast (spy against Orléans heretics),
    96, 97
Arianism, 64, 76, 83
Arius, 1, 57, 59–60, 61–62, 65
    and Council of Nicaea, 63, 80
    as elite, 102
    later conflicts reminiscent of, 169,
        254
Arminians, 210
Armstrong, John, 181–82
Arnold, Gottfried, 234
Arnold of Brescia, 114
asceticism
    and Gnosticism, 30
    of Marcionists, 23
    of Montanists, 31, 33
Augsburg, Catholics and Protestants
        coexisting in, 223
Augustine, Saint, 74
    Bayle opposes, 231, 232, 233
    and Circumcellions, 73
    and Donatism, 73, 74–76
    on heresy, 75, 83, 217
    and original sin, 81

Backus, Isaac, 241
Bale, John, 180
Bapst, John, 273
baptism, adult
    and Anabaptists, 197–99
    Baptist banished by Peter Stuyvesant
        for, 256
Baptists, 198, 262, 289
    and Donatists, 205
    Madison in defense of, 267
    with Madison in fashioning First
        Amendment, 270
    persecuted in Boston, 254
Barnes, Robert, 173
Barton, Thomas, 262
Basilides, 25
Bauer, Walter, 45
Bayle, Pierre, 231–33, 277
    quoted, 146

Beguines, 142–45
Belloc, Hilaire, 7, 141
Berenger of Tours, 102, 191
Bernard of Clairvaux, 103, 104, 157
Beukels, Jan, 198
Béziers, massacre of Cathars in, 2,
    132–33
Bible
    Catholic reexamination of, 287
    Luther's emphasis on, 162–63
    Montanist revelations as challenge
        to, 32
    need to translate into local tongues,
        167
    See also scripture
bishop of Rome, Ignatius suggests as
        primary, 18
bishops
    in early Christianity
        Ignatius's support of, 15
        role of uncertain, 18
    Presbyterians against, 167
Black Death, 116
Blandina (martyr), 43–44
Bloody Tenent of Persecution
    (Williams), 252
Bodin, Jean, 227
Boggs, Lilburn, 275
Bogomils, and dualisms, 25, 98, 130
Bohemia, religious disaffection in, 150
Boniface VIII (pope), 122–23
Book of Common Prayer, Cotton's dis-
    like of, 244
Bradford, William, 267
Breton, Nicholas, 176
Bristow, Richard, quoted, 160
Bruno, Giordano, 212
Bucer, Martin, 174, 199
Byzantine Empire, heresy in, 85–94

Caecilian (bishop of Carthage), 70–71,
    72
Calas, Jean, 234–35
Calvert, George and Cecil, 239

Calvin, John, 85, 156, 164–65, 170, 175,
     206, 208, 210, 213
   Catholic denigration of, 188
   orthodoxy imposed by, 187
   and predestination, 164, 175, 201, 210
   and Servetus, 200–201, 204, 217
Calvinists and Calvinism, 247–48
   Massachusetts as home for, 250
   as Reformation result, 162
Campanella, Tommaso, 212
Campbellites, 274
Campion, Edmund, 217
cannibalism, charged against both
     early Christians and heretics, 99
Canossa, 119
capitalism, Catholic Church's response
     to, 285
Castellio, Sebastian, 202–3, 215, 219
Cathars, 2, 130–31, 134, 137, 191
   crusade against, 132–34
   and dualisms, 25
   Bernard Servel among, 105
   Valdes opposes, 108
Catherine of Siena, 191
Catholic Church
   apologies from for past persecu-
      tions, 298
   Donatist controversy gives rise to
      name, 72–73
   modernism opposed by, 277, 285–90
   and America, 286–87
   in 19th- and early 20th-century
      America
      inability to harm heretics, 286
      treatment of, 273
   and Reformation, 159, 167
   in response to Reformation, 184–85,
      186–87, 188, 196
      Council of Trent, 185–86
      Counter Reformation, 175, 179–80
      papal bull, 183–84
   See also Christianity
celibacy, clerical, 67
Celsus, 12, 38–39, 79, 205, 294

censorship, by Catholic Church,
     288–89
Chaderton, Henry, 177–78
Chalcedon, Council of, 65, 66, 86, 90,
     102
Channing, William Ellery, 279
Chardri, 49, 50
Charlemagne, 93
Charles I (king of England), 244
Charles II (king of England), 260
Charles V (Holy Roman emperor), 184,
     185, 208
Chelchicky, Peter, 155–56
Chillingsworth, William, 228–30
Christ
   Gnostic view of role of, 26, 29
   imminent return of, 37
   noncorporeal, 24–25
   question of identity of, 57–58
   and Arius, 59–60, 80
Christian heretics. See Heretics
Christianismi Restitutia (Servetus),
     200, 201
Christianity
   beginnings in first centuries of
      attempts to impose artificial unity
         on, 36–39, 44
      Council of Jerusalem, 21
      discord as actuality of, 17, 36, 38,
         45
      excess zeal feared as causing back-
         lash, 32
      fundamental questions in conten-
         tion for, 18–19, 46
      and Greek philosophy, 23–24
      heresy controversies essentially
         settled in, 83–84
      Ignatius's denunciation of divi-
         sions within, 15
      and Judaism, 21–22, 41
      and Madison on church without
         support of state, 269
      and noncorporeal Christ, 24
      as non-European, 69

Christianity, beginnings in first centuries of *(cont.)*
  perilous future of saved by Constantine, 47–48
  persecution of, 39, 41–44, 48, 53, 70
  Protestants appeal to as legacy, 189
  question over emergence of orthodoxy in, 45–47
  seen as pure and unified, 17
  unity as supreme goal of (Cyprian), 34
  under Constantine and successors, 48–49, 53–54, 190
  becomes only legal form of worship (381), 55
  compared to Reformation, 204–5
  Councils of Nicaea and Chalcedon, 62–64, 65–67
  pagan religions destroyed, 55–56
  and political potential of fighting heresy, 57
  and question of Christ's identity, 57–67
  and Seven Sleepers of Ephesus, 50–53
  Theodosian Code, 56–57
  uncertain evaluation of, 78
  unity of belief mandatory, 49, 56, 63
  in medieval period
  and church's need to find heretics, 126–30
  and dissatisfaction with established church, 116–23
  dissension between popes and secular rulers, 119–23
  East-West schism in, 117–18
  reform but not revolutionary Reformation desired, 157–58
  and Reformation, 161–69, 179–81 (*see also* Reformation)
  and role of heresy

Christianity illuminated by history of heresy, 12–13
  heresy as arising from inherent diversity of Christianity, 7–8, 79, 293–94
  heresy as challenge to self-examination, 8, 80–82, 136, 185, 225–26, 293
  as unified authoritative system vs. diversity of beliefs, 5
  unity as all-important for, 34–39, 56, 63, 83
  viewpoints and histories of
  Emerson's critique of, 280–81
  Foxe's history of, 190–92
  Jefferson's view of, 264–65
  Olivi's account of history of, 139–40
  Parker's critique of, 282–83
Christianity in age of religious pluralism. *See* era of religious pluralism
Christianity in America. *See* America
Christology, 58, 66
  and images of Christ, 89–90
Chrysochir, 87
church councils, 160–61
  popes' distrust of, 184
  See also specific councils
Circumcellions, 73
Clarke, John, 254
Clement V (pope), 123
Clement of Alexandria, 24, 99
Clerical supervision, as criterion of acceptability vs. heresy, 34, 35
Colet, John, 157–58
Colloquium of the Seven (Bodin), 227
Cologne of 1530s, heretics' status in, 298
Conciliarism, 118
Conrad of Marburg, 9–10
Constance, Council of, 153–54
Constans (Roman emperor), 72, 75
Constantine (Roman emperor), 54, 190
  and Arian crisis, 62

and Christianity, 48, 53, 54–55, 57, 78
    and Council of Nicaea, 62–63, 64
    and North African schism, 72, 75
Constantine (7th-century dualist), 86
Constantine V (Byzantine emperor), 90
Constantinople, Council of (381), 65, 76
Constantinople, Third Council of (680–681), 86
Constantius I (Roman emperor), 54
Constantius II (Roman emperor), 64
consubstantiation, 167
conversion experience, and predestination, 165
Coornhert, Dirck, 215
Copts, 66, 162
Corpus Christi processions, Calvin's outlawing of, 166
Coster, Francis, 1
Cotton, John, 243–44, 245, 253
council(s), church, 160–61
    popes' distrust of, 184
Council of Aachen (799), 85
Council of Chalcedon, 65, 66, 86, 90, 102
Council of Constance, 153–54
Council of Constantinople (381), 65, 76
Council of Constantinople, Third (680–681), 86
Council of Frankfurt (794), 85
Council of Jerusalem (about 50 C.E.), 21
Council of Lyon, 120–21
Council of Nicaea (325), 62–64, 67, 69, 102
Council of Pisa, 111
Council of Regensburg (792), 85
Council of Rome (798), 85
Council of Sens (1141), 103, 114
Council of Soissons, 103
Council of Trent (1545–1563), 185–86
Council of Vienne, 144
Counter Reformation, 175, 179–80

Crandall, John, 254
Cranmer, Thomas, 173, 176
Cromwell, Thomas, 173
crusade, against Cathars, 132–34
Cyprian of Carthage, 34–36, 39–40, 47, 70, 298
Cyril (patriarch of Alexandria), 65

Damian, Saint Peter, 141
Dante, 136
Darius, 75
"Dark Ages," 84
D'Ascoli, Cecco, 146
Dead Sea Scrolls, 27
Decius (Roman emperor), 48, 50, 52
De Heretico Comburendo (English statute against Lollards), 150
De nugis curialium (Courtiers' Trifles) (Map), 98
Descartes, René, 228
De unitate ecclesiae (Cyprian), 34
Dexter, Dr. (inquisitor at Andover heresy trial), 234
Dialogues Concerning Heresies (More), 1
Diocletian (Roman emperor), 48
Divine Comedy (Dante), 136
Docetism, 23, 60, 85–86
Dominic, Saint, 131
Donatism, 2, 69–73, 80–81, 83, 102, 117, 205
    Augustine on, 74–76
Douglas, William O., quoted, 238
Dryden, John, quoted, 204
dualism, 25, 130
    of Paulician, 86, 88–89
    See also Manichaeism
Dyer, Mary, 254–55, 259

Ebionites, 21, 22
ecclesiology, and popular heresy, 106
Eckhart, Meister, 142
Edict of Milan (313), 54
Edict of Nantes (1598), 224
    revocation of, 224, 232, 233

Edward VI (king of England), 174
Elipandus (archbishop of Toledo),
    84–85
Elizabeth I (queen of England), 168,
    175, 178, 182
Emerson, Ralph Waldo, 280–81
England
    Laudian ascendancy in, 244–45
    Reformation in, 173–79, 181–82
        coexistence prevalent in, 177
    Toleration Act in, 233
Enlightenment, 233–35, 264
Ephesus, 87
Epiphanius, 225
    quoted, 19
era of religious pluralism
    in America, 276
        friendly heresy trial at Andover
            Theological Seminary, 283–84
        and Parker, 283
        vs. Catholic opposition to modern-
            ism, 277, 285, 286–87, 288
    in Europe, 276–77
    heresy as concern of internal
        church discipline, 278, 279, 283,
        289
    and Unitarians, 278–79
    and World's Parliament of Religions
        (Chicago 1893), 277–78
    See also pluralism, religious; right to
        religious freedom; toleration
Erasmus, 36, 158, 217–18
Eucharist, under Protestantism, 166
    Luther on, 166–67, 210
Europe, in age of secularism, 276–77
Eusebius, 31, 63
Eusebius of Caesarea, 62
Eusebius of Nicomedia, 62
Evers, Sir Francis, 178
evil, problem of, and Gnostics, 28
excommunication, of Marcion, 24

Fagius, Paul, 174
faith, Luther's appeal to, 163
Felix (bishop of Apthungi), 70

Fetherstone (victim of English reli-
    gious quarrel), 173
Fifth Lateran Council, 161
Finch, John, 178
First Amendment, 263–64
    and Catholics, 286
    interpretation and application of
        unsettled, 271–73
    and Jefferson, 264–67, 270
    and Madison, 267–70, 271–72
First Corinthians, 81
Fisher, John, 229
flagellants, at time of Black Death, 116,
    141
Fourteenth Amendment, and religious
    freedom, 272
Fox, George, 258
Foxe, John, 168, 190–92, 217, 254
Fra Dolcino, 112, 113–14, 115, 137
France
    Edict of Nantes (1598) in, 224
        revocation of, 224, 232, 233
    Francis I's campaign against heresy,
        187
    religious conflict in, 182, 232, 234
Francis I (king of France), 184, 185, 187
Francis of Assisi, and Franciscans,
    137–40
Franck, Sebastian, 215
Frankfurt, Council of (794), 85
Frederick II (Holy Roman emperor),
    120–22
Frederick III of Saxony, 207–8
freedom, religious. See era of religious
    pluralism; pluralism, religious;
    right to religious freedom;
    toleration
Free Spirit, heresy of the, 127, 144
free will, vs. predestination, 164
French Revolution, 277
Furley, Benjamin, 9

Galileo, 212, 298
Gardiner, Stephen, 176
Garret, Thomas, 173

gender discrimination, and Anne
      Hutchinson, 249
Gentilis, Valentin, 202
Geoffrey of Auxerre, 6
German Peasants' War, 193–95
      Luther's reaction to, 195–96
Gerson, Jean, 154
Gibbons, James, 286
Gifford, George, 176
Gnosticism, 12, 25–30, 45–46, 80–81, 205
      Clement of Alexandria on, 99
      and dualisms, 25, 130
God, Oneness of, and argument for
      unified church, 37
Goethe, Johann Wolfgang von, on tol-
      erance, 268
good works, Council of Trent on, 185
Goslar, Germany, heretics executed in,
      97, 98
Gottschalk (theologian), 85
Great Awakening, 262
Great Case of Liberty of Conscience, The
      (Penn), 259
Great Schism (late 14th and early 15th
      centuries, 118
Greek philosophy, 23–24, 46
      and Christology, 58
      in Gnosticism, 27, 28
      and Nicene Creed, 64
Green, John, 275
Gregorian Reform, 117
Gregory II (pope), 91
Gregory VII (pope), 119
Gregory IX (pope), 120, 298
Gregory of Nyssa, 66
Grosseteste, Robert, 3, 4
Guibert of Nogent, 98
Guzman, Dominic, 131

Hall, Edward, 173
Hallaj, al-, 292
Hamerstan, Mr. (Catholic preferring
      prison to Protestants), 168
Hans (beggar of Augsburg), 105
"heathens," 76

Hecker, Isaac, 286
Henry, Patrick, 269
Henry IV (Holy Roman emperor), 119
Henry VIII (king of England), 173
Henry of Lausanne, 111–12
heresy, 6–7, 83, 298
      adult baptism as, 198
      Catholic viewpoint on, 289
      "Americanism" seen as, 286
      and modernism as "synthesis of
            all heresies," 287
      Protestantism seen as, 168
      as challenge to self-examination, 8,
            79, 80–82, 136, 185, 225–26, 293
      coercion against, 67–68, 73–74
      Aquinas on, 137
      Augustine on, 75, 83, 217
      contention over means of (caritas
            vs. potestas), 68–69, 76–77
      by Inquisition, 128–29
      legal executions for heresy in 16th
            century (number of), 181
      papal decree authorizes torture,
            128
      through partnership of religious
            and secular power, 276
      and coexistence from pragmatic
            necessity, 10–11
      definitions and occasions of
      conditions of (Directorium
            Inquisitorum), 291
      as engendered by accusations of
            heresy, 84, 127
      as opposition to victorious ortho-
            doxy, 5–6
      refusal of clerical supervision as
            test of, 34, 35, 109, 142
      and Enlightenment, 234
      Erasmus on misuse of, 36, 217–18
      as existing without Christianity, 300
      future of, 300–301
      vs. inventive speculation, 213–14
      and Judaism, 292–93
      and magic, 148–49
      and modern values, 9–10, 11–12

heresy *(cont.)*
  outrageous examples of, 6
  pre-Christian meaning of, 291
  in present times, 297, 298–300
  Protestants' pursuit of, 196, 199,
    204
  as pursuing accepted notions in new
    ways, 30
  Scotland of 1540s obsessed with,
    297–98
  and social and political order
    heresy as divisive, 3, 222–23
    pursuit of heresy as divisive, 223,
      233
    unity as all-important, 34–39, 56,
      63, 83
  softening of into tourist attraction,
    258
  of Sufi thinker, 292
  Thomistic themes among those
    condemned as, 103–4
  Voltaire on, 291
heresy in historical view
  and early church, 18, 45–47, 83–84
    Cyprian on, 35
    and dualistic theories, 25
    and Gnostics, 28–29
    Ignatius on, 15
    and Jewish Christianity, 22
    as pursuing accepted notions in
      new ways, 30
  after Constantine, 49
    as convenient target for post-
      Constantine emperors, 57
  in early medieval period
    in Byzantine Empire, 85–94
    lack of pursuers in West, 84–85
  in medieval period, 97, 99–100,
    135
    church sees renewal of old battles,
      98
    codification of attacks on, 129
    and crusade against Cathars,
      132–34

    diabolical activities associated
      with
    heretics, 98–99
    as golden age of heresy, 94
    intellectual heresy, 102–5
    Knights Templar accused of,
      123–24
    as obsessive fear, 135–36
    Orléans discovery and executions,
      95–97
    popular participation in, 101–2,
      105–6, 110–11 (*see also* popular
      heresy)
    portrayal of the heretic missing
      from art, 136
    and power, 100–101, 120, 127–28
    and problem of distinguishing,
      137, 140–42
    Thomas Aquinas on, 136–37
  and Reformation, 169, 172, 180–83
    (*see also* Reformation)
    and Luther's reaction to Peasant
      Revolt, 195–96
    mutual Catholic-Protestant accu-
      sations of, 169
    and Protestant riposte to Catholic
      critique, 192
  in America, 240–41
    and friendly trial at Andover
      Theological Seminary, 283–84
    and Mormons, 275
    New England, 241, 245, 246, 250
    and Quakers, 257–58
  and era of religious pluralism,
    276–77 (*see also* era of religious
    pluralism)
    Catholic power against heresy
      limited, 285–86
    as concern of internal church dis-
      cipline, 278, 279, 283, 289
heretics, 1
  definition of, 3, 4, 9
  famous 17th-century trials of, 212
  Ignatius on, 15–16

in New England
  Dyer, 254–55
  Hutchinson, 250
  Parker, 283
  Willliams, 252
persecution of, 1–2
as political traitor (post-Constan-
    tine), 56
and problem of good Christians
    lapsed from orthodoxy,
    78–80
in Protestant view of early church,
    189
rough correction of attempted, 2–3
as setting up own church, 66
as threat to Christendom, 3–5,
Hezekiah, 75
Hippolytus, 29, 32–33
history of Christian heresy
  examination of, 294–96
  gap in, 84
  objectivity needed in, 302
  Olympian judgments unjustified
    on, 296
  and recognition of past world-
    views, 295, 302
Hodgson, Robert, 256
Hogarde, Miles, 168, 192
Holland
  pragmatic resolution of religious
    differences in, 224–25
  Reformation Wonder Year in, 182
Holmes, Obadiah, 254, 281
Holy Roman Empire, religious division
    within, 224, 271
Hubmaier, Balthasar, 197
Huguenots, 224, 232
Humanism, 158, 170
Humiliati, 141
Hus, Jan, 106, 149–50, 151, 152–54, 190,
    192
Hussitism, 154–56
Hutchinson, Anne, 245–50, 253–54
Hypostatic union, 66, 86

iconoclasm, 89–94
Ignatius (bishop of Antioch), 14–16, 17,
    18–19, 22, 32, 35, 36, 39, 41, 47, 60,
    190, 242
  quoted, 14
incest, charged of both early Christians
    and heretics, 99
indulgences, 150, 153, 157
Innocent III (pope), 117, 132
Innocent IV (pope), 121
Innocent VIII (pope), 149
Inquisition, 128–29
  and Calvin's Geneva, 202
  against Cathars, 133
  Spanish, 277
interpretation of history of Christian
    heresy, 294–96
intolerance on part of heretical move-
    ments as well as established
    church, 11
invading tribes, Arianism pacticed by,
    64
Ireland, John, 286
Irenaeus of Lyon, 29
Irene (Byzantine empress), 92, 93
Islam, 291–92

James V (king of Scotland), 297
Jefferson, Thomas, 264–67, 270
  quoted, 238
  on tax support for churches, 269
  and "wall of separation between
    church and state," 265
Jerome, Saint, 33, 141
Jerome, William, 173
Jerusalem, Council of (about 50 C.E.),
    21
Joan of Arc, 149, 155
John XXII (pope), 148
Jovinian, 141
Judaism
  and Christianity, 21–22, 41
  and heresy, 292–93
Julianists, 85–86

Julian of Norwich, 142
Justin Martyr, 42

Kant, Immanuel, 287
Keith, George, 261
Kennedy, John, 274
Kent, James, 272–73
Kerry, John, 299
King, Karen, 27
Knights Templar, 123–24, 298
Know-Nothing political party, 274
Koran, Servetus studies, 201
Krieg, Blesy, 194–95
Kyteler, Alice, 147–48

Latitudinarianism, 228
Laud, William, 245
Laudian ascendancy, 244
lay investiture, 119
Lazarus (painter of sacred images), 93
Ledrede, Richard de, 148
Leland, John, 270
Le Mans, revolution ignited in, 111
Leo III (Byzantine emperor), 90, 91, 92
Leo IV (Byzantine emperor), 92
Leo V (Byzantine emperor), 92
Leutard of Vertus, 6
Libanius, 55
Libra Extra (Gregory IX), 298
life-beliefs, heresy as accompaniment
    of, 301–2
Lipsius, Justus, 226
Locke, John, 219, 230–31, 235, 262, 264,
    265
Lollards, 152, 162, 206
London, Edward, 186
Louis IX (king of France), 143
low-hanging fruit syndrome, 209
Luke, Gospel of, 76, 77
Luther, Martin, 156, 162–64, 192–93,
    206
    Catholic denigration of, 188
    Erasmus on, 218–19
    on Eucharist, 166–67, 210
    on "heretics" of early church, 189

orthodoxy imposed by, 187
papal bull against, 183
and Peasants' Revolt, 195–96
quoted, 160
and Vitrier's teachings, 157
Lutherans, as Reformation result, 162
Lyon, Council of, 120–21
Lyon and Vienne, martyrs in, 43–44

Macarius (imperial envoy to North
    Africa), 72
Madison, James, 219, 267–70,
    271–72
magic, 148–49
Majorinus, 71
Malleus Maleficarum (The Hammer of
    Witches), 149
Manichaeism, 74, 83
Map, Walter, 98
Marcion, 20–21, 22–23, 24, 60, 81
    banished from Rome, 46
    and dualism, 130
    as elite, 102
    and Gnostics, 25, 26
    and Paul, 163
Marculus (Donatist bishop), 72
Marcus Aurelius, 42
Marcus Cornelius Fronto, 42
Marsilius of Paduja, 221
martyrdom
    of Anabaptists, 197
    and Christian unity, 39, 44
    of Circumcellions, 73
    commitment exhibited by, 43
    as counterproductive to persecu-
        tors, 217
    in Ephesus, 50
    and heretics, 2
    of Hus, 154
    of Ignatius of Antioch, 15, 16
    and Montanists, 31–32, 34
Mary I (queen of England), 174–75,
    176, 182
Maryland, as Catholic refuge, 239
Mason, George, 268

Massachuetts, 278, 280

Mathijs, Jan, 198

Maxentius, 54

Maximilia, 31, 32, 34

Memorial and Remonstrance
    (Madison), 269

Mennonites, 239

Methodists, 205

Methodius (Byzantine patriarch), 93

millennial expectations, 37

Millerites, 274

Milvian Bridge, battle of, 54

Mirror of Simple Souls, The (Porete),
    144

modernism
    Catholic Church opposes, 277, 285,
        286–87, 288
        as "synthesis of all heresies," 287
    and Catholic modernism, 286–87

Molinos, Miguel de, 234

Monarchianism, 60

Monforte, heretics executed in, 97

Monophysitism, 65–66, 86

Monothelitism, 86

Montanism, 19–20, 30–34, 70, 80–81

Montanus, 30–31

Moravians, 156, 239

More, Thomas, 1, 214

Morison, Sir Richard, 174

Mormonism, 274–75

Morning Star of Reformation,
    Hussitism seen as, 156

Morse, Samuel, 274

Muggleton, Lodowick, 261

Münster, Anabaptist extremists in con-
    trol of, 198–99

Nag Hammadi, Gnostic tests found
    near, 27

Napper, George, 178

Nashe, Thomas, 178

Near Eastern religious movements, in
    Gnosticism, 28

Nebuchadnezzar, 75

Neo-Platonism, and Arius, 59

Nero (Roman emperor), 43

Nestorius and Nestorians, 65, 66, 78,
    80, 102, 162

Netherlands. *See* Holland

New Age movement, 28

New England, 241–45, 246, 250
    Baptists and Quakers in, 254–55
    Dyer in, 254–55
    Anne Hutchinson in, 245–50,
        253–54
    Parker in, 283
    Roger Williams in, 251–53

Newman, John Henry, 82

New Netherland, Stuyvesant rebuffed
    in, 255–57

New Testament
    as source of Christian dogma, 3
    See also Bible

Nicaea, 87

Nicaea, Council of (325), 62–64, 67, 69,
    102

Nicene Creed, 63, 64

Nicomedia, 87

North African church, schism in, 70–73

Norton, Andrews, 281

objectivity, 295–96, 302

obstinacy, as defining feature of her-
    etic, 4

Old Testament
    Marcion's renunciation of, 20
    Paulicians reject, 87
    See also Bible

Olivi, Peter John, 139–40, 141

Origen, 24, 38–39, 79–80, 141, 213
    and Arius, 59

original sin
    Henry of Lausanne on, 112
    Pelagius's denial of, 81

Orléans, heresy uncovered in (1022),
    95–97, 98, 101

orthodoxy
    myth of imposed, 36–39
    as theological anchor, 5–6

Outlawe, William, 147

Pantheism, Meister Eckhart suspected of, 142

parable of guests compelled to come to feast, 77

Paraclete, 32, 33

Parker, Theodore, 281–83

Paul, Apostle, 5, 21
  and Calvin, 164
  in history of heresy, 163
  and Luther's realization of faith, 163

Paulician sect, 86–88, 130

Paulus (imperial envoy to North Africa), 72

Pelagius, 81

Penn, William, 240, 259–61
  quoted, 255

Pennsylvania, 239
  Madison's praise of, 267
  religious freedom and haven for Quakers in, 259–61, 262

People v. Ruggles, 272

pertinacity, as defining feature of heretic, 4

Peter, Saint, 18, 35

Peter of Bruis, 111, 115

Peter of Castelnau, 131–32

Philip IV (king of France), 122, 123, 143

Pietists, 239

Pisa, Council of, 111

pluralism, religious, 212
  assertion of heretical views not based on (contrary to modern viewpoint), 213–15, 216
  growth of (19th century), 278 (*see also* era of religious pluralism)
  question of strength of, 299
  and tolerance vs. religious freedom, 268
  See also era of religious pluralism; right to religious freedom; toleration

polytheism, and Arius's criticism of orthodox view, 60

Pontus, Tertullian's diatribes against, 20

Poor Clares, 138

Poor of Lyon, 108

Pope(s)
  competition among claimants (Great Schism), 118
  denounced as Antichrist, 122, 153, 190
  denounced by Arnold of Brescia, 114
  Olivi's followers on, 140
  Papal infallibility asserted, 285
  Wyclif's teachings hostile to, 152

popular heresy, 101–2, 105–6, 110–11, 135
  of Arnold of Bescia, 114
  explanations for, 114–15
    caution called for in judgments on, 124–25
    dissatisfaction with established church, 116–23
    as rallying point for church and secular rulers, 126–30
    social and economic readjustments, 115–16
  of Fra Dolcino and Apostolici, 112–14
  and Henry of Lausanne, 111–12
  of Valdes and Waldensians, 107–9

Porete, Marguerite, 144

poverty
  of Beguines, 143
  Francis insistent on, 138, 140
  of Valdes, 107–8

poverty of Christ, in charge of heresy, 140

Powell (victim of English religious battle), 173

power
  and accusations of heresy, 100–101, 120, 127–28
  as motive for asserting orthodoxy, 36–37
  of orthodoxy post-Constantine, 57

Prades, Jean Martin de, 234
pragmatism
    and First Amendment, 271
    toleration emerges from, 221–25,
        226–27, 235
Prague, religious disaffection in, 150
predestination, 85, 164, 175, 201, 210
    Unitarian denial of, 279
Presbyterians, 167, 289
priesthood
    of all believers, 164
    Colet's criticism of, 157
    Jefferson on, 264
    and Montanists, 33
    as only true intermediary between
        God and humanity, 108
    Protestant questioning of, 166
Primian (bishop), 72
print revolution, Reformation aided
    by, 206
Priscilla (or Prisca), 31, 32, 34, 147
Protestant Episcopal Church, and
    Philadelphia, 261
proto-orthodoxy, 45, 46
Purgatory, 151, 166

Quakers, 205, 257–59
    in Massachusetts, 254
    New Netherland defense of,
        256–57
    and Penn, 259–61

Ramihrdus, 141
Raymond, count of Toulouse,
    131–33
Raymond-Roger (viscount of
    Trecaval), 132
Reformation, 161–69, 179–81
    Catholics see as heretical excres-
        cence, 159
    Church's response to, 184–85, 186–87,
        188, 196
        Council of Trent, 185–86
        papal bull, 183–84

and colonial America, 241 (*see also*
    America)
as complex, unclear, and confusing
    process, 169–71
and popular understanding of
    leaders' dogma, 171–72
and disaffection of German peas-
    antry, 194
early church compared with, 204–5
in England, 173–79, 181–82
    coexistence prevalent, 177
and Fifth Lateran Council, 161
as generating pragmatic rationale
    for toleration, 222, 223
as heretical event par excellence,
    169, 172
hope for imposition of orthodoxy
    shattered by, 226
as inexplicable, 158–59
number of 16th-century legal execu-
    tions, 181
as political transformation, 167–68
Protestant positions
    and Anabaptists, 196–99
    Calvin's harsh rule in Geneva, 202
    and Castellio's questioning prac-
        tice of persecuting heretics,
        202–3, 204
    control to squelch dissent and
        heresy (post–Peasants' Revolt),
        195–96
    and John Foxe's account, 190–92
    Luther's original support for free-
        dom of conscience, 192–93
    mytho-history of Christian ori-
        gins, 188–90
    orthodoxy affirmed, 187–88
    and Servetus, 199–202, 203,
        204
and question of Protestantism's fail-
    ure to abolish divisions, 209–11
and question of Reformation's sur-
    vival, 205–9
    and print revolution, 206

Reformation *(cont.)*
  and translation of Bible into ver-
    nacular, 167
  violent activities in, 180–83
Regensburg, Council of (792), 85
*Religion of Protestants, The: A Safe Way
  to Salvation* (Chillingsworth),
  229
Revolutionary War, 263
right to religious freedom
  assertion of heretical views not
    based on, 10, 180, 213–15, 216
  and First Amendment, 263–64
  Jefferson on, 265–67
  See also era of religious pluralism;
    pluralism, religious; toleration
Robert II (king of France), 95, 100
Robinson, William, 254
Roman Empire
  Christian condemnation of, 40, 41,
    42
  Christianity established by, 53,
    77–78
    by Constantine, 48, 53
    in Seven Sleepers of Ephesus, 52
  Christianity slandered in, 42–43
  fall of, 84
Rome, Arnold of Brescia occupies, 114
Rome, bishop of, Ignatius suggests as
  primary, 18
Rome, Council of (798), 85
Romulus Augustulus (Roman em-
  peror), 84

Sabellius, 60–61
Sacraments, Council of Trent on, 185
Saint Bartholomew's Day Massacre,
  182
Saints, 106–7
Sandy Foundation Shaken, The (Penn),
  259
Satan
  in Bale's polemic, 181
  heretics seen as minions of, 4
  as instigator of heresy, 83, 100, 147

New England's fear of, 246, 247
  and witches, 149
Sattler, Michael, 197
Schismatics, 35
Schwenkenfelders, 239
Scotland, heresy strictly persecuted in,
  297–98
scripture
  Calvin on, 165
  Council of Trent on, 185
  Luther's emphasis on, 162–63
  and pulpit for Protestants, 166
  See also Bible
second coming, Montanus sees visions
  of, 31
Second Council of Nicaea, 92, 93–94
Second Vatican Council, 289–90
Seculus, Petrus, 87–88
Segarelli, Gerardo, 112–13
Sens, Council of (1141), 103, 114
Sergius, 87, 88
Servel, Bernard, 105
Servetus, Michael, 199–202, 203, 204,
  205, 215, 216
Seven Sleepers of Ephesus, 49, 50–53
Shakers, 274
Shepard, Thomas, 249
Siger of Brabant, 102
Sigismund (king of Bohemia), 155
significant commitments, heresy as
  accompaniment of, 301–2
Simon de Montfort, 133
Simony, 151
Skelton, Samuel, 251
Smith, Al, 274
Smith, Ralph, 251
Smyth, Egbert Coffin, 283, 284
social justice
  as Circumcellions demand, 73
  German peasants see Gospel as tool
    of, 194
Society of Friends. *See* Quakers
Soissons, heretics in, 98
Soissons, Council of, 103
Spinoza, Baruch, 228, 293

Spirituals (Zelantii), 139
Staplehill, Walter, 177
Stevenson, Marmaduke, 254
Story, John, 241
Stradigotto, 105
Stuyvesant, Peter, 256–57
subordinationism, 61
Sufism, 292
Syllabus of Errors, 285
Sylvester I (pope), 69
Symmes, Zachariah, 247

Tacitus, 43
Tanchelm of Antwerp, 6
Tertullian, 19–20, 80
    and escape from world, 40–41, 42
    vs. Gnosticism, 29
    and Greek philosophy, 23
    on heresies, 81–82
    vs. Marcion, 20, 22, 25
    and Montanism, 30, 33, 78–79
    and North African, 70
Testwood, Robert, 181
Theodora (Byzantine empress), 93
Theodosian Code, 56
Theodosius (Roman emperor), 52–53
Theodosius II (Roman Emperor), 56
Theophilus (Byzantine emperor), 92
Third Council of Constantinople
    (680–681), 86
Thirty Years' War, 231
Thomas Aquinas, 103–4
    attempt to reinvigorate legacy of,
        285
    on heresy, 136–37
    modernists push aside, 287
Thrace, Paulicians in, 88–89
toleration, 211
    emergence of, 212, 219–21
        and Chilllingsworth, 228–30
        from doubt over possibility of
            certainty in belief, 227–28
        and Enlightenment, 233–35
        and Locke, 230–31
        Penn argues for, 259

    as possible veneer, 220, 235–36
    from pragmatism, 221–25, 226–27,
        235
    snags in, 234
    Williams argues for, 253
    vs. "free exercise" (First
        Amendment), 268
    as guarantor of social stability
        (Bayle), 233
    and modern outlook, 236
    premodern variants of, 212–16
        on assumption that open discus-
            sion leads to one true belief,
            214–15
        and distinction between mere
            pursuit of heretics and barbaric
            treatment, 216–17
        and Erasmus on trivialities,
            217–19
        self-interest as basis, 214
        and solitary Reformation apolo-
            gists for tolerance, 215–16
    See also era of religious pluralism;
        pluralism, religious; right to
        religious freedom
Toleration Act, England, 233
Toleration Act, Maryland, 239
torture, papal decree sanctions, 128
Tradition, Council of Trent on, 185
Traditors, 70
Trajan (Roman emperor), 14, 18–19,
    42
Transcendentalism, 280, 281
transubstantiation
    and Berengar of Tours, 102
    Calvinists' denial of, 166
    Wyclif's denial of, 151, 152
Trent, Council of (1545–1563), 185–86
Trinity, 61
    Abelard on, 103
    Calvin on, 201
    Cyril on, 65
    and early years of Christianity, 19
    Penn questions, 259
    Sabellius sees as "modes," 60

Trinity *(cont.)*
  and Servetus, 200
  Unitarian denial of, 279

Unam Sanctum (papal bull), 122
Unitarianism, 58, 278, 282
Unity of Brethren, 156
Utopia (More), 214
Utraquist Church, 155

Valdes of Lyon, 106, 107–9, 110, 115, 137
  and St. Francis, 138, 140–41, 142
Valentinus, 25
Vane, Henry, 77
Vanini, Giulio Cesare, 2
vegetarianism
  among Cathars, 131
  suspicion of heresy from, 97
Vermigli, Peter Martyr, 182
Vernacular scripture, and Reformation,
  167, 170, 206–7
Vie des Set Dormanz, La (Chardri), 50
Vienne, Council of, 144
Vincent of Lérins, 5, 66, 78–79
Viterbo, townspeople interrupt papal
  conclave in, 118–19
Vitrier, Jean, 156–57
Vitry, Jacques de, 143
Voltaire, 219, 234–35, 235, 261

Waldensians, 106, 108–10, 162, 206
Ward, Nathaniel, 247
Ware, Henry, 279
Wenceslas IV (king of Bohemia), 152,
  155
Weston, William, 168
White, Richard, 169
Wibald of Corvey, 98
Wickendon, William, 256
Wightman, Edward, 277
William of Conches, 104
Williams, Roger, 77–78, 239, 240,
  251–53, 255
  and Penn, 259
  on tax-supported churches, 269
  as Winthrop nightmare, 245
Winthrop, John, 242, 243, 245, 246
  and Anne Hutchinson, 253–54
  and Roger Williams, 251
witchcraft, 100, 147–49
  and witch craze in New England,
  247
Woodman, Richard, 182
World's Parliament of Religions
  (Chicago 1893), 277–78
Wyclif, John, 106, 151–52, 190,
  191–92

Zwingli, Ulrich, 167, 188, 197, 210